Conquering Complexity In Your Business

How Wal-Mart, Toyota, and Other
Top Companies Are Breaking Through
the Ceiling on Profits and Growth

Michael L. George
Stephen A. Wilson

McGraw-Hill

New York   Chicago   San Francisco   Lisbon   London
Madrid   Mexico City   Milan   New Delhi   San Juan
Seoul   Singapore   Sydney   Toronto

The **McGraw·Hill** Companies

1 2 3 4 5 6 7 8 9 0 DOC/DOC 0 9 8 7 6 5 4

ISBN 0-07-143508-5

This publication is designed to provide accurate and authoritative information in regard to the subject matter covered. It is sold with the understanding that neither the author nor the publisher is engaged in rendering legal, accounting, or other professional services. If legal advice or other expert assistance is required, the services of a competent professional person should be sought.

—From a Declaration of Principles jointly adopted by a Committee of the American Bar Association and a Committee of Publishers

McGraw-Hill books are available at special quantity discounts to use as premiums and sales promotions, or for use in corporate training programs. For more information, please write to the Director of Special Sales, McGraw-Hill, 2 Penn Plaza, New York, NY 10121. Or contact your local bookstore.

This book is printed on recycled, acid-free paper containing a minimum of 50% recycled de-inked fiber

Contents

PART II
Complexity Analysis:
Quantifying and Prioritizing Your Complexity Opportunities

PART III
Implementing Complexity Agendas

About the Authors

Michael George, Chairman and CEO of George Group Consulting, has worked personally with CEOs and executive teams at major corporations worldwide. His primary emphasis is on the creation of shareholder value through application of process improvement initiatives including Lean Six Sigma, Lean Manufacturing, and Complexity Reduction. He is the author of *Lean Six Sigma* (McGraw-Hill, 2002) and *Lean Six Sigma for Service* (M-H, 2003). Mr. George began his career at Texas Instruments in 1964 as an engineer. In 1969, he founded the venture startup International Power Machines (IPM), which he subsequently took public and sold to a division of Rolls Royce in 1984. This enabled him to study the Toyota Production System and TQM first hand in Japan, resulting in the book *America Can Compete*, which led to the founding of George Group in 1986.

Stephen Wilson is the Director of the Conquering Complexity practice at George Group. He works with companies to drive improvements in shareholder value through the application of Conquering Complexity methodologies and strategies. He has worked internationally and his experience spans multiple industries, including consumer goods, financial services, technology and manufacturing. Additionally, Mr. Wilson has expertise in strategic assessments and strategy development, Value Based Management, and Lean Six Sigma, the process improvement methodology. Previously, he worked at Marakon Associates, a strategy consulting company. His education includes an MBA in Finance and Strategic Management from The Wharton School.

Acknowledgements

We would like to thank our clients who have generously supported our efforts in understanding what it will take to conquer complexity, including: Lou Giuliano and ITT Industries, Anne Mulcahy and Xerox, Chris Cool of Northrup-Grumman; and Geoff Turk of Caterpillar. We also thank Jim Patell (Herbert Hoover Professor of Public and Private Management, Graduate School of Business at Stanford University), and Lars Maasdeivaag, Kimberly Watson-Hemphill, James Works, Bill Zeeb, and the Officer Team (all of George Group) for their many contributions to this area of study. We greatly appreciate the work of Sue Reynard (editor and ghostwriter), Brenda Quinn, Tonya Schilling, and Kim Bruce for producing the book.

Preface

By Mike George

Over the past two decades, my colleagues and I have helped many businesses create shareholder value primarily through process improvement. But we often found that clients who restricted their efforts to improvement approaches such as Lean and/or Six Sigma would hit a ceiling in profit generation: though progress was significant, there was only so much they could accomplish through process improvement.

Where did this ceiling come from? Our most recent research and our experience over the last few years led us to a startling conclusion: that there is an entirely separate dimension to operating improvement that often presents the single largest opportunity for cost reduction and the most significant hurdle to profitable growth in most companies.

What is this mysterious force? **Complexity**.

Here's a guarantee: Somewhere in your business, there is too much complexity—more product offerings than your customers want, more services than your markets can support with positive Economic Profit, too many ways of accomplishing the same output, etc. This kind of complexity generates huge non-value-add costs, work your customers wouldn't want to pay for if they had an alterative. These costs are enormous in terms of lost profit *and* growth, and are hidden in overhead—a hidden profit pool of huge potential.

It's also possible that there may be places in your business with too little complexity in your offerings, where you're missing opportunities by having too few options for your customers. And there's another contributor to the hidden profit pool: revenues you could easily generate if you understood what your customers value and are willing to pay for.

Every CEO and senior executive who has seen the data presented in this book has responded *"We know we have complexity. We know it's a big problem. We want to know more."* Supplying the "more" is one purpose of this book.

The primary goal, however, is to provide you with the tools you need to **conquer** complexity in your own business. We'll show you how to…

- Identify the offering and process complexity in your business
- Quantify the cost impact of that complexity
- Decide which complexity you want to keep and exploit, and which you should eliminate
- Select specific approaches to eliminate different kinds of complexity

Together, this knowledge will enable significant improvement in your ability to grow profit, revenue, and shareholder value.

The Struggle to Quantify Complexity

Back in the mid-1980s, International Power Machines (IPM), a company I founded, had reached a crisis. IPM produced uninterruptible power supplies (used mostly to protect mainframe computer systems from power failure), and had reached a point of offering hundreds of different product designs, each consisting of unique parts. The complexity associated with supporting all these unique products prevented us from earning the cost of capital; the internal inefficiency throttled our growth despite an expanding market.

We solved the problem by standardizing designs and slashing the number of different internal components by nearly 70%. The resulting simplicity of our operations led to a doubling of gross margin and revenue growth, which ultimately allowed me to sell the company to a division of Rolls-Royce for seven times book value. (You'll find more details on this story in Chapter 1.)

This personal experience made me aware of complexity in ways I hadn't seen previously. The lessons I learned were bolstered by later experiences with clients and by examples I saw in the marketplace that demonstrated just how big an opportunity existed that was not being exploited. For example, by applying complexity principles, a heavy-equipment manufacturer was able to cut material, labor, and overhead costs by 11% and cut development time from 36 to 14 months. Lockheed Martin's application of complexity reduction techniques to its procurement operations contributed significantly to a 50+% reduction in costs (you'll find several of their cases in Chapter 12).

Other examples abound, especially in some of the most successful companies operating today: Wal-Mart offers more than 100,000 different Stock Keeping Units (SKUs), ensuring a full variety of offerings from the customers' perspective, yet has attained a dominant cost position. Capital One has become a market leader by being able to tailor an attractive credit offering to each customer by creatively conquering the cost of complexity using information technology. Dell Computer has achieved a similar stunning success by conquering complexity in its supply chain, keeping costs low while tailoring the offering to the customers' needs.

Yet despite these and other examples of companies conquering complexity, my colleagues and I kept running into another barrier. Yes, there were success stories, featuring the intuition, judgment, and personal insight of people like Michael Dell, Herb Kelleher, Sam Walton. Each had a brilliant hunch that led to an offering with the right level of complexity at the right cost, and a value proposition that created explosive demand.

But there wasn't much more beyond these success stories. When we looked for books, papers, or other advice on conquering complexity, we were surprised at the lack of substance. Most importantly, there was no way to *quantitatively* evaluate the size of complexity profit opportunities or compare them to competing investment opportunities. (A decade ago people praised the merits of "mass customization" without any estimate of the benefits that would result.) The lack of rigor reminded me of a passage from Goethe's *Faust*:

> *That I may recognize what holds*
> *the world together in its inmost essence,*
> *behold the driving force and source of everything,*
> *and rummage no more in empty words.*
>
> —*J. W. von Goethe, Faust*[1]

Ultimately, most discussions of complexity we found did little more than "rummage in empty words." The only "technique" we could find for conquering complexity was to have smart people review some business information and hope for a brilliant hunch that would expose a complexity problem.

While I have no doubts as to the intelligence of most business people, a strategy of relying on personal insight or brilliant hunches seems at best an unpredictable method for attacking such an important strategic issue. We did find that the tools to eliminate the costs of complexity were relatively well known. But applying these tools costs time, money, and scarce resources—and there we could find no bridge from a vague "we think we have a complexity problem" to an operating plan with specifics ("In Division X, we need to attack product/service line Y with the following tools…to achieve Z amount of profit").

This led us to launch a major development effort involving our own experts and those from academia,[2] and help from our clients, to find a way to bring more rigor to the analysis of complexity. Our first fruits are reported in this book.

Our goal is clear: **to provide companies with a systematic method for eliminating the costs associated with complexity while enjoying its market benefits (through diverse offerings and customer satisfaction).** The strategic questions are:

- Where is complexity (or its lack) silently killing your business?

- How will conquering complexity give you a competitive advantage?

- What is it worth to solve the problem?

- How do you solve it?

To answer these questions, we developed approaches for identifying complexity opportunities, *quantifying* the size and impact of those opportunities, and deciding which opportunities to pursue. The core of our method is the Complexity Equation, which relates complexity to cost data (*see* Chapter 2 for details). It provides the quantitative foundation every company needs. You'll find out how to determine if shareholder value will be optimized by more or less complexity in the markets you serve, and how to calculate the benefits of conquering the cost of complexity relative to complementary initiatives such as Six Sigma (to improve quality) and/or Lean (to improve process speed). You'll find these approaches described for the first time in this book, along with both established and innovative strategies for taking action on those opportunities (described in Part III).

Structure of Conquering Complexity In Your Business

Part I lays out the case for conquering complexity. You'll find evidence of where complexity initiatives have worked and where they haven't, along with explanations of *why* and an overview of how you can start to conquer complexity in your own business.

Part II provides the rigor that's missing from most other approaches to conquering complexity. You'll find methods for calculating which of your value streams are most complex, which should be eliminated, and which can be improved with various complexity strategies.

Part III reviews strategies for identifying the complexity your customers will value and removing anything they won't.

Part IV provides examples of how to truly leverage your investments in conquering complexity through building the right cultural support infrastructure, extending the use of complexity strategies to your supply chain, and increasing the success of high-impact actions such as mergers and acquisitions.

Putting Complexity On *Your* Agenda

Companies such as Wal-Mart, Dell, Southwest Airlines, Capital One, and Toyota owe much of their success to their conquest of complexity, as you'll see later in this book. Growing numbers of prominent business leaders are seeing what they can gain from having a rigorous means of evaluating and conquering complexity:

> *"I am really intrigued with the idea of measuring the impact of complexity, and then BEING ABLE TO DO SOMETHING ABOUT IT! I have long recognized that complexity is a big*

problem, but those units with the biggest problem act like Gordian knots. It would be terrific to have a new approach to solving these problems."

– Lou Giuliano, CEO, ITT Industries

"As we tackle the most resistant issues in the company, it is clear that complexity is a key causal. For companies like Xerox who have aggressively reduced cost, the cost of complexity is the next big opportunity. The challenge is getting our arms around the cost of complexity. Being able to size the opportunity creates a compelling call to action."

– Anne Mulcahy, CEO, Xerox

"It has become apparent there is a large contributing source of the waste called complexity. While I have known this intuitively, it is critical that the study and analysis you and the George Group have done gets out to a wider audience on how this complexity occurs and more importantly, how to both attack it and prevent it."

– Chris Cool, VP, Northrop-Grumman

Unless your company grapples with both the growth opportunities and the costs of your own complexity, you will be unable to pierce the ceiling of profit and revenue growth under which you labor. Taking the time to understand complexity and developing strategies for conquering it in your own business can turn lackluster performance into dazzling success. The evidence is here before you.

Endnotes

1 In the original German: Das ich erkenne, was die Welt / Im Innersten zusammen-hält / Schau' alle Wirkenskraft und Samen / Und tu' nicht mehr in Worten Kramen. From Part I, Act I, Scene I, Lines 382-385. I am indebted to F. Reif, Professor of Physics, UC Berkeley for the translation.

2 The derivation of the Complexity Equation is straightforward and is contained in the Appendix. The full equation is derived in a patent by George, Maaseidvaag and Sherman of the George Group and Jim Patell, Professor at the Stanford Graduate School of Business.

PART I

Complexity:
The Silent Killer
of Profits and Growth

CHAPTER 1

The Overwhelming Case for Conquering Complexity

What do Southwest Airlines, Capital One, Dell Computer, Wal-Mart, ALDI International, Scania Trucks, Ford (in 1914), GM (in 1923), and Toyota (today) have in common? Each of these companies outperformed or is outperforming its competition, as reflected in their stock price. How did they do it?

In each case, they conquered complexity. The winning strategies were based on either supplying a *very low* level of complexity to the marketplace (products/services with few options or variations), or targeting customers who were willing to pay an adequate premium for *higher complexity*—and delivering that high complexity at a low cost.

These companies have firm control over how many different products or services they offer. They've avoided the uncontrolled proliferation common in their competitors. They know how to minimize complexity in their internal operations. These companies have offered the "right" level of complexity to meet customer requirements while at the same time benefiting shareholders. And they've enjoyed the benefits of this control—their lower costs and improved market position precipitated the downfall of initially more powerful competitors who failed to respond in time and quickly lost their seemingly impregnable positions.

The experience of these companies and many others prove that **portfolio and process complexity is often a larger drag on profits and growth than any other single factor in the business.** Every business has too much or too little of *something*... too many service offerings than can be reasonably sustained, too few product lines to be competitive, or too many different ways of doing the same kind of work.

The potential represented by conquering complexity—making explicit decisions about what complexity to keep and exploit, and what to get rid of—is enormous. There is a huge profit pool hidden by complexity that every company can exploit to its advantage. To prove it to you, this chapter presents some famous and not-so-famous examples of conquering complexity that did nothing less than lead to market dominance. Later chapters will then delve deeper into understanding what complexity is, where it comes from, what it costs, and what it will take to conquer it in your business.

A Tale of Two Companies

Complexity reduction reached its first milestone in the early part of the twentieth century. Henry Ford was just starting his automobile career by *failing* in two ventures targeted at building fancy cars (one of which later became Cadillac). At the time, cars were the toys of the rich—the volume leader in 1908 was the luxurious Buick. President Woodrow Wilson decried the conspicuous display as a mark of class distinction and an encouragement to the growth of Socialism. Ford saw the unfilled need for utility transportation for the masses, and the Model T was born, available in "any color you want so long as it is black."

The Model T, the ultimate in product simplicity, resulted in low cost due to vertically integrated production in stupendous volumes... and made Ford the richest man in the world. He was able to transform iron ore into an automobile in just 33 hours. Table 1.A shows Ford's financial results:

Table 1.A: Ford's Financial Results

Year	Price of Model T $	Total Revenue $ in millions	Net Income $ in millions
1908	850	4.7	1.1
1909	750	9.0	3.0
1910	680	16.7	4.1
1911	590	24.6	7.8
1912	525	42.5	13.5
1913	500	89.1	27.1
1914	440	119.4	33.0
1915	390	121.1	30.0
1916	345	206.8	57.0

By 1921, Ford had taken 65% of the low-cost market while rival GM was teetering on the brink of bankruptcy. Alfred Sloan, GM's new President, was confronted with a ragtag collection of more than 20 different car companies that had nothing in common except that they had been acquired by his predecessor.

Sloan's great insight was in realizing that he could defeat Ford's value proposition of providing low cost through zero complexity. Sloan saw that the market was changing. The demand for utility transportation, upon which the Model T was founded, was increasingly being served by the rising tide of *used* Model Ts. Many consumers had grown beyond just wanting utility transportation. They had more money, they wanted cars in different colors, cars with roofs, cars with more powerful engines, etc. And *they were willing to pay a slightly higher price* than Ford was asking for the Model T.

Sloan took action. He ordered the design of the Chevrolet Model "K."[1] He hired one of Ford's best production executives. He also *reduced* over-all complexity by eliminating 15 of GM's 20 brands; the remaining 5 brands all had distinct price/performance differences. But he also *increased* complexity to stimulate demand by introducing the "model year" concept, adding attractive new features and styling. So now there was a new value proposition: a car for every purse.

By 1925, and even though GM's cost always remained higher than Ford's, Sloan's strategy was working. He commented: "Ford's precious volume, upon which all depended, began slipping." Ford responded by cutting prices to the bone, to no avail: the fact was that even at this price, the Model T no longer provided an attractive value proposition to the customer, and by 1928 was driven from the market.[2]

The Three Rules of Complexity

The experience of Ford and GM created several rules of complexity we can still apply today and that we'll explore in the rest of this chapter:

1) Eliminate complexity that customers will not pay for

2) Exploit the complexity customers will pay for

3) Minimize the costs of the complexity you offer

Complexity Rule #1: Eliminate complexity that customers will not pay for

Most businesses today find themselves carrying more products and services (or variations on them) than their customers really want. Getting rid of that complexity not only removes a source of wasted costs, but can also lead to an enviable competitive position, as described in the following case.

Case #1: The story of Southwest Airlines vs. American Airlines

If you ask people why it is that Southwest Airlines can remain profitable in what is now a commodity industry, most will credit low labor cost or an incredible and unique culture. But there's another part to the story that is usually overlooked: Southwest recognized that their market would not pay any of the typical costs of complexity seen in the air travel business. So they designed out the complexity that customers won't pay for.

Southwest, for example, operates only Boeing 737 aircraft. American Airlines, in contrast, has historically supported a lot of internal complexity—operating as many as 14 aircraft types—to address what it thought were different markets with different needs. The resulting cost structure of these airlines is shown in Figure 1.1. The difference in results stemmed from American's older cost structure that arose from supporting 14 types of aircraft, which means 14 spares depots, 14 sets of mechanic and pilot training, 14 kinds of FAA certification, and the cost of an information factory to schedule and maintain it all... none of which is value-add to the customer.

The dynamics of the market were such that customers did not value American's differentiating features enough to pay an adequate return. As American's president & CEO, Gerard Arpey, remarked shortly after he took over, "The cost of complexity isn't offset by what you can charge."

Figure 1.1: Airline Performance (1996 – 2001)

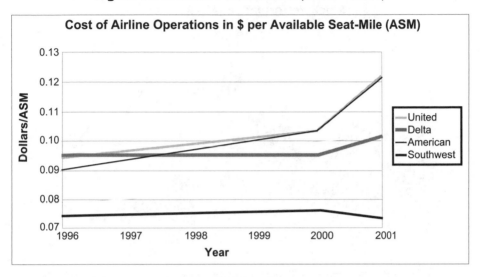

As you can see, Southwest's cost structure has always been significantly lower than those of other airlines. They even managed to lower costs at a time when costs for other airlines were skyrocketing.

In addition to the lower complexity, Southwest has a far faster and more reliable landing/take-off turnaround time and can generate profit much more quickly than American by making more revenue flights per day for each unit of equipment investment. In addition to complexity reduction, Southwest has trained their ticket agents to multi-task as baggage handlers, keeps their planes in the air 14 to16 hours per day versus the standard 12 hours, turns them around in 30 minutes, and listens carefully to the customer. Over the past five years Southwest's share price has doubled while American's has sunk near zero (*see* Figure 1.2, next page).

Southwest's low complexity has made it possible for excellent management to achieve low labor cost and enabled them to deliberately create an environment of happy employees. They've gradually expanded from their Texas niche to approach a national presence as a no-frill airline. One must never confuse cause and effect.[3]

You might think the argument is specious because American is in a very different business than Southwest. But American CEO Arpey doesn't

Figure 1.2: Southwest (LUV) vs. American Airlines (AMR) Stock Performance (1999 – 2003)

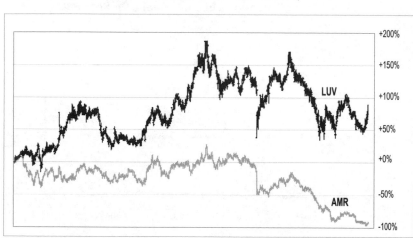

Southwest's cost advantage, provided in large part by low complexity, has contributed to strong market performance, especially compared to high-cost competitors such as American Airlines.

consider it so: "One of the reasons Southwest is so successful is because they promise something very simple and they deliver that very consistently," he said at a conference in 2004. "I think that's a better paradigm than where we've been historically and where we need to move to."

Also consider the cases of two other airlines: British Airways and Continental. British Airways CEO Rod Eddington in 2002 declared that "our whole business is too complicated." The airline was losing out to low-fare carriers, he said, because of too much complexity—complexity in pricing, in operations, in the supply chain, in IT. Continental had reached the same conclusion in the nineties and had embarked on a similar tack. Said Continental CEO Gordon Bethune[4]:

> *The point is, you'd better figure out what your customers— the customers you want—value. Because that's what they'll buy. Anything else is a waste of their money, and they'll figure that out in a hurry.*"

Continental deliberately reduced the number of aircraft types to five and got rid of several Airbus models that *could never* earn their cost of capital on Continental routes.

The message has taken root at American under Arpey's tenure. He said in February 2004, "If you look back at the history of American, there was a focus really on driving, or be willing to accept, complexity in the desire to maximize revenue. And because of that sort of focus, we evolved our network in ways that allowed a lot of complexity: multiple fleet types and multiple configurations within fleet types."[5] Not only were there 14 different fleet types, but more than 35 different configurations, tailored to different markets like Asia or Europe.

"The complexity gave us the ability to optimize revenue within unique markets," he said. "But we believe the world fundamentally in this business has changed and we have to move more in the other direction: which is to move away from complexity, drive towards simplicity, to drive efficiency, because we can no longer get the revenue benefits for that complexity to justify the cost." American has reduced its fleet types from 14 to 6 and is focused on standardizing the configurations with a focus on profitability rather than on revenue.

Complexity Rule #2: Exploit the complexity customers will pay for

"I have this simple law of economic redemption—and it suggests that if you do something that's valuable, you should be able to make a profit," said Michael Dell at a conference in 2003. "And there are not a lot of companies in our business that do anything that's valuable."[6]

One key message of this book is that *conquering* complexity does not always mean eliminating it. In some cases, businesses can get a market edge by *adding* complexity, as Capital One discovered.

Case #2: Capital One vs. MBNA, Bank of America, et al.

The dynamics of some markets may reward the creation of a highly complex offering *if it can be delivered at a cost that provides an attractive value proposition.* Capital One's early success is one such example. Capital One noticed that most credit cards were issued at zero complexity: a single offering at an interest rate of 19.8% regardless of the creditworthiness of the customer. Competitors acted like the market only needed one product to fit all risk profiles! Thus customers with good credit profiles paid a high rate (that supported deadbeats), and generated a handsome return to the banks. This cost of deadbeats was borne by good customers—was "non-value-added" in their view—which created a market opportunity for a differentiated and highly attractive offering.

By building up private databases of credit information and developing proprietary algorithms, Capital One was able to tailor significantly lower rates for lower-risk cardholders, and to deny credit to higher-risk applicants. How could they afford *adding* complexity, offering *more* options than competitors at a lower price? Their investment in technology: by the third ring of a customer phone call, the computer recognizes the customer's telephone number, identifies the most likely reason for calling, routes the call to the appropriate associate, and then populates the associate's computer screen with products and services that the caller may be interested in purchasing.

In this case, the cost of complexity was low due to a smart investment in information technology, product design, and testing. So Capital One could provide a highly desirable offering, which afforded them a 40% compound growth rate per year with the highest ROE and lowest charge-off rate in the industry. Their stock price grew three times more than the industry average over a five-year period (*see* Figure 1.3, next page).

The single offering of 19.8% interest rate, offered by most financial companies, supported large non-value-add costs from the customer's perspective and opened up a complexity-driven profit opportunity. As Capital One lured away the most profitable customers (high recurring balances and very low default risk) and built up a successful business, competitors not only lost share but were left with an increased proportion of economically unprofitable customers.

The incumbents scrambled to make up for the economically attractive customers lost to Capital One's strategy. Some competitors raised prices on their remaining customers, falling into a "death spiral."[7] By raising

Figure 1.3: Capital One's Share Price vs. Competition (1995 – 2002)

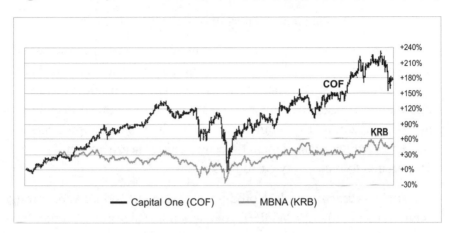

The comparison of Capital One's share price versus that of MBNA illustrates the benefits of targeted increases in complexity (the right rate for the right customer) done at low cost. MBNA, a very well-run organization, suffers by comparison. The takeaway: to reach breakthrough profit and growth levels requires more than being operationally excellent.

prices, they effectively ordained a whole new set of customers as economically attractive to Capital One, who could then come in with a profitable rate that was nonetheless attractive to the customer relative to what competitors were offering. Eventually, Capital One's competitors counterattacked, but it took them nearly five years to respond.

Complexity Rule #3: Minimize the costs of the complexity you offer

Whether you're getting rid of complexity or adding it, you have to make sure whatever complexity you keep is provided at the lowest possible cost. This mandate requires a rigorous analysis of every element of your service or product: Does it add value that the customer will pay for? Is the value worth the cost? There are a lot of approaches for delivering complexity efficiently; specifics are covered in Part III of this book. But we can see the principles in operation through Toyota's impressive achievements in the past few decades.

Case #3: The real secret of Toyota

Creating a new model of complexity at low cost

A major advance in complexity achievements was made by Toyota in the 1960s when they created a system to simultaneously achieve Ford's high process velocity (which yields low cost) with Sloan's product complexity and market appeal. Toyota used a complexity reduction strategy known as standardization to eliminate waste in their *internal* products and processes, which enabled them to easily produce nearly one million vehicle variants to meet every customer's needs.

This process reached back to product development and forward through manufacturing to sales. While Toyota uses internal standardization techniques to minimize complexity, it retains a culture of deep functional expertise and excellence in design through its organizational structure. It has never eliminated complexity at the expense of the customer's desire for quality and variety. And in fact, of 200,000 total monthly units of production, approximately 40,000 variants are actually produced at or near the lowest cost in the world. Yet despite this complexity (which is valued by customers), the internal complexity and cost of Toyota is far less than Ford or GM. Ford is now taking action:

> [Ford's] new emphasis is on sharing parts, systems and engineering across all the vehicles teams. This should reduce the number of platforms that Ford uses to 12 by 2010 from the current 18. Some Ford executives say the company was too proud to learn from what many regarded as a second-tier auto maker [Toyota].
>
> —*Wall Street Journal, April 16, 2003*

There is another aspect to Toyota's standardization. They currently build their complete variety of cars and trucks (Toyota and Lexus) on just 13 platforms—foundational designs that can easily be customized to specific products. Each platform in turn derives its subassemblies and parts from a book of standardized designs, each of which is used across many platforms. With more sharing of parts and assemblies, any quality problems solved or lessons learned in any one area are likely applicable to many other areas—accelerating the information flow *between*

Low Cost AND Differentiated? How Wal-Mart and Toyota destroy the Porter Paradigm

Michael Porter, author of *Competitive Strategy* (1980),defined two principles for strategic advantage: 1. Overall cost leadership **or** 2. differentiation.[8] Moreover, he argued, the hesitation to commit to **just one** of these strategies leaves companies in danger of being "stuck in the middle." Such a firm would lose the high-volume customers who demand low prices and would lose high-margin customers who demand unique features and service.

But many companies that have conquered complexity have destroyed the constraint of this paradigm. How is this possible?

The implicit assumptions in Porter's theory are **1) that differentiation is expensive** and **2) that customers function in a very black-and-white way**, seeking either the lowest cost or the most features, instead of making purchases on a sliding scale, a spectrum of choices with different balances of price vs. features.

The first assumption is theoretically true—imagine two processes with 100% efficiency; the first produces the basic version, the second produces the premium version with more features and therefore more cost. But that belies the fact that **differentiation is more expensive for some companies than for others.** For example, Toyota can deliver more customer value-add features than Ford or General Motors and still produce at lower cost. Scania Trucks has achieved the same phenomenon in competition with Mercedes-Benz. High levels of differentiation can be delivered at low cost by conquering complexity! The Porter model labors under the artificial constraint that the cost of complexity inherently cannot be conquered. But complexity is not necessarily high in cost.

The second assumption has also unraveled over time. We no longer have to make the "lowest cost vs. most features" choice.

So what is the right approach for today's market? We would add a twist to Porter, borne out by our analysis. Companies should seek:

1. Cost advantage relative to peers in markets where they can generate value, **and**

2. Optimized differentiation, optimizing the level of features and services to maximize value

platforms, something that rarely happens in other organizations. Toyota's lower cost basis provides a share price bonanza during good times and protection during down markets. Over the last four years Toyota shares have held steady whereas Ford lost 75%, and GM lost 50% of value.

At the other end of the volume spectrum is Scania Trucks of Sweden. They have the same truck lineup as Mercedes-Benz, but with fewer than half the part numbers. Their internal design processes ensure that use of common parts is driven through engineering. European-based Scania dominates sales in countries as far flung as Brazil. They have achieved an unrivaled world record of 34 years of continuously profitable operations.

Case #4: Experience bought, not taught

As mentioned in the preface, coauthor Mike George was the CEO of International Power Machines (IPM), a company he founded. IPM designed and produced uninterruptible power supplies that protect critical computers and instrumentation from AC power failures. The IPM systems protected computers of the NYSE, Depository Trust, Merrill-Lynch, to name but a few applications.

IPM began with just one product offering, a 5 kw unit. Then, like most companies, they fell prey to exploding market demand and started developing additional power units (eventually up to 300 kw) to satisfy customer needs. Over the years, this drive to grow power ratings resulted in over a dozen different products built on seven separate mechanical designs and scores of electrical designs in just the 10 kw to 80 kw range, with few fabricated or purchased parts in common.

At that point, the products in that power range generated a gross profit margin (GPM) of 15%, which resulted in breakeven performance at best. In desperation, Mike went to the public library and read, among other things, about Toyota's drive to make many different final products out of a small number of common subassemblies. Toyota also applied what are now called Lean and Six Sigma process improvements to achieve high velocity and high quality. The cost benefits and revenue growth reported were amazing. But he also read of the disaster caused by the low complexity that led to the "lookalike" cars that GM was producing.

Clearly the best approach to IPM's problem was to standardize internal processes and simplify its designs but still satisfy a variety of customer needs at low cost and high velocity. Thus any "transparent" component or subassembly (one that customers wouldn't notice) across the 10 kw to 80 kw range was a candidate for design simplification.

IPM examined the variation in electrical design and found that 98% of the wiring could in fact be across all products. Ultimately, they combined all mechanical and electrical designs into a single platform used initially for all power ratings from 10 kw to 80 kw, and eventually up to 200 kw. All custom items were relegated to a secondary wiring list.

What had been a nightmare of hundreds of products became more manageable with more than 75% of components in common on average. By making the designs less complex, they eliminated a lot of internal costs and time. Because the same parts were used so often, they virtually eliminated what manufacturers call "setup times" (delays caused by having to switch production lines from one configuration to another).

Figure 1.4: IPM's Results

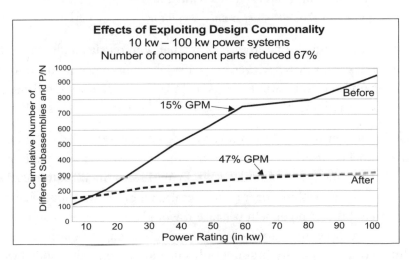

The upper line represents IPM's original complexity, with rapid growth in part numbers (at first, there were virtually no parts common to different power ratings). The lower line shows the slow growth of part numbers after design simplification. With more than 75% of all parts now common to multiple designs, IPM could add new products without dramatically increasing the number of parts.

GPM for the lower power ratings went from 15% to 47% (overall company GPM rose from 18% to 37%, as shown in Table 1.B). Return on Invested Capital (ROIC) went from a *negative 6%* to *plus 33%*, and IPM was subsequently sold to a division of Rolls-Royce for 7.2 times book value.

Table 1.B: Corporate-wide Impact of Complexity Reduction at IPM*

Year	1	2	3	4
Gross Profit	18%	25%	31%	37%
Operating Profit	-3%	6%	17%	20%

(* as % of revenue; ref. SEC Registration 2-68861).

Most of the cost reduction was reflected in managerial accounting as lower overhead costs (which is where most non-value-add cost is hidden). Other firms have arrived at the same conclusion[9]:

> *Part proliferation is expensive. A Tektronix study determined that half of all overhead costs related in some way to the number of different part numbers handled.*

For IPM, of equal importance was that complexity reduction also reduced test time, lowered warranty cost, and eliminated a host of other costs that provided no value to customers. These gains were reflected in a revenue growth rate of 20% per year for five years.

Here's a lesson from IPM that's critical to companies today: IPM could have knocked itself out for years trying one improvement tactic after another—fixing quality problems, applying Lean principles to speed up the process, everything people are being taught about "improvement" today—to little or no benefit because it would still have been stuck with all the complexity imposed by having seven different designs. **Eliminating complexity first** not only cut a lot of non-value-added work immediately, it also allowed IPM to focus all their subsequent Lean and quality improvement efforts on the (far fewer) remaining processes.

Getting the big gains from complexity reduction

When a former United Technologies Automotive division began deliberately reducing complexity they discovered an interesting pattern in their cost reductions, as shown in Figure 1.5.

Figure 1.5: Pushing for Big Gains from Complexity Reduction

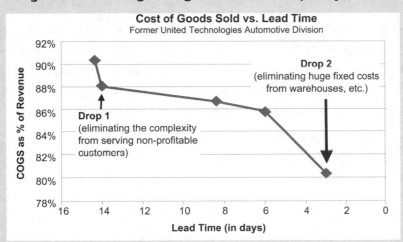

Drop 1 occurred when they decided to stop making products for several customers—i.e., they reduced complexity in the product line by eliminating products that could not generate positive Economic Profit because of the cost of doing business with those customers. Subsequently, they could focus their process improvement efforts on fewer products, and were able to complete numerous projects built around specific Lean, Six Sigma, and internal complexity targets. That led to substantial reductions in lead time (their processes got faster and faster).

Drop 2, which occurred when lead time approached 3 days, may be more surprising. This drop occurred when the company could finally remove **fixed** costs that were non-value-added. For example, how much does it cost to operate a half-full warehouse? The same as it does a full warehouse! But a warehouse that has ceased to exist costs nothing. In this case, the company could eliminate a warehouse and a satellite facility only after they achieved a 3-day lead time—which illustrates the ripple effect that eliminating complexity can have on your bottom line.

Finding the Right Combination of External and Internal Complexity

The Toyota and Scania cases showed that reduction of internal complexity through design simplification ("commonization") can allow the low-cost production of highly complex and desirable offerings from the customer's perspective. Here are more examples of this strategy:

Wal-Mart, like Capital One, delivers complexity at very low cost, offering more than 100,000 Stock Keeping Units (SKUs) that cover everything from groceries and apparel to jewelry, pharmaceuticals, and beauty aids. Their challenge: How to deliver all this complexity at a low cost that can be passed along to consumers to win dominant market share?

Part of the answer is that they can purchase in huge volumes that drive very low costs from their suppliers. But this is again an effect not a cause. The essence of Wal-Mart is the internal application of commonization, much like Toyota, on an even grander scale. *Every* grocery distribution center is a *carbon copy* of every other one, whether it handles perishable or dry goods. The design of distribution centers is controlled out of Bentonville, Arkansas. (In complexity terms, they are applying standardization in areas that are completely transparent to the customer.)

By making all processes and software standard, Wal-Mart has been able to scale up the number of distribution centers from 10 to 28 in under four years (from 1999 to March 2003). Standardization makes the training and systems very supportable, dependable, and provides a level of redundancy and reliability. Standardization is the engine that has allowed Wal-Mart to continue to reduce lead times and grow inventories at half the rate of sales growth.

"Stovepipe" or "rogue" systems unique to a region are not tolerated. The drive to standardization will one day make *all* distribution centers carbon copies of one another, whether they supply groceries or tires, with standard modules to address the variation in application. Thus the standardization effort can be expected to yield continuing gains.

As another example, Lockheed Martin consolidated various procurement operations into one location that served 14 different divisions. The task of each commodity buyer in the centralized group was very complex because he or she had to deal with numerous legacy computer systems, part-numbering systems, purchasing procedures, etc.

Reducing the complexity of the offering itself was not an option—Lockheed Martin wasn't about to stop producing any of its current products and thought that trying to force engineers to use standard parts across all of its operations would be too huge a task to tackle at the time. But they were able to standardize the purchasing process *without* requiring the divisions to reduce complexity. The result was that the total cost of the procurement operation was reduced by 50% and factory productivity increased 20% due to fewer shortages. (More details on this case are in Chapter 12.)

In the 1980s Compaq seized the commanding heights of personal computer (PC) sales from a slow-to-react IBM, and appeared impregnable. Compaq focused on advancing technology and led the industry in innovation. Dell Computer recognized that the exploding number of features and increasing customization of PC configurations had created an added layer of internal manufacturing cost and downstream distribution cost and dealer markups. Compaq's supply chain included significant non-value-add costs as perceived by customers. Dealers effectively compensated for the manufacturer's complexity and lead time delay by keeping ever-increasing inventories of PCs in burgeoning and theoretically infinite variety. These layers of internal and external non-value-add cost could be stripped away if Dell could produce what customers wanted when they wanted it... in less than a week.

So Dell reduced internal complexity and improved flexibility such that it could produce any model with any feature in less than 3 days. Dell applied web and telephone sales to replace the dealer's cost in their entirety, which, with internal complexity reduction, allowed their total cost to approach *half* that of their competitors. A portion of the savings on the whole infrastructure of internal and external cost was passed on to the consumer, delivering more value per dollar. Dell has continued to grow faster than any of the markets which it serves, increasing the breadth and complexity of its offering while simultaneously increasing flexibility and process speed to prevent the layer of cost borne by its competitors.

The emphasis on internal complexity reduction, flexibility, and speed enabled Dell to quickly counter Compaq innovations. In essence, they overwhelmed Compaq with their decisive cost advantage and speed, proving that it is often better to be fast than first.

But that's not the end of the story. Dell carefully watched the varieties of PCs actually being purchased, and found that a few models generated 80% of sales. By training marketing staff to guide customers from a pure custom configuration to one of these high-volume models, they increased that volume from 80% to 95%. Thus they enjoy the reputation for "what you want when you want it" together with the benefits of high volume. Compaq did not respond in time, and lost the race in sales, in shareholder value, and ultimately in independence. (There's more to the Dell story, as you'll find out in Chapter 3.)

The Complexity Value Proposition

If you look at stock performance graphs throughout this chapter and compare the share performance of companies that conquered complexity versus those who did not, you will see the increase in operating profit and ROIC resulted in share price growth *three to five times* that of competitors (at least of those who survived). More importantly, conquering complexity was a breakthrough strategy that built great companies of global significance as well as little jewels like IPM and Scania.

Customers who have unique demands for which they will pay a *value creating* price are far more loyal than customers who simply buy commodities at the lowest price. When serving demanding customers, companies with a low cost of complexity such as Dell, Toyota, and Capital One will aggressively *increase* complexity in response to the Voice of the Customer.

> *Producers of undifferentiated products in capital intensive industries must earn inadequate returns except under conditions of tight supply or real shortage. As long as excess capacity exists, prices tend to reflect operating costs rather than capital employed.*

> —*Berkshire Hathaway Annual Report, 1978*

... a product that cannot be differentiated in any meaningful way. In such an environment, only a very low cost operator or someone operating in a niche can sustain high levels of profitability.

—*Berkshire Hathaway Annual Report, 1987*

A differentiation strategy is not limited to consumer products and services. It applies to everything from high tech companies (Intel and Microsoft), to aerospace companies (Lockheed Martin), to financial companies (Capital One, Charles Schwab) and beyond. Less-nimble competitors are forced into high volume "plain vanilla" commodity products where customers are loyal only to the lowest price and yield low ROIC and hence low shareholder value.

There is room for *one* very low-cost operator (Southwest Airlines, Henry Ford, etc.) in a market; undifferentiated competitors with higher cost will be destroyed. But there is room in each market for businesses that offer customer-driven complexity with a favorable value proposition.

Conclusion: The competitive advantage of conquering complexity

The stories above illustrate the importance of understanding the difference between two kinds of complexity:

- **Deliberate complexity**: There probably isn't any market in which customer power has not grown significantly in the last 20 years. The internet now provides customers with more information and buying choices. Speed and intensity of global competition have increased, resulting in a more intense focus on delivering unique products and services to capture specific customer segments. The result? Companies make deliberate decisions to increase complexity, to expand their product and service lines, to constantly modify and redesign existing products/services. The net impact is more and more product/service variations chasing limited dollars, which are growing more slowly than the rate of proliferation. Many companies are now choked by the complexity they offer to customers.

- **Unmanaged proliferation**: Much of the complexity in businesses is unintentional. New products or services are often designed without consideration for what already exists; new activities are added to processes without thought to whether existing activities could be used or adapted; acquisitions are integrated with no thought to the resulting cost of complexity. Many new products are introduced without a business case that shows that revenue will support the true "complexity adjusted" cost of the new product. This kind of complexity isn't the fault of any individual. It's simply that no one has understood how incremental decisions made in isolation can result in very high complexity-related costs over time. And in general, no system exists for high-level managers or executives to coordinate design and implementation decisions to *minimize* complexity.

Conquering complexity means taking control over both of these sources. We need to...

1) Understand that complexity is neither good nor bad when evaluated in isolation. It can be labeled only when compared to customer needs and the value it adds to your business through Economic Profit.

2) Know how to diagnose the complexity in a business:
   - Identify which complexity creates value and which destroys value
   - Quantify the costs this complexity imposes on your business
   - Expose the underlying cause of the complexity (is it market driven? customer driven? product/service design driven? process driven?)

3) Develop rational strategies for building onto value-added complexity (minimizing the costs associated with complexity that customers will pay a premium for) and eliminating or minimizing non-value-add complexity.

4) Know how to evaluate whether potential new products/services will be worth the complexity they'll introduce into systems.

A few standout firms have made valiant attempts to catch up with the complexity success companies. GM has tried the hardest to catch up with Toyota. They formed a joint venture with Toyota (NUMMI in California) to learn their process, created Saturn in its model, etc. GM has in consequence outperformed Ford and Daimler-Chrysler, *but still significantly lags behind Toyota.*[10] Why? Because while competitors will copy your products, your physical and IT investments, they virtually *never copy your intellectual capital or process.* And why is this? Because true intellectual capital that is woven into your business processes and instilled within your people becomes a culture that is nearly impossible to copy.

At a minimum, conquering complexity will provide your company with significant cost advantages over your competitors as you tap into the hidden profit pool. And it may do more. Learning how to exploit external complexity—the kind that customers see—can help you achieve a market dominance that your competitors are unlikely to copy. The winners and losers in the next decades may well be separated by a single factor: those that conquer complexity and those that do not.

Endnotes

1 Alfred Sloan, *My Years with General Motors* (New York: Doubleday, 1990).

2 *Ibid.*

3 I can't resist telling the story of the English journalist who was sent to America in 1906 to write about the success of Andrew Carnegie (who had by this time sold out to J.P. Morgan) The journalist wrote back to London: "You'll never believe the money that's to be made from Libraries!" Definitely libraries were an effect of his wealth, not a cause.

4 Gordon Bethune, *From Worst to First: Behind the Scenes of Continental's Remarkable Comeback*, with Scott Huler (New York: John Wiley and Sons, 1998), 67-68.

5 Goldman Sachs *19th Annual Transportation Conference*, February 5, 2004.

6 Michael Dell, proceedings from *The Future in Review* conference, San Diego, CA, May 20, 2003).

7 Eric Clemons and Matt Thatcher, "Capital One: Exploiting an Information-based Strategy in Newly Vulnerable Markets" (proceedings of the *31st Hawaii International Conference on System Sciences* (HICSS '98), IEEE Computer Society, 1998).

8 The 3rd often cited, Focus, is simply referring to segment targeting, but employing the same two competitive strategies.

9 David M. Anderson, *Build to Order and Mass Customization: The Ultimate Supply Chain Management and Lean Manufacturing Strategy for Low-Cost On-Demand Production Without Forecasts or Inventory* (Cambria, CA: CIM Press, 2002), p. 114.

10 But GM has imperfectly applied these principles. This is proven by what we will see in Chapter 2 is a key metric: their inventory turns still lag far behind Toyota.

CHAPTER 2

Exposing the Silent Killer

How (and how much) complexity drains time and resources in your business

If your company takes too long to deliver products and services, your customers will tell you. If your quality is poor, you will receive instant and often threatening feedback from customers. These are "loud" problems that get noticed and dealt with.

Complexity, in contrast, is a silent killer like high blood pressure: a patient with the condition can feel fine for months or years before even moderate symptoms like shortness of breath and tired performance appear. Often it takes a potentially fatal event such as a heart attack, stroke, or kidney failure to signal the severity of the condition. By then it is often too late.

So it is with complexity. If high complexity means that products and services do not generate positive Economic Profit, you receive no outside signal that will cause prompt corrective action. If complexity is destroying profits and revenue growth, it won't show up in managerial accounting and is hidden from GAAP accounting. The demands of the market will actually push you even further down the path of complexity proliferation—and all you may exhibit is a "shortness of profit" and "tired stock prices."

The arrival of a competitor who has conquered the cost and resource drain of complexity can jeopardize your company's very existence. Their arrival may signal management that a catastrophe has occurred. By then it may be too late.

The best remedy for silent killers like high blood pressure and complexity is prevention. The next best is early diagnosis—before irreversible damage is done—and a regimen to reverse the problem and prevent catastrophe.

There are tools for eliminating complexity once it is recognized that are already in wide use (*see* Part III), but few methods for prevention or early diagnosis. To identify and understand the complexity in our organizations, we need to take a tip from Lord Kelvin:

> *When you can measure what you are speaking about, and express it in numbers, you know something about it, but when you cannot measure it, when you cannot express it in numbers, our knowledge is of a meagre and unsatisfactory kind.*

As mentioned in the preface, the problem with complexity reduction strategies such as "mass customization" was that they offered no quantitative means of computing the benefits of reducing complexity. In the absence of numbers, our "knowledge is of a meager and unsatisfactory kind." The tools necessary to quantify the impact of complexity are introduced in this chapter.

How Complexity Silently Kills Profits and Drains Resources

Suppose that your business starts out like Ford in 1914 when it was producing only black Model Ts: offering just one product or service to customers, with each employee performing only one task. Employees have to learn about only one set of components or one set of service instructions. There's no reason to expedite one order ahead of another because each product or service is exactly the same as the one before it and the one after it.

Now, in response to some new marketing data, you decide to add a second offering. And you find that going from 1 to 2 offerings has a dramatic impact. You now have...

- **Setup (or "changeover") time**: Even if the new product/service (let's call it "Y") is just a variant on the original offering ("X"), staff will have a **learning curve** because workers will have to deal with two sets of instructions, and switch between the two at the drop of a hat. The more different Y is from the original X, the greater the loss of productivity. If the switch requires a changeover of equipment, materials, computer programs, etc., there may be a period of zero output. In manufacturing, learning curve effects and changeover delays are all called **setup time** (service functions have similar delays but no one calls them setup time—they're usually just accepted as part of the process required to deliver multiple services).

- **Delays:** Once any process has to handle more than one type of product or service, the natural tendency is for people to perform the work **based on convenience not customer demand**. For instance, say that the changeover from service X to service Y takes a long time. What we would all do is produce a lot of Y before going back to X so we didn't have to do that setup very often. (*Lean Six Sigma for Service* gives an example of this situation at the Lockheed Martin MAC-MAR procurement center. *See* Chapter 2, p. 42). If we're working on Y, that means orders for X are sitting around waiting to be worked on.

- **Inventory:** If you have delays, you also have **inventory**, which in manufacturing appears as piles of physical components, parts, assemblies, or materials, and in service functions shows up as filled in-boxes and email overload. You'll need physical or virtual space to store the inventory. (Of course, you could add a separate production line or work group to deal with offering Y, but then you'd have the extra cost of people, materials, equipment, etc.)

- **Demand for scheduling capability:** Unless you have a Pull system, where the process is paced to "pull" work along at the type and rate demanded by customers (*see Lean Six Sigma for Service,* Chapter 2, p. 31), you need to develop more complex scheduling systems that will tell an operator how much of X to produce, how much of Y to produce, how much extra product to put in stock, how much to send on, where to send it, etc.

- **Greater opportunity for errors or defects:** While it's unlikely that people would make many errors with just two offerings, it's *more* likely than it was with just one offering. The chances of making errors increases rapidly as the number of different tasks increases.

- **Various collateral impacts:** You'll have to create and update all your marketing media (print, website, packaging, etc.), work instructions, test procedures, field service training, warranty procedures, and customer satisfaction procedures.

… And the list goes on. In short, adding even a single additional offering adds **time and non-value-add cost** to your delivery systems, which are likely operating at low efficiencies already! You have to invest in systems. You have to train staff. You may need to add staff. If an order for product or service Y comes in while everyone is involved in X, you need to be able to expedite the new order or run the risk of alienating customers who have to wait. None of these costs adds a form, feature, or function of value to the customer. (If the additional gross profit generated by the new offering more than offsets the non-value-add cost created by complexity, well and good. But as we will see in Chapter 4, cost accounting procedures need to be modified to correctly estimate these costs.)

Extrapolating this impact to the real world where you need to manage dozens, hundreds, or even thousands of products, services, features, options. etc., and you can begin to appreciate the ubiquitous costs that complexity imposes on a business. Each additional feature, each new service option, each component or new set of instructions adds more "stuff" that your company has to deal with and manage. In manufacturing it leads to complex and expensive tracking systems and a hidden factory that diverts energy away from process improvement and productive functions. The net impact is that the unit costs for multi-line items can be 25% to 45% higher than the theoretical cost of producing only the most popular item of the family.[1] This doesn't mean you should never add complexity to your business, it just means you should know if customers are paying enough to earn more than your cost of capital.

Conq

Process Cycle Efficiency: The f dation for quantifying comple

The discussion in the previous section demonstrated that complexity has its most direct effect at the micro-level—at the point where an extra product or service, an extra feature or option causes delays in delivering value-added work. **And it's the accumulation of all these small disturbances that causes some products or services to destroy value.**

So how do we quantify these "disturbances" caused by complexity? Start by imagining a perfect process in which 100% of the time is spent on value-added work—no time is wasted on rework, delays, errors, etc. In real life, we know that no process is 100% efficient; some of the process time will be "wasted" from our customers' viewpoint. The metric used to gauge how well a process works is called **Process Cycle Efficiency** (PCE), which gives you a ratio or percent of value-add time compared to the total process time (called **lead time**), as shown in Equation 2.1:

Equation 2.1: Basic PCE Equation

$$\text{Process Cycle Efficiency} = \frac{\text{Value-add Time}}{\text{Total Lead Time}}$$

Math disclaimer

One of the main reasons we wrote this book was to get people excited about the ability to go beyond mere arm waving to put actual numbers on the impact that complexity has on their businesses. Naturally, that's going to involve some equations and math. The remainder of this chapter explores the structure of and factors in several key equations. In Part II, we'll revisit these equations and show examples of the calculations. (You can find detailed derivations in the Appendix.) If math is not your strong point, don't worry. In practice, the equations we use can be programmed into spreadsheets so you don't have to perform the calculations manually. However, because the output of equations will be used as the basis for strategic decisions, it's important that you have at least some appreciation for the factors built into the equations so you'll understand what the numbers mean.

Data from hosts of companies in every business sector show that most processes have PCEs of less than 10%, indicating that they contain a lot of waste. Think about all the non-value-added time spent in most processes—rework, supervision, scheduling, information technology, setup time, downtime, tracking down information to complete an order—and the low PCEs should come as no surprise. In fact, administrative and engineering processes are even worse, typically having a PCE of less than 5% (meaning people put in only 5 hours of value-add time for every 100 hours of process time). A world-class PCE level for service processes is 20%. Manufacturing processes range from PCEs of 1% for machining to 10% for assembly, versus world-class levels of 10% and 30% respectively.

An example of PCE in action

Consider the Hose and Fittings Division of United Technologies Automotive (introduced in Chapter 1, see p. 17). It originally produced coupled hose fitting products for GM, Ford, Chrysler, Toyota, and International Truck. The company was generating an 11% Gross Profit Margin, and barely earned their cost of capital. The average product had less than 4 hours of value-add-time and a total lead time of about 12 to 14 days, which equates to a 4% PCE.

The first thing this division did was eliminate some product offerings that were destroying value. Then they focused their improvement efforts on the remaining systems and drove the lead time down to 3 days, resulting in a PCE near 17% and a doubling of gross profit margin. (*See* Figure 2.1, next page.)

Largely as a consequence of removing complexity and then implementing Lean, work started moving directly from value-add activity to value-add activity (think Model T efficient production). The gains in PCE reflected diverse improvements:

- The cost of the scheduling process was cut by more than 50%
- Scrap and rework costs fell from 2% of revenue to near zero
- Faster lead time led to revenue growth of 30% per year by outperforming competition in supplying desired variety

Figure 2.1: Relationship of PCE and Gross Profit Margin

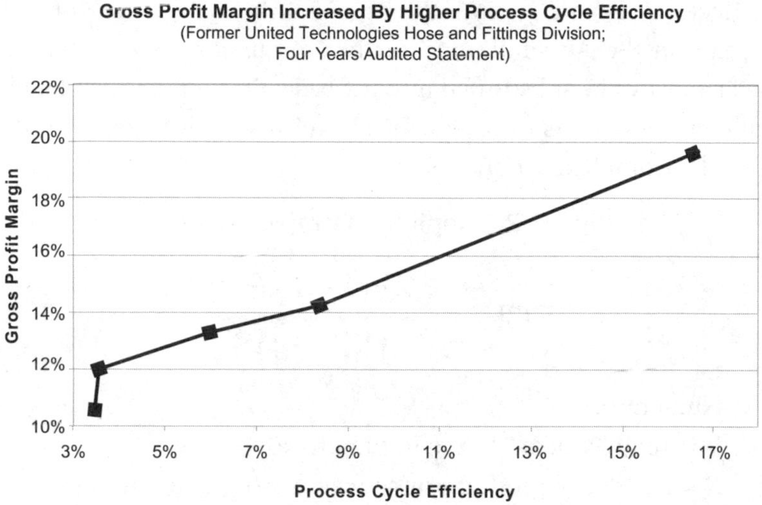

Gross Profit Margin Increased By Higher Process Cycle Efficiency
(Former United Technologies Hose and Fittings Division;
Four Years Audited Statement)

Process Cycle Efficiency

This data from United Technologies shows how Gross Profit Margin increased as PCE increased. It should be noted that this graph shows only a small portion of the PCE curve (from 3% to 17%). It will flatten out as the amount of non-value-add cost that can be affected is exhausted (i.e., the curve is linear only over the small range of values shown).[2]

- Direct labor and manufacturing overhead cost, originally at 24% of revenue, dropped to about 18% (in consequence, the cost of goods sold fell by about 8%)

As you can see, **PCE serves as a good indicator of overall process health.** As noted in Chapter 1, the company was eventually able to close a satellite manufacturing facility and finished goods warehouse when lead time approached 3 days.

Quantifying What Affects PCE: The Complexity Equation

PCE is a very useful metric because it is affected by nearly everything, good or bad, that can happen to a process—adding or taking away workload, increases or decreases in quality problems, long setup times that cause delays (or removal of them), and so on. For that reason, it becomes a critical metric when tracking the effects of complexity.

The key to quantifying complexity is to dissect PCE into all of the factors that affect it. We won't go into the details of the math here (you'll find a derivation in the Appendix and further discussion in Chapter 8), but these factors can be substituted into the basic PCE equation to let us link specific process effects to complexity. Here's a simplified version of what we call the Complexity Equation[3]:

Equation 2.2: Simplified Complexity Equation

$$PCE = \frac{2V(1-X-PD)}{N(2A+1)S}$$

Numerator

V = Total value-add time in the process

X = Percent of products or services with quality defects

P = Processing time per unit

D = Total demand of products and services

> Note: often times, processing (P) is the only or at least the primary value-add time. That means, as a proxy, you can simply multiply processing time by the number of activities to estimate V (so V = AP).

Denominator

N = Number of different tasks performed at an activity

A = Number of activities or steps in the process

S = Longest setup time in the process

The Complexity Equation shows the key factors that influence Process Cycle Efficiency. Notice that it includes factors that are influenced by **quality** (percent defective), **speed** (setup time and processing time), **customers** (demand), and both process and offering **complexity** (number of activities and number of tasks).

We call it simplified because this version assumes that all products and offerings have the same demand, the same processing time per unit, the same setup time, etc. The actual equation and associated analysis we use in practice (and which appears in the Appendix) allows us to account for unique demand, different processing times, etc.—and variation in demand—for different offerings.

For those of you who aren't used to working with equations, we'd like to point out the factors in the lower portion of the equation (the denominator):

N the number of different tasks, which is a function of the variety in product/service types and options

A the number of activities in the process

S setup time

Because they're in the denominator, these factors all have a powerful *inverse* relationship to PCE: If they increase, PCE goes down (along with profit!). If they decrease, PCE goes up (along with profit!). In other words, doubling N (through uncontrolled product proliferation, for instance) will cut PCE in half. Or alternatively, cutting N in half (through complexity reduction) will let you double PCE. When IPM, the power supply company, reduced the internal complexity of the product by a factor of 6, PCE *increased* by a factor of 6! The same type of relationship is true of the other denominator factors.

United Technologies data applied to the Complexity Equation

As you can tell from the examples in Chapter 1 and this chapter, removing the costs imposed by complexity represents a huge profit pool that is generally hidden from view. There are a number of ways to quantify this profit pool, one of which is to use the Complexity Equation and PCE. Here's an example drawn from United Technologies, the automotive supply company, that was able to make the following gains:

* The number of parts (N) was reduced by 10%

* Quality defects (X%) went from 10% to near zero

* Number of activities (A) dropped by 20%

* Setup times (S) reduced by 50%

The company operated at 71% of theoretical capacity (determined by multiplying process time by demand, P*D = 0.71).

Plugging these numbers into the equation we find that the PCE has been increased by a factor of 5 (from about 3.4% to 17%):

$$\text{PCE Improvement} = \frac{\text{PCE}_{After}}{\text{PCE}_{Before}} = \frac{\dfrac{2V(1-0-0.71)}{(0.6N)[(2*0.8A)+1](.5S)}}{\dfrac{2V(1-0.1-0.71)}{(N)(2A+1)(S)}} \approx 5$$

The result was an increase in Gross Profit Margin from 11% to 19%, from mediocre to stellar performance as a Tier II supplier.

The 7 Deadly Sins of Complexity

Complexity plays a dominant role in PCE through its 7 Deadly Sins. Complexity increases...

1. Number of different offerings (N)

2. Number of tasks in the process (A)

3. Opportunity for errors (X%)

4. Variation in processing time (not shown explicitly in the equation, but it has a systemic effect)

5. Setup time (S) in several ways: first, the reason we have to change over from one offering to another is because of having multiple offerings (complexity); second, the complexity of the process may induce long setup times

6. Processing time (P)

7. Variability in demand (D)

How Variation in Mix Destroys PCE and Profit

As we noted above, we used a simplified Complexity Equation here to illustrate the basic elements. But this version assumes that demand for different offerings is constant. In practice, we know that some offerings will have high-volume demand and others low-volume demand. Because they tend to go from "nothing" to "something," low-volume offerings also tend to have a wider variation in demand relative to high-volume offerings.

To illustrate the impact that variation in demand can have, we've created and graphed a simulation that begins with three high-volume offerings, then adds increasing numbers of low-demand offerings (*see* Figure 2.2). For our purposes, we assume that each low-volume offering accounts for

Figure 2.2: The Impact of Low-volume Offerings

PCE for *all* offerings plummets as more low-volume offerings are added, an effect exacerbated by increased variation in demand. Here, we assumed that each of the high-volume offerings has about a 25% variation in demand above and below the average. Experience shows that low-volume offerings have a much higher variation in demand, often 100% of the mean—you're more likely to find yourself towards the front the graph than near the back! And the more complexity you have—the more varieties of products, services, options, features, etc.—the more likely it is that you'll have a large number of low-volume offerings.

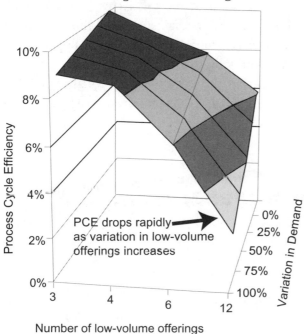

2% of total demand, and the three high-volume offerings divide up the balance equally. (E.g., five low-demand offerings would account for 10% of total demand, so the high-volume offerings would each account for 1/3rd of 90%, or 30% of demand.)

The reason that low-volume offerings have such an adverse impact on PCE is most visible in manufacturing: Low-volume products have about the same setup time as the high-volume products and about the same startup scrap rate (which are fixed costs). Most companies therefore tend to run low-volume products in relatively large batches (say, a six-month supply, so they don't have to run it often), which ties up warehouse costs, increases the odds of obsolescence, and so on. In service applications, the result of low-volume offerings is far less obvious, but just as potent. Having high variation in service mix and demand means that staff are constantly challenged by the learning curve. Subsequent delays and non-value-add costs are also high but masked by managerial cost accounting.

Complexity and ABC

The Complexity Equation clearly identifies the drivers of low PCE and hence high non-value-add cost. In principal, Activity Based Costing (ABC) attempts to find these drivers, and given enough time and insight, probably would. However, practitioners of ABC would be the first to point out that it would be unlikely that they could find the functional form (the Complexity Equation) by which the drivers affect PCE and high cost. ABC was created to enhance conventional cost accounting and is discussed further in Chapter 5.

What Lever to Pull?: Advice on improving PCE

Look again at the basic PCE equation:

$$\text{Process Cycle Efficiency} = \frac{\text{Value-add Time}}{\text{Total Lead Time}}$$

What levers can we pull to improve PCE? Think about these tv

- *Most* process time is spent on non-value-add work

- It's easier and cheaper to remove non-value-add work than to speed up value-add work

That means the greater leverage lies in reducing total lead time, *not* in focusing on value-add time. How can we improve lead time? An equation for the lead time of *any* process, known as Little's Law (named for the mathematician who proved it), shows that the two key factors are the number of "things" or "work" in process (called TIP or WIP) and how quickly you can get work done (the average completion rate):

Equation 2.3: Little's Law

$$\text{Total Lead Time} = \frac{\text{Number of Things in Process}}{\text{Average Completion Rate}}$$

Obviously, to reduce lead time you have one of two choices:

1) Increase the average completion rate

2) Reduce the number of Things-in-Process (TIP)

Choice 1 generally requires *financial capital* investment to increase capacity, i.e., increase the average completion rate of the facility. This means investing in more people, more equipment, more machines. But if this capacity is in excess of market demand, the investment is in fact a waste of shareholders' money. Our studies of capital equipment budgets over the last 15 years indicates that as much as 50% of capex is in fact wasted.

TIP by any other name

TIP (Things-in-Process) is more commonly called WIP (Work-in-Process) in manufacturing. The terms are synonymous. Being "in process" means the work or things have entered a process but not yet exited. The "work" can be anything: materials, components, sales orders, projects, customer inquiries, checks, phone calls to return, reports, suppliers to qualify, repair orders, emails waiting to be answered, and so on.

Choice 2 requires *intellectual capital* investment to reduce the number of Things-in-Process. The Complexity Equation tells us that we can increase PCE and reduce lead time by reducing the complexity of the product (or service), the complexity of the process, and the setup time, and by improving quality. This avoids the waste of unnecessary financial investment of Choice 1, delivering more ROIC and hence shareholder value per revenue dollar of profit. (You'll find suggestions on how to simplify product, service, and process design in Part III.)

The simplest, fastest, and most effective route to improving lead time, and hence PCE, is to reduce TIP or WIP. Lean practices describe a number of ways to reduce the amount of work "in process" *without* reducing the completion rate—meaning you can still meet customer demands. You'll find them described in a lot of books (including our previous publications, *Lean Six Sigma* and *Lean Six Sigma for Service*).

What causes a high level of TIP? Part of it is management policies of just dumping too much work on the process. But another part is simply needing a minimum level of Things-in-Process to maintain workflow in today's currently inefficient processes (that level can be reduced only with process improvement). In manufacturing, for example, the amount of time it takes to switch from one product or configuration to another (**setup** or **changeover time**) has a big impact on batch size. If setup time is long, you have to produce in bigger batches simply because you won't meet total demand if the batch is too small. And setup time is just one factor in the Complexity Equation.

The Power of Numbers

Lack of a quantitative understanding of the drivers of the cost of complexity has caused companies to make very bad decisions. One European car company decided to build focused factories to reduce the cost of complexity, building one model in Germany and a different model in Spain. Unfortunately, the demand for the model built in Spain lagged and resulted in layoffs, while the model built in Germany exceeded all forecasts and the factory worked beyond capacity at high cost. Had the company understood and removed the cost of complexity, it could have built two mixed-model facilities and more effectively responded to what actually happened in the marketplace.

With the Complexity Equation, we have the quantitative power we need to make rational decisions about whether the complexity we're trying to support is worth the impact it has on the organization. Tearing apart these different factors will not only let us diagnose the impact of complexity, but also evaluate which tools—complexity reduction, Six Sigma, or Lean—we should use and in which order to reduce cost. Thus this simplified Complexity Equation provides an excellent shorthand for executive action. If the strategy is to grow revenue through product proliferation of 15% per year, you must have a plan to eliminate 15% of existing products or reduce average setup times by 15%, etc.

The unification of Complexity, Lean, and Six Sigma in one equation makes two major contributions to shareholder value:

- **Magnitude and Speed of Results:** The ability to prioritize projects based on their ability to increase PCE will allow management to proceed with a clear eye and sure hand. Management can make rational

Reducing demand variability (an aside for the statistically inclined)

For those of you familiar with statistics, if this European car company could have decreased total demand fluctuation by $1/\sqrt{2}$, each plant would have operated within design capacity. Corporate profits would have increased and human capital and relations preserved.

All that was required was to design the process so that the process parameters would have compensated for the increased product complexity. In this case, if the company wants to double the number of products (N), they will have to design the changeover time from model to model to be near zero. This is feasible in assembly plants, and in fact Toyota typically runs four models in a mixed line. Again, it's a choice of intellectual or financial capital.

investments much as they do with capital expenditures—"If I invest $X in complexity reduction I will get $Y back every year" and "How much Economic Profit will be generated by launching new products, and what actions are necessary to preserve PCE?" Management is then far more motivated to accept responsibility for continuous improvement execution, just as they do revenue and profit.

- **"Clarity and precision…. beyond prejudice and opinion"**: These are the words Napoleon used to explain his love of mathematics and dislike of philosophy. As you'll see in Part II, the Complexity Equation can provide clarity around any number of strategic business options, such as launching a host of new offerings or products, incorporating an acquisition, adding complexity reduction projects to your mix of improvement opportunities, etc. Many companies have invested in one option or another based on past experience or opinion. By making a quantitative estimate of impact, managers can coalesce around a balanced integrated set of initiatives, showing the impact of each that is "beyond prejudice or opinion."

Conclusion

The cumulative effect of conquering complexity on market strength was demonstrated by the cases in Chapter 1. But the origin of that impact lies in the very specific and direct effects that complexity has on slowing down a process, creating non-value-add cost, increasing the chances for errors and delays, and so on. This understanding of complexity's impact at the process level and on PCE and cost forms the foundation for the complexity analyses we'll explore in more detail later in the book.

Endnotes

1 John A. Quelch and David Kenny, "Extend Profits, Not Product Lines," *Harvard Business Review*, September-October 1994.

2 The S-1 registration that details this financial performance is available from the authors upon request.

3 The Complexity Equation is protected by US Patents 5,195,041 and 5,351,195 and patents pending. Contact George Group for details.

CHAPTER 3

How Complexity Slows the
Flow of Critical Information

*It's a key part of why rivals have had great difficulty
competing with Dell... the way the information from
the customer flows all the way through manufacturing to our
customers... the kind of coordination of information that used
to be possible only in vertically integrated companies.*

—Michael Dell, CEO of Dell

Having discussed how, and how much, complexity drains your
company's time, resources, and profits, it may come as no surprise that complexity also slows your information flow. Yet its effects in
this area are often overlooked. To exemplar companies, however, information velocity—the ease and speed with which you gather, process, and
respond to information—is a critical strategic issue. John Chambers,
CEO of Cisco Systems, once said:

> *Products commoditize so quickly that in the end, the only sus-
> tainable competitive advantages you have are speed, talent
> and brand.*

Perhaps no company is more publicly attuned to the impact and power
of information velocity than Dell. Says COO Kevin Rollins[1]:

> *Life cycles in our business are measured in months, not years,
> and if you don't move fast, you're out of the game. Managing
> velocity is about managing information—using a constant
> flow of information to drive operating practices, from the per-
> formance measures we track to how we work with suppliers.*

On Performance Metrics: From the balance sheet, we track three cash-flow measures very closely. We look at weekly updates of how many days of inventory we have, broken out by product component. We can then work closely with our suppliers so we end up with the right inventory.

We also track and manage receivables and payables very tightly… The payoff is that we have negative cash-conversion cycle of five days—that is, we get paid before we have to pay our suppliers. Since our competitors usually have to support their resellers by offering them credit, the direct model gives us an inherent cost advantage.

On Working with Suppliers: The key to making it work is information. The right information flows allow us to work with our partners in ways that enhance speed, either directly by improving logistics or indirectly by improving quality.

Another company to focus on information flows is Capital One, which conducts thousands and thousands of actuarial tests to learn how to customize products to individual consumers. The driving idea: the only sustainable advantage they have is their ability to innovate better and more quickly (through better information flows) than their competitors. Capital One decentralizes this testing process, which eliminates time-wasting decision-making bureaucracies, limits risk, and encourages entrepreneurial behavior.

As Dell, Cisco, and Capital One have shown, the new competitive giants will be those who can use information the fastest. Yet horror stories about poor information flow abound in the workplace (you've likely lived through some of them yourself). At one end of the scale is a division of a large healthcare organization that got in trouble because it completely missed the fact that competitors were building three new plants to compete with its products. At the smaller end is the Engineering Change Notice (ECN) approval process at one company. Each ECN required signatures from all seven managers—and it could take weeks for the forms to make it through all seven in-baskets. Meanwhile, manufacturing was still performing rework on old versions of the products.

What's seldom appreciated is that the complexity of the decision process—the delays caused by a lot of handoffs, the noise generated by having to deal with so many "things-in-process"—is often the underlying reason for these misses. As the last chapter illustrated, complexity adds waste, cost, and *time* to all processes. These effects are compounded when complexity is interfering with strategically critical information (such as what your competitors are up to) or decisions (such as how you will respond to a new market opportunity). In those situations, slow information velocity can be a death knell.

In this chapter, we'll look more closely at the impact of complexity on information flow and speed, and explore some ways to counteract those effects.

Information Flow Complexity = Too Long to Reach Decision Makers

Consider the decision-making process within your company: How long does it take for a strategic decision to be implemented and affect customers? How quickly do hiring and firing decisions get made? How long is your decision lead time? How long does it take emails and paperwork to flow through your processes, attain "value" through managerial discussions and actions, and lead to changes that affect customers?

Any color you want so long as it's... green

In the 1920s, the Ford Model T commanded more than 60% of the low-cost market with one color: black. But with the rise of a used car market and the burgeoning desire for cars available in a wide variety of colors, Ford lost out to GM.

So why in the 1990s, did Volvo see a surge in the production cars in one specific color (green)? Was green the new black? No, the answer is poor information velocity.

From *The Economist,* Jan 31st 2002:

"The Swedish car manufacturer found itself with excessive stocks of green cars. To move them along, the sales and marketing departments began offering attractive special deals, so green cars started to sell. But nobody had told the manufacturing department about the promotions. It noted the increase in sales, read it as a sign that consumers had started to like green, and ramped up production."

It is very common for small entrepreneurial companies to flourish because they have a decision value stream that has only two to three layers, nodes, or activities in it. As the company grows in management layers and offering complexity, the decision value stream lengthens out to a dozen or more activities or decision points between the initial thought and impact on a customer.

One large company we know had a saying: "I need 34 'yes' answers on this product development proposal, and it just takes one 'no' to kill it." Consider the probability that a great idea will be rejected by any one decision maker in your organization. Even if the chance of acceptance is 90% every step along the way, if you had, say, 20 decision makers in the process the overall probability of getting a final "yes" decision is only $0.9^{20} = 28\%$ (so almost 3 in 4 ideas will get rejected).

As a company grows in complexity and management levels, the lead time of the decision process is dramatically increased. Patrick Haggerty, the CEO of Texas Instruments during their days of glory, clearly understood this when he created the Product Customer Center, essentially scores of little P&L centers dedicated to a tightly defined market and technology. His successors chose to centralize manufacturing into Fabrication Customer Centers with all other functions, slowing down the process of decision making by adding layers to the structure. This played no small part in the company falling behind the upstart Intel.

We can find the levers that affect decision lead time by "solving" the Complexity Equation (introduced in the last chapter) for lead time, and using "decisions" as the "thing in process." What we get is…

$$\text{Lead Time to Make a Decision} \quad = \quad \frac{N(2A+1)S}{2(1 - X - PD)}$$

For this purpose, N is the number of decisions that need to be made, A is the number of levels or Activities the decision must pass through, S the preparation time to make the decision.

Your company's decision-making process has some lead time required to transform a strategic input to an operational output. If you add more decisions (N) to your process without reducing the number of levels (A) through which the decision must flow, decision-making velocity will be dramatically reduced. In short, the more decisions in process, the longer it will take to arrive at a decision. As we learned from the original discussion of the Complexity Equation in Chapter 2, if you increase complexity you can maintain lead time *only if* you reduce the number of layers in the decision process or reduce the number of decisions (N).

The fact is that many companies have improved the lead time for decisions by examining a process- or value-stream map of the steps in making past decisions, determining which steps are value-added. They've gotten closer to their customers, reduced the number of non-value-added "nodes" in the decision process, and also removed a lot of non-value-added steps. The result? Significantly faster decision making.

Dell deliberately limits the number of decision nodes for this very reason. Says Michael Dell:

> *"We turn our inventory 96 times per year. If you look at the complexity and the diversity of our product line, there's no way we could do that unless we had credible information about what the customer is actually buying. It's a key part of why rivals have had great difficulty competing with Dell... the way information from the customer flows all the way through manufacturing to our suppliers."* Compressing that flow is critical, he adds. *"The longer the distance, the more intermediary channels you add, the less likely it is you will have good information about demand—so you will end up with more variability, more inventory, higher costs, and more risk."*[2]

The impact of complexity on the quality of strategic decisions

These quantitative predictions of slower decisions with more complexity are borne out by intuition, and confirmed in studies of human behavior. One study looked at the impact of complexity on managers' ability to correctly assess and respond to the threat of potential entrants.[3] The researchers found that the increased complexity of a competitive situation negatively affected the decision process and outcome. Not only does complexity slow the decision process, it can worsen the quality of the decision.

Complexity Creates Noise in Information Systems

The more complex your organization, the more noise you will have in your decision-making and information processes. The data overload obscures critical information and increases the likelihood that important messages will be ignored and not acted upon.

In a company with an unfocused portfolio of offerings, experience shows that 15% of the offerings drive 95% of ROIC. The rest is noncore and undifferentiated. But the presence of so many offerings obscures this fact, with two potentially disastrous consequences: First, management is unaware of what drives value for the company and so underinvests in the 15% with potential. Failure to understand how a company creates value leads to underinvestment and an inability to respond to market changes. Second, the perception that the company's portfolio is sturdier than it really is, which breeds complacency.

A thorough analysis of Economic Profit might lead management to divest noncore holdings. That requires an understanding of where and how you are creating value, and reducing or relocating the complexity that is consuming management capacity. Not all customers are equally valuable, nor are all product or service lines equally profitable. Having a simpler, more-focused portfolio concentrates management attention on the customer sets served by the 15% of your offerings that are your true value generators.

To escape this quagmire, you have to be capable of separating critical information from non-critical noise. What that takes will be different for each organization. But all of us must take a look at which kinds of information are currently getting through the process and which aren't, and make deliberate decisions about whether and how to change that reality.

Probability vs. information content

Critical information is usually associated with what a mathematician would call a low-probability event. The fact that a new competitor is entering the marketplace is a different type of information from finding out that an existing customer is placing another order. It happens far less frequently. Why is that important? Because the amount of information conveyed by an event is **greater** the less probable the event. Telling someone in Texas that it's hot on July 4th conveys a lot less information than if you said it was July 4th and snowing! The latter would be front-page news.

If the probability is high, the information content is low. If the probability is low, the information content is high. A new competitor entering the market is perhaps a very low-probability event, but one that conveys a lot of information and should cause a proportional response, such as planning a reactive strategy, new operational initiatives, or a change in marketing and pricing. However, due to the impact of complexity, these low-probability events may be regarded as "noise" in an overloaded decision process and may simply be ignored. The critical information may not survive a complex process flow. And if it does, the information flow from management back to the market (its strategic response) may not.

Dell and Compaq: Better to be fast than first

No example of information velocity is more stunning than the demise of Compaq at the hands of Dell. Compaq was well known for being the innovator; Dell for being fast. Consider Figure 3.1 (next page), which depicts "Work-In-Process (WIP) inventory turns," a metric common in manufacturing used to gauge speed and efficiency (higher numbers are better). (For our manufacturing readers, WIP turns are higher than total turns because raw material and finished goods are not included.)

The figure shows that Dell's WIP turns increased rapidly at a time when competitors' turns remained steady. If you have low WIP turns, that means you have lots of inventory sitting around consuming capital and generating no revenue. You will also have a long lead time and low PCE

Figure 3.1: Dell's Speed Advantage

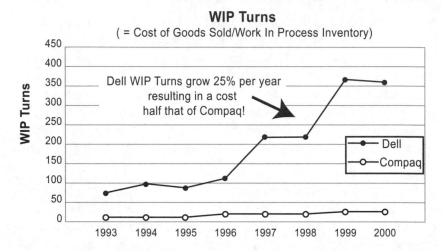

WIP Turns

(= Cost of Goods Sold/Work In Process Inventory)

By increasing WIP turns, Dell reduced costs far beyond what Compaq could achieve. Lead time is inversely proportional to WIP turns, meaning lead time goes up (gets longer) when WIP turns go down. Since lead time is a key driver of PCE, you want lead time to go down so PCE can rise (in other words, removing non-value-add time to improve lead time causes an improved PCE).

(both are inversely proportional to WIP turns—lead time goes down when WIP goes up and vice versa).

What's one of the biggest contributors to excess inventory? Product and process complexity. Simplification leads to an enormous reduction in cost, which explains why Michael Dell announced in an interview that his costs are half that of the competition and that he intended to cut prices to gain market share. That a leading competitor would suddenly increase inventory turns at such a rate is an incredible low-probability event conveying huge information that should have triggered a response from Compaq, but no response occurred.

How Does Dell Achieve Fast Information Flow?

Dell is physically fast, without question, but how do they do it? Start with the business model. Dell sells its product directly to its customers. That fact alone has a lot of implications, not the least of which is that Dell is able to *receive information quickly and accurately* on what the customer wants and is willing to pay for. Dell has exploited this direct model to convince customers that the company will build the computer exactly to the customer's specifications. Wow! If you are the customer, this is the best kind of complexity: infinite variety that allows you to completely personalize your PC.

But wait… wouldn't the Complexity Equation tell us that "infinite variety" should result in a crippling level of complexity inside Dell? Their secret lies in combining fast information processing with several standard product design and packaging techniques to exploit what they call "naturally occurring configurations." Here's how it works:

When Dell introduces a new product, the company is able to quickly gather and respond to actual data on which configurations are selling most effectively. They then create special pricing for and heavily advertise those high sellers to steer volume to a smaller set of configurations. In theory, Dell could still produce any configuration, but customers are steered towards slightly lower-priced standard configurations that have nearly all of the features they requested (as compared to opting for higher-priced custom configurations).

The reality is that Dell offers truly custom configurations only in the very beginning of the product life cycle. At one point, as soon as Dell realized that customers were ordering two basic configurations 80% of the time, they then began to market/promote those basic configurations heavily. That drove the order rate up to 95%.

Another example of increased inventory turns

Toyota has steadily increased its inventory turns from 15 – 50 to 100 – 200 per year. That increased PCE and decreased cost and lead time—resulting in major competitive advantage. You can respond to that kind of performance only if information flows quickly and easily through the organization. As we noted previously, GM tried to implement Toyota's methods and we applaud them for making the strongest effort of any U.S. car company in the last decade. But after 20 years, a huge gap still exists in PCE and in the underlying costs. Why? GM never integrated information velocity into its culture, and culture always wins out.

So Dell's ability to exploit its information velocity allows it to get the brand position of "built-to-order" PCs, while having the complexity and cost of delivering cookie-cutter PCs.

Compaq's go-to-market model has always rested on dealer and retail distribution channels. The complexity of this distribution model (a) separated them from their customers, and (b) kept them from reacting as quickly as Dell because they'd have to "bleed inventory" out of the channel before introducing a new configuration. If the market changes and certain configurations are no longer selling due to a new technology, a company like Dell can change with the market (and does so fast) while highly complex organizations are still spinning their wheels.

Dell's strategy can be summed up by saying that "it is better to be fast than first." Dell really does not care about creating a new technology to bring to market. Dell is essentially a financial company that knows it can move quickly enough to catch up to a competitor's innovations and ensure they are applied effectively to meeting customers' needs.

Compaq, on the other hand, believed that technology was the answer and that being first to market with an exciting new technology could and would win the day. The simple reality is that developing new technologies and managing "industry standards" is enormously complex and time consuming. Unless you have a market monopoly, it is not possible to innovate fast enough to overcome the slower velocity of information. This occurs because the sum total of resources that "the market" can and will bring to bear on any real opportunity/innovation is more than a single innovator can muster—the brief head start the innovator gets is quickly overwhelmed by the tsunami of competitive investment.

Structure also plays a part. Dell has historically defined success for a division as growing to a point that the business needs to be split. Once a division reaches a billion dollars in size, the unit is split in two. For example, the large accounts division might be split into corporate and government, and then later the large corporate accounts division would be split into *Fortune* 200 and *Fortune* 200-500, and so on. Why? To eliminate layers of management between the boss and the people talking to the customer. **Fewer layers of management means faster flow of information.** A business that is focused on a more tightly defined group of customers and offerings can make better decisions. Customer needs are easier to understand and the product/service and marketing decisions are much more straightforward.

Conclusion: Cumulative effect of complexity on strategic decision making

The overall impact of complexity is to hinder management's ability to identify, collect, and respond to information that is strategically critical to the business. For example:

- Managing all the non-value-added "stuff" caused by complexity consumes management resources, which are finite.

- It can be hard to identify the true value drivers (offerings that contribute most to shareholder value). For example, clutter or noise can obscure a significant Pareto effect—that only 20% of offerings are driving 80% of ROIC, and the remaining 80% of the product or service lines essentially are filler. Missing that kind of pattern would cause management to underinvest in value generators and overinvest in value destroyers.

- Carrying a lot of product or service offerings gives the impression of having a diverse and sturdy portfolio. But if many of those offerings are value-destroying, that impression is misleading. A crowded portfolio can obscure a real crisis and delay reactions, with potentially fatal outcomes.

- Even if management can pick up on critical information, the complexity of the decision-making process itself can make them slow to respond. The information flow from strategy through operations may be swamped by existing operational priorities and never affect the market.

Endnotes

1 Michael Dell and Joan Magretta, "The Power of Virtual Integration: An Interview with Dell Computer's Michael Dell," *HBR OnPoint*, 2001.

2 *Ibid*

3 Bruce R. Klemz and Thomas S. Gruca, "Dueling or the Battle Royale? The Impact of Task Complexity on Evaluation of Entry Threat," *Psychology and Marketing*, Volume 20, Issue 11, November 2003.

CHAPTER 4

How Conquering Complexity Drives Shareholder Value

We continue to believe that the ratio of operating earnings to shareholder equity is the best measure of performance. Earnings per share... is an invalid measure.

—Berkshire Hathaway Annual Report, 1979

The best business to own is one that over an extended period can employ large amounts of incremental capital at very high rates of return.

—Berkshire Hathaway Annual Report, 1992

In 1964, General Motors management inherited the edifice that Alfred Sloan had built. They presided over the fortunes of the largest, most successful company in history, operating in the economy's largest industry. They guided GM into the most catastrophic loss of market share in business history. What metric did management use to guide GM into the chasm?

"I look at the bottom line. It tells me what to do."

—Roger B. Smith

As your awareness of complexity increases, you begin to appreciate that a focus on earnings alone can lead management to make decisions that can destroy corporate value. GM's approach to conquering complexity in the 1980s was to build lookalike cars to reduce cost in a market that valued differentiation. The primary result was the acceleration of loss of market share. Toyota, Dell, and many other companies have taken the opposite tack of emphasizing a differentiated offering that maximizes operating profit and minimizes invested capital. Southwest has recognized that their markets do not value differentiation sufficiently to earn an adequate return on capital, which has guided strategic and operating decisions. These strategies maximize Economic Profit (EP), the difference between return of invested capital and cost of capital. Clearly it is important to understand the relationship between complexity and shareholder value in conformance with Buffett's principles.

GM's experience is hardly unique. As described in the previous chapters, few companies appreciate the true benefit that increased complexity can have on their business *if* accompanied by appropriate process improvement. Those few that do have achieved remarkable results.

All companies will benefit from a means to quantify the impact of complexity, because traditional cost accounting practices and measures of value do not include a complexity/customer component. In short, business leaders have trouble making good decisions because the old metrics don't tell them what they need to know. One of the creators of Activity Based Costing wrote:

> *Management Accounting Put American Businesses in the Dark:*
> *Management accounting practices adopted in American businesses after World War II motivated companies to make decisions that systematically put them at a disadvantage compared to focused and flexible competitors that began to appear, mainly from overseas, during the late 1960s. These practices concerned primarily the handling of indirect costs, or overhead.*

> *—H. Thomas Johnson, Relevance Regained, p. 44*

Remember, our argument is not with GAAP, which doesn't care how costs are allocated among products and services. Our issue is with managerial accounting. Separating fact from fiction is the first step to value creation. That means objectively evaluating products and businesses through the lens of their impact on Process Cycle Efficiency and Economic Profit. This analysis includes all offerings—those that appear to have historically performed well (and to which, as a result, management harbors an emotional attachment) and those that everyone thinks are bad performers.

The discussions in this chapter are targeted primarily at executive-level managers, company leaders, Board members—anyone with sufficient scope and authority to influence a company's shareholder value. However, other readers may want to review the content so they can understand what factors are going to influence strategic decisions about a company and its portfolio of offerings.

Be forewarned: the approaches described here frequently produce surprising and potentially unwelcome results. A company may find its "identity" business units are consuming capital—and destroying value for the corporation. Kimberly-Clark confronted this reality when former CEO Darwin E. Smith and his team concluded that the traditional core business (coated paper) was doomed to mediocrity. They made the most dramatic decision in the company's history: sell the mills. That's complexity reduction on a massive scale.

Your business may not face anything that drastic, but Kimberly-Clark's strategy is worth noting. They didn't just reallocate resources from the paper business to the consumer business. They completely eliminated the paper business, sold the mills, and invested all the money into the emerging consumer business, which was creating value. And that's the kind of decision making that's discussed in this chapter—how you can tell whether the complexity caused by multiple business units, product/services lines, or value streams is creating or destroying value, and what options you have.

The Challenges of Accounting for Complexity

As outlined in Chapter 2, complexity is responsible for a number of insidious costs in your business, primarily contained in overhead costs and low labor productivity. The most obvious example is manufacturing overhead cost, but you'll also see it in things like large procurement costs and constant task switching—e.g., the setup and downtime on production lines as they switch between products, the lag time in service functions as people try to process a confusing number of options, etc.

Unfortunately, current accounting methods aren't set up to identify those hidden costs. As has been proven by Robert Kaplan et al.,[1] traditional cost accounting procedures do a very poor job of making an accurate allocation of overhead cost to specific services, products, and processes. GAAP accounting, for example, does a good job of computing the profit of a whole organization over long periods of time, but does a poor job of properly allocating overhead costs to each offering and fails to recognize low direct labor productivity. Since overhead cost—be it SG&A and direct or manufacturing overhead—often amounts to 30% of total cost, this is a gigantic miss.

When these erroneous data are used to guide operations management, disastrous consequences can follow. The shortcomings of traditional costing systems have been eloquently analyzed in the book *Relevance Lost*,[2] and led to the rise of Activity Based Costing (ABC), which seeks

Cost accounting problems

One major problem with cost allocation that relates to complexity is the fact that many costs allocated to overhead are scale independent. To illustrate that concept, think about a production line that handles two different products. The time and cost needed to change from producing one product to the other product are the same regardless of whether you build one unit or ten thousand units. Yet the overhead cost applied often is based on a % of direct labor, i.e., it depends on how many you build.

This means that high-volume offerings are allocated too much cost, and low-volume products are allocated too little. In his *Introduction to Activity Based Costing*, Robert Kaplan notes: "Traditional cost systems... will systematically and grossly under estimate the cost of resources required for specialty, low-volume products and will over estimate the resource cost of high volume, standard products."[3]

Since one of the themes of this book is assigning the true cost to complexity, the conventional approach is obviously inadequate.

to remedy the problems outlined above but has often proved to be a cumbersome approach.[4,5] ABC attempts to find the true drivers of cost by, for example, tracing setup time and cost back to each low-volume product or service and appropriately increasing its unit cost and reducing the allocation made to the unit cost of a higher-volume product or service. (For example, an ABC effort might discover that some products require a disproportionate amount of engineering support, and make suitable additions/reductions.) The result is a corrected Gross Profit per product or service line.

How big can the correction be? Let's look at an example: One of our early engagements was at a company that principally produced wall coverings but, due to their ability to extrude and roll sheets, also produced rubber sound deadeners for automobile doors (they give doors a nice solid "clunk" when closed). The Gross Profit Margin on the door product was reported as 40% vs. only 22% for the wall coverings. No wonder the sound deadeners were widely considered as one of the company's winners. Marketing had incentives to sell more automotive products.

This company had about 22 equipment and quality engineers on staff whose time was charged to manufacturing overhead, then allocated out based on volume. Because wall coverings accounted for more than 90% of the volume, these high-volume products carried 90% of the engineering cost. However, it was found that the automotive products *consumed more than half of the engineering cost.* Much of an engineer's time was spent on the automotive products in unscheduled phone calls, quality audits, handling returned material, creating test data, etc.—things that are difficult to capture on a time card and yet are completely non-value-added from the customers' perspective.

In short, the tasks that an engineer faced working on automotive products were vastly more *complex* than those related to wallcoverings. Likewise, the automotive products required special capital equipment for mixing and rolling material, and therefore should have had a much higher depreciated cost per unit than did wall covering. But depreciation, like engineering time, was rolled into overhead cost and charged out based on volume. When all these costs were properly applied to the automotive product, the company realized that product line was destroying value. (And their calculations didn't even account for the opportunity cost being lost in the wallcovering business.)

Making Decisions That Benefit Shareholders: Earnings Per Share vs. Economic Profit

The challenges of accounting for or valuing complexity begin at the product-by-product, service-by-service level, and extend corporatewide. As noted previously, few businesses can evaluate the true costs of complexity. The direct impact of complexity is seen in things like lots of work-in-process (high WIP), slow processes, and low PCE—things that don't show up in divisional Income Statements. The impact of complexity is also absent from the most common metric used to evaluate shareholder value: Earnings Per Share (EPS).

Of course, to believe that EPS is the primary driver of value assumes that *capital is free*—that *the investment required* to produce a given return is not a relative factor. But producing $1 million profit on $5 million investment is better than producing $1 million on $100 million investment. And empirical data proves that there is very low correlation between share price and EPS.[6]

The bottom line is that managing to maximize EPS can lead you to decisions that are not in the interests of shareholders. Value is a good performance measure because it requires complete information. To understand value creation, you need to use a long-term, strategic point of view, actively manage cash flows and the balance sheet, and be able to understand the impact of time and risk on your cash flows.

The fundamentals that drive shareholder value have been much debated since the 19th century. Notwithstanding a few well-known aberrations (J.P. Morgan watering U.S. Steel's balance sheet with $400 million of goodwill; more recent widely publicized criminal behavior), a discipline of valuation based primarily on Discounted Cash Flows (DCF) has emerged over the last few decades and quietly gained acceptance.

First observed in *Security Analysis* by Benjamin Graham in 1934, and then in John Burr Williams' *Theory of Investment Value* in 1938,[7] DCF's best-known practitioner today is Warren Buffett, Graham's former protégé. The underlying concepts are well represented within Berkshire Hathaway annual reports:

> *The value of any stock, bond, or business today is determined by the cash inflows and outflows—discounted at an appropriate interest rate—that can be expected to occur during the remaining life of the asset.*

> —*Berkshire Hathaway Annual Report, 1992*

This theoretical Discounted Cash Flow that Buffett labels the *intrinsic value* of a company is consistent with empirical studies of actual stock prices. In Copeland's *Valuation*,[8] we can see that stock market values are 92% statistically "explained" by their respective Discounted Cash Flows (*see* Figure 4.1).

Figure 4.1: Correlation of Market Value and Discounted Cash Flow

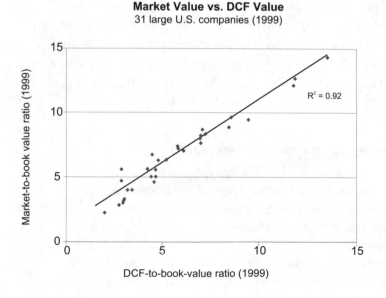

Market Value vs. DCF Value
31 large U.S. companies (1999)

$R^2 = 0.92$

Market-to-book value ratio (1999)

DCF-to-book-value ratio (1999)

However, predicting future cash flows presents some challenges. Copeland chooses to use a *single-period* metric for understanding valuation: Economic Profit (EP).[9]

EP = (ROIC% – Cost of Capital%) * Invested capital

It can also be expressed as a percentage:

EP% = ROIC% – WACC%

EP is gaining wider acceptance—and is particularly relevant in complexity decisions—because it is the *real* profit after taking into account *all* of the resources the company has consumed, both operating cost and capital. EP is also better than EPS because it more closely aligns with the way investors see the world—as a set of portfolio choices where opportunity costs matter. EP is a better indicator of profitability, as it takes into account the opportunity cost of the inputs used to generate the revenue, thus aligning management actions with investors' interests.

For these reasons EP is more useful in driving corporate behavior, helping us adopt actions and select projects that will drive the biggest increase in shareholder value. Its main limitation is that it is typically calculated as a single-year "snapshot." While we don't have to worry about future cash flows in developing the model—and it circumvents the largely fatal tendency to develop "hockey stick" growth projections—long but valid payback projects would fare poorly from an EP perspective. That said, EP is still a much better metric than current alternatives, so you'll see it used throughout this book.

Accounting profits vs. Economic Profit

While accounting profit represents the difference between a business's revenue and its accounting expenses, it frequently has little relationship to a company's Economic Profit because of the difference between accounting expense and what we might call the production opportunity cost. Some accounting expense is not an opportunity cost and some opportunity costs do not show up as accounting expenses. Bottom line: EPS is an accounting measure, but often **not** an indicator of value creation.

EP and stock prices

We've plotted some empirical stock market data in Figure 4.2 to show how shareholder value is correlated with:

- Return on Invested Capital (ROIC) minus the Weighted Average Cost of Capital (WACC), which is the return that could have been earned from alternative investments—the opportunity cost for investors.

- Good growth, that is, growth that fuels the proliferation of value-add products and services that are generating positive Economic Profit (the x-axis in Figure 4.2)

Figure 4.2: Stock Price Performance and Complexity

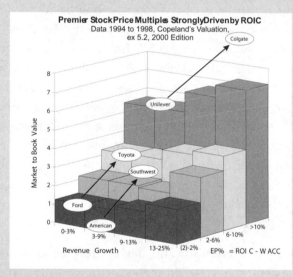

Premier Stock Price Multiples Strongly Driven by ROIC
Data 1994 to 1998, Copeland's Valuation, ex 5.2, 2000 Edition

EP% is graphed along the axis going back into the page, while revenue growth % is along the front axis. The vertical axis represents the market view (Market to Book ratio). You'll notice that companies like Ford whose ROIC% is less than its cost of capital, trade at around book value (lower left corner).

Conversely, companies like Colgate Palmolive (with an ROIC of 27%) are off the scale and receive high price premiums.

As you can see in the chart:

- Values rise most steeply along the EP% axis, meaning that EP% (or equivalently, Discounted Cash Flow) is the most powerful driver of share price

- Revenue Growth, the darling of the internet bubble, is only of sustained value when EP is greater than 2%

Key Lessons About EP and Growth

Because Economic Profit accounts for costs as well as returns, it holds a critical lesson for us that other metrics overlook: Most of us have been trained to think of growth as a good thing, but growth will actually accelerate the *destruction* of shareholder value *if Economic Profit is negative.* Understand that for every shareholder dollar invested by the corporation in projects that yield below the cost of capital, the investor has suffered economic losses; growth simply magnifies this shareholder loss.[10]

Figure 4.3 shows an example of how this happens. The chart shows the stock performance of Value City (VCD—now owned by parent company Retail Ventures, Inc, which also owns DSW Shoe Warehouse and Filene's Basement stores), Kohl's (KSS), and May Department Stores Co. (MAY), all department store chains, versus the S&P 500 Index. Both Value City and Kohl's saw revenue growth rates of about 20%. But from 1999 to 2004, Value City saw negative ROIC, while Kohl's remained at a solid 13%. This is reflected in the value of the shares. Value City was thus valued at *less* than book value. May Co., on the other hand, while maintaining a relatively robust ROIC of 9.7%, had an anemic growth rate of 0.83%. Its market-to-book ratio, while better than Value City's, is only 1.88. The market performer had strong growth rates working to leverage its strong return on capital. For Value City, growth served only to magnify the value destruction.

In short, **growth can be an accelerant to value destruction,** a conclusion not too surprising to people who are attuned to the true impact of complexity on costs and speed.

The Complexity Imperative in Fast Markets

The call to action is made imperative by the ferocity of global competition. We are now operating in fast, vast markets. ABN-AMRO, a Netherlands-based multinational commercial and investment bank with roots back to Dutch colonial times, lost ground to competitors in the late

Figure 4.3: Stock Performance of Kohl's, May's, and Value City Department Stores

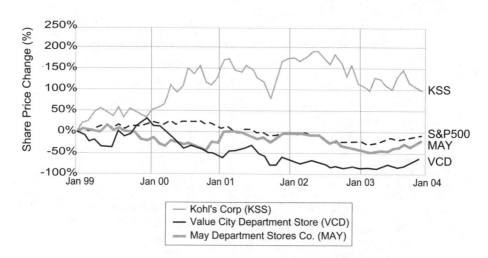

Over the last five years, an investment in Kohl's would have yielded a doubling of shareholder value, due to its strong Economic Profit and growth records. An investment in May's would have barely broken even—this is consistent with an Economic Profit of approximately zero. Value City, despite a growth bonanza (or rather because of it) has yielded negative returns for investors in that time period.

nineties as the financial markets transformed around it into a global marketplace, while ABN-AMRO remained true to its tradition of being a "universal bank"—offering all investment as well as savings and loans services. The bank's focus on earnings and growth, rather than value, led to its complex offering portfolio with many services generating negative Economic Profit.

When a new chairman, Rijkman Groenink, was appointed in mid-2000, one of his first actions was to redefine the set of competitors that formed its frames of reference, emphasizing the point that while the consensus-driven management of the bank remained very Dutch in style, the pressures it was facing were global and unrelenting, coming from competitors such as Citigroup, Bank One, Barclays and Wells Fargo. It had to change from its universal approach to being selective in which parts of the value chain it focused on, eliminating much of the complexity in its portfolio, and freeing up a lot of assets tied to unprofitable operations.

> *The review process has led to a substantial reorganization of the institution with an explicit emphasis on Economic Profit. It has also marked the end of the 'Universal Banking concept.' We have set ourselves the objective of attaining a top 5 position in a peer group of 20 financial institutions within a four year period.*
>
> — *ABN-AMRO 2000 Annual Report*

Figure 4.4: ABN-AMRO Performance vs. Citigroup, Wells Fargo, Barclays

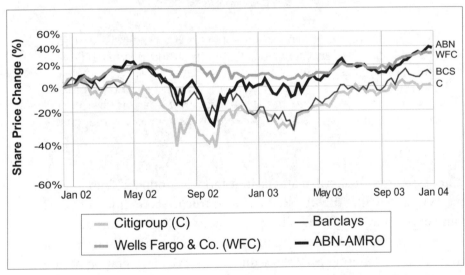

ABN-AMRO remained true to much of its banking traditions throughout the 1990s, even as the global banking marketplace underwent huge transformation. It had to redefine its set of competitors and adopt a value-view to regain competitive position.

The nature—and extent—of proliferation itself has changed. "Product life cycles are getting shorter and shorter," the founders of Capital One wrote to shareholders in 1998. The intensification of competition and increased customer power has compressed life cycles, in turn spurring companies to launch more and more new products/services and extensions. For some, this has become a strategy: 3M dictates that 30% of its revenues will come from new products every year. In 2000, 3M made 60,000 products.

Each new offering brings with it new levels of complexity, which must be compensated for by adequate margins. However, the complexity costs of an "SKU explosion" (however that translates to your business) can overwhelm the additional value from more choice. John Vegter, a vice president of logistics at SUPERVALUE, a *Fortune* 100 grocer and wholesaler, said that when one distribution center increased SKUs by 67%, sales rose only 10.2%.[11] The more capital tied up by slow moving products and offerings, the greater the risk that complexity will destroy value. The faster the market, the higher the stakes for conquering complexity.

No market better encapsulates the fast market than the PC industry. While it saw record growth through the 1990s, it was also prey to extremely compressed product life cycles. Moore's Law[12]—that processing power would double every couple of years—was less a law than a shot across the bows to Intel's lesser competitors warning that there would be the blistering pace of change in a punishing industry. Figure 4.5 shows that despite economies of scale with gargantuan increases in unit sales, revenue per unit stays largely flat.

Figure 4.5: Revenue Per Unit in PC Industry

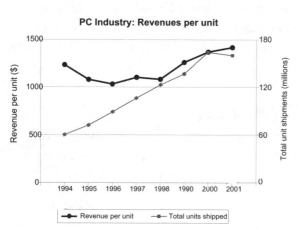

Revenue per unit has hardly changed at all in the PC industry despite a huge increase in overall volume. This type of dynamic makes it imperative that players stay on top of market needs and provide only the kinds of complexity that customers are willing to pay for.

The implication is that players in fast markets such as the PC industry cannot afford high levels of non-value-add complexity **because slow-moving products in fast markets never maximize ROIC**. Their "shelf-life" is limited: the company is left with obsolescence costs or the products' Cost of Goods Sold is inflated. The component cost of personal computers erodes in keeping with Moore's law of capacity expansion, hence, Dell's zealous focus on minimizing inventory levels.

The Links between Complexity and Value

Look again at the two forms of the Economic Profit (EP):

EP = (ROIC% – Cost of Capital%) * Invested capital

EP% = ROIC% – WACC%

The link between value creation and capital allocation (invested capital) becomes clearer. "Blind" capital allocation processes that do not make a distinction between accounting profits and Economic Profits will end up investing capital in businesses that do not warrant it, while simultaneously underinvesting in value-creating businesses. Strong capital allocation processes will do just the opposite: feed the strong and starve the weak. Decisions about a firm's business portfolio directly affect its ability to create wealth for the shareholders. The decision to broaden product/service lines and add new brands and offerings—to increase complexity—can drive revenues, build customer loyalty and steal market share. But doing so also consumes capital and creates complexity costs.

In essence, businesses face twin pressures: (1) how to grow (exploiting the complexity that customers value), while methodically (2) pruning away dead branches (the value-destroyers and non-value-add complexity). What is clear: doing one and not the other is insufficient.

With broadening markets from globalization and deregulation, there is still a growth land-grab; and as we've seen, the market rewards good growth. Thus guarding EP margins is paramount. Empirical evidence points to the fact that in most firms 100% of value is concentrated in less than 50% of the capital employed.[13] That means companies need to root out and eliminate the invested capital that isn't producing positive EP and focus their efforts on the 50% that is.

This principle is ubiquitous and represents a profit opportunity. A leading mortgage provider recently told us that out of 100 mortgage products offered, 5% constituted 90% of the value; another study estimated that in retail banking, the profit generated by the best 20% of customers is harmed by those that destroy value—so profits could actually be higher if banks focused on the 20%.[14] As discussed in Chapter 1, Capital One, which outperforms its competitors and has conquered complexity, understands this principle well. Long before anyone else, the firm understood that some customers were more profitable than others based on their consumption behavior and risk profile. Another example, from a construction equipment manufacturer, is shown in Figure 4.6.[15]

Figure 4.6: What Offerings Contribute to Earnings?

This chart illustrates how the majority of profits at a construction

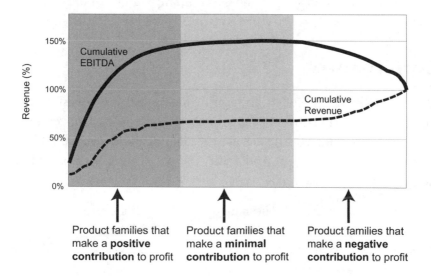

equipment manufacturer are concentrated within a small portion of the product line (left side of the graph). EBITDA measures earnings before interest, tax, depreciation, and amortization, which is a proxy for cash flow from operations.

These examples underscore the following: **the prerequisite to value creation is good information.**

Many corporations do not have income statements and balance sheets by business unit, or the information for calculating EP by division. There is an investment in time to understand if Customer A is driving value, or if Customer B, while bringing in strong revenues, is actually economically unprofitable. The nonintuitive impact of complexity on profits and growth, the subject of this book, is the final nail in the coffin of management by instinct. Rather: **Quantifying the impact of complexity on your offering is a critical first step to value creation in an increasingly fast market.** For...

> *"Nothing has such power to broaden the mind as the ability*
> *to investigate systematically and truly all that comes under*
> *thy observation in life."*

—*Marcus Aurelius*[16]

Without this understanding, management is operating largely in the dark; corporate strategy is "hopeful groping"; and better informed competitors are free to cherry-pick the pockets of value creation.

Conclusion

We agree with Warren Buffett, the world's most successful investor: high rates of return are the driver of superior shareholder value. Conventional cost accounting, unfortunately, has proven to be an ineffective tool for understanding these drivers. And while ABC accounting attempts to find the true drivers of cost, it has proven cumbersome in practice.

Chapter 2 showed that the best metric of operating performance was PCE and its drivers as defined by the Complexity Equation. This chapter built on that foundation to show that the best single-period measure of corporate performance is Economic Profit, the difference between ROIC% and Weighted Average Cost of Capital%. Later chapters of this book will combine the notions of PCE and Economic Profit to determine the value created or destroyed by each offering.

Endnotes

1 H. Thomas Johnson and Robert S. Kaplan, *Relevance Lost: The Rise and Fall of Management Accounting* (Boston: Harvard Business School Press, 1987).

2 *Ibid.*

3 Robert S. Kaplan, "Introduction to Activity Based Costing," *Harvard Business Review*, February 19, 1997, revised July 5, 2001.

4 *Ibid.*

5 H. Thomas Johnson, *Relevance Regained: From Top-Down Control to Bottom-up Empowerment* (New York: Free Press, 1992), pp. 131 and 154.

6 In "Do Appearances Matter? The Impact of EPS Accretion and Dilution on Stock Prices" (working paper, Harvard Business School, 1999), Harvard Business School Professor Gregor Andrade addresses the question of whether deals that reduce EPS affect share prices, independent of impact of actual cash flows. In practice, acquisitions often go ahead only on the basis of being accretive to EPS (i.e., increasing EPS). But in the study, which considered more than 200 transactions between 1975 and 1994, Andrade found that EPS accretion/dilution has only a marginal impact on share performance and then only for a period of up to 18 months following the deal, with zero impact thereafter (marginal: a 0.3% increase in share price for each 1% increase in expected earnings yield—or ratio of projected EPS to current stock price). The magnitude of this effect is higher for firms with lower ownership by institutional investors, i.e., with a larger percentage of unsophisticated investors. In sum, the impact is far smaller than popularly believed by practitioners' views.

7 Williams is responsible for creating the Dividend Discount Model, still widely used today.

8 McKinsey and Company, Inc., Tom Copeland, Tim Koller, Jack Murrin, *Valuation: Measuring and Managing the Value of Companies, Third Edition* (New York: John Wiley and Sons, 2000), pp. 76-77. Copeland's book makes valuation accessible to those who do not have an MBA. ROIC ia an appropriate metric for the majority of companies, but we use Return In Equity for banks and other financial institutions.

9 More background on the link between DCF and EP is available from the authors upon request.

10 This can be seen quantitatively in Gordon's Constant Growth Model, a version of the dividend discount model in which dividends are assumed to grow at a constant rate. The model is: $P0 = Div1/(k - g)$, where g = growth rate, k = cost of capital or expected return. You can see from the model that P is positive as long as $k > g$; conversely, it is negative when $g > k$. Clearly, runaway growth with poor returns is value destroying.

11 "SKU'd again, or Why Excess SKUs are killing our efficiency," *2000 Food Industry Productivity Convention*, Minneapolis, MN, October 22-25, 2000).

12 In 1965, Gordon Moore, a cofounder of Intel, predicted that the capacity of PCs would double every 18 months.

13 James McTaggert et al., *The Value Imperative* (New York: The Free Press, 1994).

14 Clemons and Thatcher, "Capital One" (see chap. 1, n.7).

15 Rebwar Taha and Gary Mitchell, "How Complexity Costs Associated with Product Portfolio Proliferation Impact Economic Profit" (proceedings from *International Mechanical Engineering Congress and Exposition*, Nashville, TN, November 14-19, 1999).

16 Marcus Aurelius Antoninus, A.D.121-180, Roman Emperor AD 161-180. From his *Meditations iii. 11*

CHAPTER 5

Complexity as a Strategic Weapon

"However beautiful the strategy, you should occasionally look at the results."

—*Sir Winston Churchill*

L eading companies including Wal-Mart and Toyota understand that market strategy cannot be viewed separately from operating strategy. Portfolio decisions regarding customers and offerings, and operational decisions regarding service, delivery, and production have direct impact on each other. In other words, strategy is a tool, not a jewel—the means for charting the path forward, which then must be executed through the company. The interactions between corporate strategy decisions and operations are the pivot points of complexity in your organization. How you exploit or conquer those points of complexity will determine the next great profit breakthrough.

At its most basic level, your options are straightforward. All decisions related to complexity fall into three categories:

1. **Change your existing portfolio of offerings**
   - Increase complexity by adding new products/services or by expanding existing brand lines, and/or
   - Decrease complexity by eliminating products, services, brands, options, etc.

2. **Improve the profitability of existing offerings**, strengthening positive Economic Profit (EP) or counteracting negative EP

3. **Minimize internal complexity** of support functions so that corporate resources can be shifted towards value-add activities

It's a given that we should all pursue options 2 and 3, making our internal costs and support operations as efficient as possible. The devil lies in deciding how best to use option 1 for your particular business. Where will providing more of the complexity that customers want allow you to grow value without reducing Process Cycle Efficiency (PCE), depressing margins, and diluting your focus with low-performing products and services? Where is it a good idea to provide less complexity? Which offerings should you leave be?

Finding answers that are right for your business is part quantitative analysis, part a change in mindset. You'll find details on the quantitative elements in Parts II and III of this book. (Part II walks you through how to get the data you need to use the Complexity Equation to determine where complexity is draining resources, and whether the solution lies in quality-, speed-, or complexity-related initiatives. Part III presents the strategies you can use to act on the results of your complexity analysis.) The focus in this chapter is on the mindset required to *think* strategically about complexity and use it as a weapon for smart growth and improved profitability.

Six Precepts For Strategic Use of Complexity

There are six precepts that drive strategic thinking about complexity:

#1: Customers define value

#2: The biggest gains from conquering complexity come from step-change improvements

#3: Focus on what matters most—100% of your value creation probably resides in only 20% to 50% of your offerings

#4: Think *value* share instead of *market* share

#5: Growth results from value-driven application of *finite* resources

#6: *First* eliminate offerings that *can never* generate positive EP, *then* attack internal complexity

Precept #1: Customers define value

Dedication to customer needs has become a byword in business over the past decade. Nowhere is it more relevant than in conquering complexity. You will never be able to make good decisions about complexity unless you know at a very detailed level what *is* and is *not* value-add from the customer's perspective (adding form, feature, or function for which the customer would be willing to pay).

The corollary to this statement is that *all* internal complexity transparent to the customer is non-value-add. It is work that your customers don't know about, don't care about, and won't pay for. Customers never see your internal complexity, but they indirectly pay the price for it in numerous ways: long wait times, higher prices, poor quality. Who pays for it directly? If you're in a market where a competitor has eliminated such non-value-add costs, your shareholders do.

There is a large body of knowledge surrounding ways to gather and interpret customer data. In Chapter 10, we'll focus on those that specifically relate to complexity decisions (*how much* of *what* is value-add).

Precept #2: The biggest gains from conquering complexity come from step-change improvements

One of the reasons why conquering complexity enables companies to break through profit and growth ceilings is because it releases committed resources or fixed costs that can then be better used to generate positive EP. For example, it is an article of faith that we should always try to meet or exceed customer expectations for quality, cost, and delivery. But complexity analysis shows that the greatest cost savings usually occur only when you push gains in PCE and associated lead times far beyond the level required to meet customer needs.

Why? In part because so many non-value-add costs are quantized, meaning there is a break point below which you can eliminate the cost entirely and above which you have some base level of cost. You might recall the discussion of Figure 1.5 (reproduced [below]) that showed how costs could drop dramatically once lead time for this operation approached 3 days. That sharp drop reflected the fact that the company could now close down a warehouse and satellite manufacturing facility. Note that the company was meeting customer expectations even before the 3-day lead time; but going beyond that limit is what allowed them to provide offering complexity with much less cost.

Figure 1.5: (Reproduced from Chapter 1)

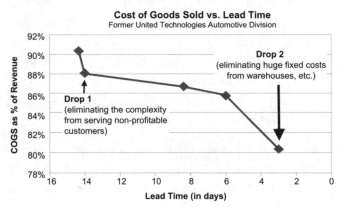

Here's another example in consumer goods: large outlays for advertising are freed up not with the withdrawal of a single product but with the withdrawal of a brand. When Procter & Gamble shifted marketing revenues away from a broad base of brands to focus on core brands, total market share increased from 24.5% to 28%.

What this means at a practical level is that once you start including complexity thinking in your strategic planning, you *may* well start setting improvement goals that are step-change in nature, and exceed those based on customer needs alone.

Precept #3: Focus on what matters most—100% of your value creation probably resides in only 20% to 50% of your offerings

The Pareto principle generally states that the majority of an effect is due to a minority of causes (the 80/20 rule). It has become ubiquitous in corporate life largely because the Pareto effect is everywhere. To an increasing degree, corporate leaders are recognizing that applying Pareto thinking to a thorough analysis of their offering portfolio yields critical insights. An assessment of EP by offering will often show that management time and corporate resources are being squandered on offerings that do not earn a positive EP.

A portion of your portfolio may act as a loss-leader and help to strategically support the brand—typically, such offerings are far fewer than is generally believed. Without a conscious focus on value, a product/ service line strategy can be a chief cause of non-value-add complexity and *diminish* the value of brilliant, highly innovative customer offerings. The good news is that attention to this precept also provides enormous leverage and focus in your shareholder returns, your growth rate, and your improvement efforts (e.g., Capital One). The alternative is dilution of profits and focus, as your competitors cherry-pick the pockets of value. (You'll find more details on portfolio assessment in Part II.)

Precept #4: Think value share instead of market share

Procter & Gamble embarked on a SKU-slashing program in the mid-nineties during which they focused on premium brands at the expense of lower-potential secondary brands. Many believed that revenues would decrease, independent of any cost savings. However, as mentioned above, *total market share increased.* P&G's share price outperformed the DJIA by nearly 50% from 1995 to 1998. How did this happen? Not only was management focus more concentrated and marketing expenditures more effective, but the effectiveness of the retailers' promotions and merchandizing increased with less complexity.

Put alternatively: P&G set as their goal *value share* (the % of total potential value creation in a given market or industry), rather than *market share.* And while the two metrics are not *necessarily* in opposition, using market share as a key metric will drive different behaviors and strategies than using value share. The difference between them often represents the difference between smart growth and dumb growth.[1] Differences in customer profitability and micro-segmentation profitability can lead to the same market yielding many different profit profiles.

The traditional, sometimes misleading, rationale is that profits follow revenues. And while management fundamentally may understand that this idea is sometimes false, management policies and strategies almost always encourage revenue without regard to profit. The question that needs to be asked is: Where is value created within this industry, within this value chain?

Figure 5.1 illustrates a study in *Harvard Business Review* showing operating margins by value chain segment in the auto industry. One lesson is that rather than yearn for more gross market share, companies may want to consider fragmenting the value chain. Toyota, for example, keeps in-house the processes and production it deems of strategic importance and outsources the rest. It has pinpointed—and focused upon—the areas in which to claim a stake to value share.

Figure 5.1: Operating Margin vs. Segment Revenue (Automotive Industry)

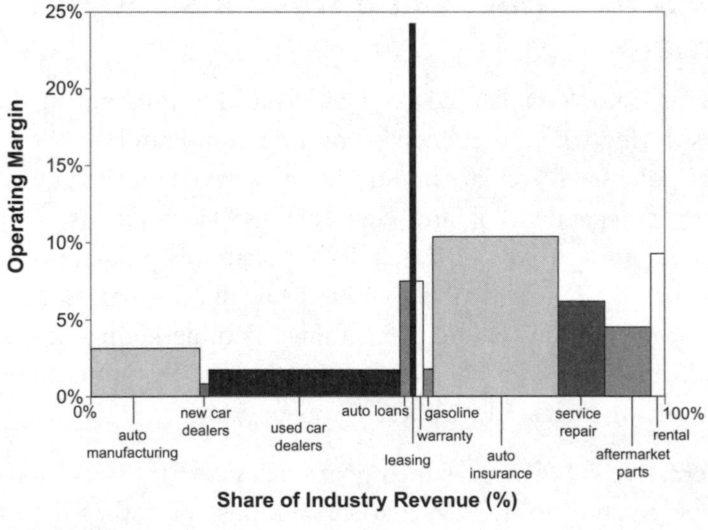

This bar chart illustrates how profits do not always follow revenue. As you can see, leasing contributes very little overall to the auto industry's profit pool (its bar is very narrow), but it does generate significant operating margins (the bar is very tall). Conversely, used car sales generate substantial revenue (its bar is very wide), but do not generate much margin (the bar is short).

Growing towards a value position is often possible by building to adjacent positions in more profitable segments, leveraging your core business; or by absenting your company from the least profitable segments while maintaining industry brand position.

One company that has practiced the pursuit of value share is Virgin Atlantic Airways, under CEO Richard Branson. Having established and continuing to uphold an outstanding brand, particularly in the U.K. and Europe, Branson leads his company into numerous industries such as cosmetics, insurance, banking, and credit cards, in many cases limiting the company's role to being a brand and publicity provider, while a partner puts up the capital. As producers enter the fray, the economics of the

What to do with the "losers"

Every company is going to find some products or services that are losers from an EP and value viewpoint. That does NOT mean the company should immediately target that offering for elimination. Experience has shown that process improvements can eliminate the cost of complexity of many of these offerings and make them value creators. Some of the new-found "losers" may have good growth opportunities.

We can extend this process to deliberately fragment the market around unique needs to create customer loyalty and higher margins (the Capital One, Toyota model). Other offerings have such a high intrinsic cost compared to the price customers are willing to pay that even reducing their contribution to overhead cost or raising prices to the maximum the market will bear will not allow these offerings to earn their cost of capital. In such an instance we can follow Greg Brennaman's advice during the turnaround at Continental Airlines: "Well, why don't we just stop doing things that lose money?"

Remember that not all customers are profitable customers. Chapter 1 described how Southwest reduced internal complexity by using common equipment, creating a multifunction work force, etc., but they also reduced external complexity by selecting routes that could earn money, a process Continental pursued just as aggressively. Part II of this book will help you identify offerings that are currently losers, but explore use of the techniques described in Part III to see if you can improve their economic position before abandoning them.

upstream production come under pressure. Virgin, however, seizes on the final and most valuable component of the value stream—in this case, the customer contact and brand—and uses those assets to win favorable partnership terms.

Precept #5: Growth results from value-driven application of finite resources

> *Growth is simply a component—usually a plus, sometimes a minus—in the value equation... Market commentators and investment managers who glibly refer to "growth" and "value" styles as contrasting approaches to investment are displaying their ignorance, not their sophistication.*
>
> —*Warren Buffett, in a letter to shareholders, 2000*

Nearly every business will place "good growth" (growth through value-add products and services that generate positive Economic Profit) high on its list of strategic priorities. Value-add products and services are, by definition, the kind of complexity *that customers want and will pay for*— it means your offering is differentiated and unique enough to warrant a premium.

However, just as capital is not free, neither is time and management focus. Value-based organizations understand this and, similar to the process of asset allocation, will allocate time to the highest-value activities. The practice is implemented from the office or shopfloor up to the Board room, where Board meeting time is apportioned depending on how much value is at stake with each decision. Complexity imposes not only a capital production cost but also consumes a portion of the (finite) marketing budget, dilutes the focus of the sales force, and competes for ever-diminishing management focus.

The implication is that one of the first constraints you will face as an organization is management talent. Aligning that talent with your highest value opportunities increases the chances of success. For example, Unilever, a leading consumer goods company, decided in the late 1990s to redo the product strategy. Said Niall Fitzgerald, Unilever's co-chairman at that time, "We dissipate our energy and resources on far too many brands. We currently have around 1,600 brands, between 5,000 and 10,000 stock-keeping units per business group, and fragmented delivery systems to our customers."

The company decided to focus its $6 billion advertising budget on just 400 key brands that commanded a price premium, had an edge in distribution, and had global scale. It staffed these power brands with its best management talent and focused resources in distribution, advertising, and marketing on these key high-EP items. Thus, Dove was expanded from 13 countries to 75 (its sales doubled), while other lesser brands were folded.[2]

Precept #6: **First** eliminate offerings that can never generate positive Economic Profit, **then** attack internal complexity

There's a simple logic behind this precept: you'll be wasting time and money if you invest in trying to improve processes that are supporting products or services or tasks that can never earn more than their cost of capital, and hence can only destroy shareholder value. This holds true at all levels. If you decide that you can't salvage a low-EP offering, get rid of it first, then focus your improvement efforts on the higher-EP offerings that remain. If you're trying to improve internal operations, get rid of the complexity of those operations first before launching specific Six Sigma or Lean initiatives.

It is always difficult to leave a business that defines your culture, as Intel found when they exited the commodity memory business. The competition was selling these chips at a lower cost that Intel could *ever* achieve. Andy Grove chronicles this gut-wrenching decision in his wonderful book, *Only the Paranoid Survive*. This freed the company to focus on creating a highly differentiated microprocessor business... the most successful semiconductor company in history. Some businesses are not for you. Remember Buffett's comment:

> *In a commodity business, it is difficult to be a lot smarter than your dumbest competitor.*

—*Berkshire Hathaway Annual Report, 1990*   **79**

ALDI International: A case study in strategic complexity[3]

Germany-based ALDI International, which describes itself as a "limited assortment discount international retailer," has turned its supply chain management—and its approach to conquering complexity—into a sustainable competitive advantage. The stores were founded after World War II by two brothers who built the company into a global giant with sales of around EUR 33 billion. The company has more than 5,000 stores across the world, including many in Europe, Australia, and more than 600 in the U.S.

What is unique about ALDI? It shelves 700 different items—but no more. When you consider that most supermarkets today stock anywhere from 15,000 to 40,000 different items (or 20 to 60 times more than ALDI), you can see that ALDI has a unique position in the marketplace. (Unique compared with the rest of the retail segment, but much in common with the warehouse stores, such as Costco and Wal-Mart's Sam's Club. Says Costco CFO Richard Galanti, "Our task is to sell high volume of a few items."[4])

ALDI's strategy for success: offer the most-needed, most-often-used products in the average home; strip away the complexity found at most superstores that results from a prolific number of SKUs—and be the lowest cost provider of these limited items. ALDI professes a "no frills" environment so as not to add to the product cost. There are no bagging clerks, fancy displays, check cashing, or preferred customer savings cards. ALDI's stated aim is to make it "virtually impossible" for competitors to match its combination of quality and price.

In effect, ALDI has simply excised the low-volume products from its shelves, recognizing that they cause massive complexity costs and provide little return. Indeed, according to a P&G Study, **one-quarter of all SKUs on supermarket shelves sell less than one unit per month**. Like Wal-Mart, ALDI occupies the low-cost provider position. In terms of revenues, Wal-Mart is approximately 6 times larger than ALDI. However, due to ALDI's operating strategy, it produces far higher sales per SKU, averaging a per-SKU sales of EUR 30 million, versus Wal-Mart's

global per-SKU sales of EUR 1.5 million. Compared with Wal-Mart's Germany stores, ALDI's prices were 20% lower.

Eating Away the Competition

As Figure 5.2 illustrates, ALDI's strategy has resulted in significant growth in terms of both stores and revenues. A key tenet of that growth is vigilance on price. Whenever a supplier lowers a price, ALDI immediately lowers the retail price, so that any stock in the supply chain is sold to the customer at lower prices. The customer also benefits from the speed of the checkout process. Capping the number of SKUs to 700 greatly increases the speed and reduces variation in the cashier process.

But what has the competitive impact of ALDI been? Consider:

Figure 5.2: ALDI's Growth

Year	Revenues (million Euro)	Number of Stores
1955	15	100
1975	3,100	1,000
1985	8,700	2,000
1995	14,200	3,000
1998	17,900	3,250
2002	22,500	3,700

- In Germany, ALDI holds 51% of the fruit juice market, 42% of the canned vegetables market, and 50% of the packaged and preserved meat products market

- Around 95% of ALDI SKUs are house brands *sold only at ALDI outlets*; its house brand laundry detergent has an estimated German market share of 25%

- According to Young and Rubicam in 2000, ALDI was the most well-recognized brand in Germany after Coca Cola and Nivea. And in one survey, 82% of West Germans claim to shop at ALDI vs. 27% for the next largest competitor.

ALDI understands that we primarily go to the supermarket for staple items. If a quarter of all SKUs on supermarket shelves sell less than one unit per month—very few customers buy these items—why should ALDI carry the burden of this overhead and have to pass it on to the customer in the form of higher prices? This is the equivalent of charging someone with a low-risk financial profile the same rate as someone who is high-risk.

ALDI has segmented the market *by the level of complexity incurred* and in so doing, has accelerated its learning curve: introducing its own brand of products, increasing its buying power, and limiting its complexity costs. Competitors are left with the low-volume products that sell infrequently. Once the margins of the poor sellers are adjusted to account for complexity, many are value-destroying.

ALDI's Secret of Success: Eternal watch against complexity

ALDI's other key tenet is **resistance to complexity**. Adding variety can be a temptation on paper. To add 50 new articles would easily increase sales by EUR 1 billion, according to Dieter Brandes, long-time manager at ALDI and author of a book about the stores. ALDI has resisted this temptation for decades.

Is this a typical corporate response? Definitely not. The opportunity for more revenue is normally seized upon. And it takes great discipline—and moreover, understanding the **full economic cost** required to produce that revenue—to resist.

"Experience has shown that infrastructure costs in companies grows in proportion to the number of various offerings," says Christian Homburg, Professor for Business Administration at the WHU in Koblenz. "In the decision process to add new variants, one assumes that the fixed costs are there already and will cover the new additional variant without addition."

Incremental decisions to increase complexity can result in quantum leaps in fixed costs (e.g., new warehouses, new technologies, new organizations to manage the new complexity). ALDI avoids these costs by strenuously resisting proliferation. And it simplifies supply chain management. If an item is not in stock, ALDI reorders, keeping one-week capacity for each article in the store. This very simple system worked well for many years even before computers supported the process.

In another instance, ALDI held back until recently in adding cashier scanners to the stores. As long as the stores had no computers, no phones were needed. Only after scanners were added to the cash registers were telephone lines required.

ALDI has withstood all temptations for growth that would have created complexity, including:

- expansion of the offering beyond 700 items

- diversification into other areas

- purchasing decisions based on supplier special offers

For many years, fruit, vegetables, frozen goods, and even butter were not carried, and when these were finally added, other articles were dropped to keep the total number of SKUs constant in the stores.

Conclusion (and a look ahead)

Integrating the precepts described above into your strategic and tactical thinking will help you decide how to use complexity best in your business. As noted above, though, these qualitative insights are only half of the equation—you also need quantitative tools. The elements of these tools—Economic Profit, Process Cycle Efficiency, and the Complexity Equation—have already been introduced in previous chapters. Here's a quick preview of how these elements come together in the methodology you'll find in Part II. The purpose of the quantitative methodology is to focus your attention on the largest creators and destroyers of shareholder value and help you find ways to defend the creators and reform or eliminate the destroyers. The way you get there is to...

1. **Identify strategic complexity targets:**
    - Identify Business Unit segments in which there is a value-creation opportunity
    - Assess how the market is rewarding or punishing complexity over time
    - Benchmark key data internally and externally to identify areas of complexity (Complexity Profile)

2. **Map and quantify cost impact of complexity:** Each product, service, feature, option, etc., affects a host of processes and tasks in ways that are usually invisible unless you map the workflow and collect data on key process factors (speed, quality, delays, non-value-add waste, etc.). The flow and data on multiple processes are captured in a Complexity Value Stream Map; the data gathered is used to establish baseline PCE measures.

3. **Create a Value Agenda:** The last steps in the process help you evaluate how much PCE is destroyed by each of your offerings at each key step in your value stream, and determine the best options for dealing with the very high or very low consumers of PCE. The outcome is a set of specific projects targeted at specific complexity or improvement opportunities, and associated with data-based projections of gains in Economic Profit.

Endnotes

1 Market share can be a good proxy for value share when the market yields high EP%, with good growth rates, low current market share, and an unresponsive set of incumbents.

2 Andrew Pierce, Hanna Moukanas, Rick Wise, "Brand Portfolio Economics: Harnessing a Group of Brands to Drive Profitable Growth," A Mercer Commentary, 2002.

3 The case history was compiled from German sources by William C. Zeeb, Jr., a Director for George Group in Geneva, Switzerland. His current role includes working with executives to plan and rapidly deploy Lean Six Sigma-based Continuous Improvement. Mr. Zeeb has trained more than 400 managers in Lean Six Sigma and Conquering Complexity methodologies in both transactional and manufacturing environments in 15 European countries. Prior to joining the George Group, he held leadership positions with Delphi Automotive, General Electric, Viterra Energy Services and the Adam Opel AG, where he gathered deep cultural understanding of driving change in various European environments.

4 Lorrie Grant, "Warehouse stores aren't just for those pinching pennies: Big Three set lures for upscale customers," *USA Today*, June 20, 2003.

PART II

Complexity Analysis: Quantifying and Prioritizing Your Complexity Opportunities

Executive Overview
of Complexity Analysis

Part I of this book laid out the argument that solving complexity problems can help you create enormous shareholder value. The question now is how exactly to leverage complexity to gain a larger share of the revenue and Economic Profit (EP) in your industry. The stakes are high. As the case studies in Part I proved, there's a huge payoff if you tackle the right targets but also a lot of ways to invest resources with little effect if you pick the wrong targets. So if ever there was a time when rigor is needed, this is it.

The purpose of the Complexity Analysis described in the next three chapters is to make the conquest of complexity (and its benefits) available to all competent managers through a well-defined quantitative methodology that supplements and informs business judgment. After a lot of research and analysis, we've developed the following process (also shown in Figure II.1):

- **Phase 1: Select Targets.** The goal is to focus your complexity efforts by identifying business units where there is good reason to suspect that complexity is either hindering EP or could serve to increase it. This phase relies on calculating EP and analyzing market trends to evaluate where you have the most "value-at-stake."

- **Phase 2: Map and Quantify the Impact.** These steps provide the rigorous backbone that is missing from most complexity analyses. We'll show you how to create a Complexity Value Stream Map, which depicts how the *full variety* of your offerings impacts your processes, and how to use the Complexity Equation to quantify this impact.

- **Phase 3: Build a Complexity Value Agenda.** These steps provide the segue from fact to action. The steps lead you through a process for using the quantitative information you've just generated to explore and select different options for attacking the complexity problems or opportunities specific to your business.

Figure II.1 Complexity Analysis Process

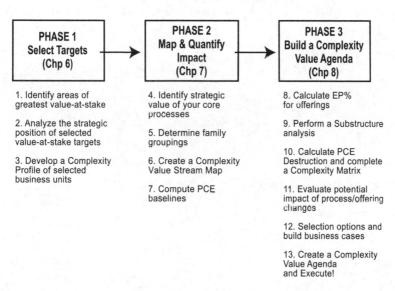

What happens if you skip any of the analytical steps? The decisions, the actions, the inactions—all the drivers that caused the issues in the first place—reassert themselves. You will generate considerable value by "conquering complexity" in the individual projects you select. But there is just as much value in *preventing* the reemergence of non-value-add complexity.

It is only through the data-based, process-focused approach that you can quantitatively identify activities that are value-destroying and those that hold promise for greater value creation. Imagine embarking on a project to reduce complexity-related costs without the process view: while you may stumble onto the right choices, that's unlikely. And moreover, you may just assume that some offerings are dogs rather than realizing it's the processes through which they pass that are the problem, leading to wrong decisions to pull a product instead of fix the process.

Data-based methodologies that reliably generate results achieve that status in part because they do *not* rely on continual heroic efforts by a few tenacious managers. Rather, they are robust because of their transparent framework for understanding and remedying company issues. This is the reason for adopting and absorbing the methodology for conquering complexity. To maintain the gains, you'll need to do more than just creating a value agenda. Therefore "conquering" complexity must become part of the culture (*see* Chapter 14: Creating the Culture to Conquer Complexity).

Which one first: Lean, Six Sigma, or conquering complexity? Ending the tool debate

A Master Black Belt from a major Aerospace company told us that the Complexity Equation and the described analytical approach nails down once and for all the issue of what to do first. He said that one of their major problems is that, in Lean Six Sigma, some Black Belts are of the opinion that they ought to apply Lean tools first then apply Six Sigma tools, while others think just the opposite. This has led to divided camps within the company. But the Complexity Equation effectively ends this debate, replacing opinion and speculation with fact and analysis. This of course drives the formulation of the Complexity Value Agenda.

CHAPTER 6

Identify Strategic Complexity Targets

(Complexity Analysis Phase 1)

With James Works[1]

This chapter walks you through three analyses that will help you figure out where and how increasing or decreasing complexity will drive strategic advantage for *your* business. You'll be looking at questions such as…

- To what degree does complexity drive our shareholder value or destroy our profits?

- How much Economic Profit (EP) are our products or services generating (or destroying)? How much *could* they generate if appropriate changes were made?

- Is the market rewarding complexity? How? How can we take advantage of it?

- How does complexity fit into our strategic goals and plans?

Subsequent chapters build on this strategic analysis by showing how to pinpoint and quantify opportunities through Complexity Value Stream Mapping and application of the Complexity Equation (Chapter 7). By looking at the value of those opportunities and exploring the impact of changes, you can build a Complexity Value Agenda that lays out specific projects with the highest potential return (Chapter 8).

Overview of Target Selection

Once you become attuned to complexity, you start seeing its impact everywhere. But the purpose here is to find areas where complexity is having the biggest impact—where too much complexity or too little variety puts a lot of shareholder value at risk. This requires a top-down approach, starting from a broad perspective then narrowing down the options based on the likelihood of a complexity effect:

Step 1. Identify areas of greatest value-at-stake

"Greatest value-at-stake" are business units or segments that are
- Destroying significant value, or
- Adding significant value *and* that warrant significant expansion or extension

You'll be using Economic Profit as an indicator of value creation, calculated from data in your income statements and balance sheets.

Graphical summary used: Waterfall chart depicting EP performance for all business units.

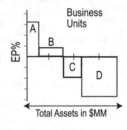

Step 2. Analyze the strategic position of selected value-at-stake targets

Before deciding how complexity can help or hurt your business, you need to understand *why* the business units/segments with a lot of value-at-stake are creating or destroying shareholder value and *how* the market is rewarding or penalizing the complexity in those units over time. The purpose here is to understand the trajectory of different business units and their markets, so you can understand what it will take to capitalize on the opportunity.

Graphical summary used: Strategic Position chart depicting the competitive position of business units with the most value-at-stake

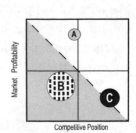

Step 3. Develop a Complexity Profile of selected business units

A Complexity Profile captures key indicators relevant to your business that are often influenced by offering and process complexity. (They are industry-specific, but include percent reuse of processes, tasks, parts; the number of different service options; the number of steps in a process, and so on). Where possible, it will help if you can compare the complexity numbers in the targeted business units with competitors (or, minimally, to other units within your business). This comparison will expose areas where the targeted business units have too much or too little complexity compared to the market—areas that should form the basis of the remaining analysis in Chapters 7 and 8.

Graphical summary used: Complexity Profile chart showing your complexity numbers and, if possible, those of competitors and/or industry standards.

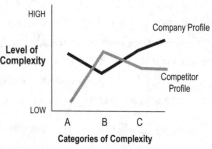

These three steps will help you determine where your investment in conquering complexity will yield the biggest gains in profits and growth.

Capitalizing on Complexity Analysis

The first two steps of this analysis are, in fact, much more than a Complexity Analysis. They will generate a lot of strategic insights for your business whether or not you have a complexity problem or opportunity. You will, in fact, be challenged to think about your business's past, present, and future. That's why it's best to have an executive-level team conduct at least this first phase of Complexity Analysis.

Step 1: Identify areas of greatest value-at-stake

Given that we want to generate the most shareholder value, the first criteria for narrowing down our focus is "which business units are creating value and which are destroying value?" In other words, after considering capital costs, identify which segments are generating positive EP (ripe for growth or expansion) and which are generating negative EP and destroying shareholder value (which we need to fix or exit).

Data You'll Need to Identify Value-at-Stake

The data you need for this analysis is EP for each of your business units, which means knowing how much capital they employ or assets they tie up (on which there is a capital charge). Because we are looking at whole business units, GAAP does a good job of supplying valid data. (The problem created by managerial accounting and the allocation of overhead costs to various offerings *within* a business unit will be discussed later.)

Look again at the Economic Profit equation from Chapter 4:

$$\text{Economic Profit (\$)} = (\text{ROIC\%} - \text{WACC\%}) * \text{Invested Capital (\$)}$$

where ROIC% = percent return on invested capital
WACC% = weighted average cost of capital

You can also see this equation represented as:

$$\text{Economic Profit (\$)} = \text{NOPAT} - \text{Capital Charge}$$

Where NOPAT = net operating profit after tax
Capital Charge = Invested Capital*WACC

Both of these equations are valid ways to calculate EP, but for our purposes here we want to use EP for *comparing* the performance of different units or segments. So it's most useful to look at *percent* EP instead of dollar figures:

$$\text{Economic Profit (\%)} = \text{ROIC\%} - \text{WACC\%}$$

The data needed to calculate EP% are usually readily available in a business unit's income statement and balance sheet.[2] For example, what is the Economic Profit of a business unit with an income statement and balance sheet like those shown in Figure 6.1?

Figure 6.1: Sample Income Statement and Balance Sheet

INCOME STATEMENT		BALANCE SHEET	
Sales	**100**	Assets	
COGS		Cash	10
Materials	58	Inventory	45
Labor	7	Accts Receivable	15
Mfg Overhead	10	PP&E	30
Total COGS	75	Other Assets	10
		Total Assets	110
Gross Profit	**25**		
R&D	5	Liabilities	
SG&A	7	Accts Payable	10
Operating Profit	13	Accrued Expenses	5
Interest Expense	2	Current Debt	5
Taxes	4	Other Current Liabilities	10
Net Income	7	Long-term Debt	45
		Total Liabilities	75
		Shareholders' Equity	35
		Total Liabilities + Equity	110

All figures in thousands of dollars

WACC = 10% (figure provided from other sources)
Total Assets = 110 − 10 = 100
Current Liabilities = 10+ 5 + 5 + 10 = 30
Invested Capital (IC) = Total Assets − Current Liabilities = 70

$$EP = \text{Net Operating Profit After Taxes (NOPAT)} - \text{Cost of Capital}$$
$$= (\text{Operating Profit} - \text{Taxes}) - (\text{WACC} \times \text{Invested Capital})$$
$$= (13 - 4) - [10\% \times 70] = 2$$

$$EP\% = ROIC\% - WACC\%$$
$$= (\text{NOPAT} / \text{IC}) - \text{WACC}$$
$$= (9 / 70) - 10\% = 12.9\% - 10\% = 2.9\%$$

Interpreting Economic Profit

Once you've calculated EP% for your business units or segments, it helps to plot the results on a chart like that shown in Figure 6.2. The height and direction of each bar represents the amount (in percentage) and direction of EP generation (positive is above the midline; negative below). The width of the bars represents the amount of capital tied up in that business unit. The arrangement in order from largest positive EP to largest negative EP generates the "waterfall" pattern that gives this chart its nickname.

Figure 6.2: Waterfall Chart of Financial Profiles

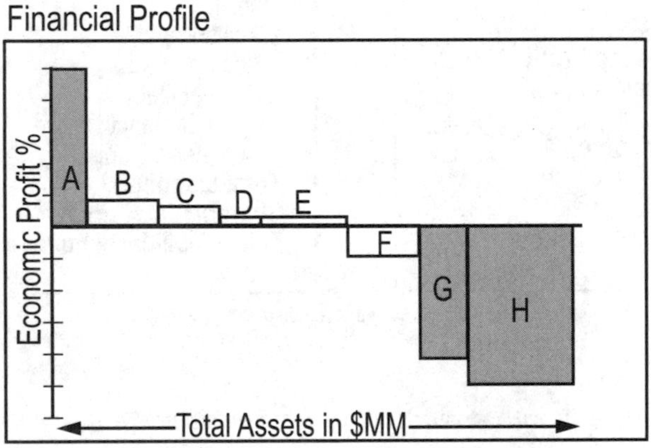

Financial Profile

This figure shows the EP plotted for the company's eight business units. The X-axis is the amount of invested capital. The Y-axis is the EP%, defined as the difference between ROIC% and the cost of capital. The width and direction of the bars indicate the total assets of each business unit and whether it is creating or destroying value. For example, the bar for Business Unit A is tall (that's good—it means a lot of positive EP) and narrow (meaning it does not consume much capital). The bar for Business Unit E is very short (not much positive EP) and very wide (it consumes a lot of capital). Likely targets identified by this chart are Unit A because it has high EP (growth or expansion may be able to capitalize on that attractiveness) and Units G and H, which are the biggest destroyers of value and therefore need to be either fixed or eliminated.

Waterfall charts provide a snapshot that indicates which business units or segments are generating positive EP and which are generating negative EP. For our purposes, the most important features in a waterfall chart are the extremes, because those are the business units that likely represent the greatest value-at-stake (places with large value creation or destruction), and so would be near the top of our list of targets for further complexity analysis. The ability to find these high-value targets is more important that the ability to finesse the marginally good or bad.

> **Another level of waterfalls**
>
> Later in the Complexity Analysis, you'll be taking the waterfall analysis down another level to look at Economic Profit for various products or services within a business unit.

Getting More From Your Waterfall Chart

As stated above, the early stages of complexity analysis serve a much broader strategic purpose. In Figure 6.2, for example, Unit G is shown to be destroying value, but internally it was seen as a fast-growing segment and potential platform for the future. This snapshot suggests that margins in G would have to be improved as volume increased and as more human and financial capital is invested.

This analysis can also highlight units that can be exploited as great engines of economic growth. For example, Unit A—while not being very asset-intensive—is nonetheless a strong value creator, so the company should look for growth opportunities there. Moreover, the company should be very alert to any competitive threat to A's position, and should have contingency plans to meet it, preferably with more differentiated products as opposed to price cutting.

By the end of this analysis, you should know how much EP is generated or destroyed by each business unit, and how they compare to each other. Select those at the extremes as your first targets for continued analysis. If you have the time, energy, and resources, you can complete the rest of the analysis for all your business units, but, again, focusing on those at the extremes is where you will likely have the biggest impact most quickly.

Step 2: Analyze the strategic position of selected value-at-stake targets

Profitability is an important metric to analyze corporate performance and locate value "pools." To capitalize on these pools, you will need to understand what is driving the current level of profitability (good or poor), how you compare to competitors, and what the shaping trends are. In other words, the financial analysis of Step 1 can tell you *where* you're creating value; a strategic position analysis can tell you *why*.

There are two outputs from this strategic analysis: knowledge about overall *market* profitability and the relative advantage or disadvantage of your business units (*competitive* position). Ideally, it helps to compare at least two points in time to understand more about the future (directions and trends) and the best actions to take.

Data You'll Need to Evaluate Strategic Position

To make meaningful decisions about complexity, you have to understand how complexity is or is not rewarded in the markets you serve.

The first piece of information you need is **market profitability**, data that will tell you if the market as a whole is profitable or if everyone struggles to make a profit.

To put a number on market profitability you must estimate EP for all the major players in the markets that your business units compete in. (It may take some digging through many balance sheets and income statements from public sources to come up with figures. Keep attuned to sources within your industry where relevant data might appear).

Another important piece of market information is **competitive position**: how well you're doing *relative to your competition*. For the purposes of this analysis, we'll calculate competitive position as your EP relative to the market average EP. (You'll use this information as the basis for discussions about whether your current levels of complexity and differentiation equate to market advantage, and, more to the point, what are the drivers of market advantage?)

Using and Interpreting Strategic Position Data

Armed with market and competitive data and a measure of revenue for each business unit, you can create a Strategic Position chart (also known as a Bubble Chart[3]) like that shown in Figure 6.3.

Figure 6.3: Strategic Position Chart

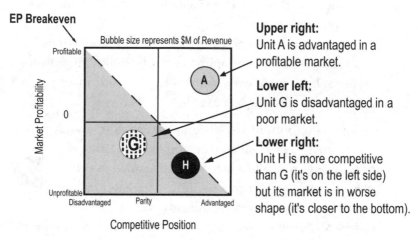

Upper right:
Unit A is advantaged in a profitable market.

Lower left:
Unit G is disadvantaged in a poor market.

Lower right:
Unit H is more competitive than G (it's on the left side) but its market is in worse shape (it's closer to the bottom).

The chart illustrates the strategic profile of the three biggest value-at-stake business units from the analysis in Step 1. Market profitability (vertical axis) for each segment is the average EP of all dominant players in that particular line of business. The horizontal axis indicates competitive position, and in this scenario reflects Business Unit EP relative to the market average (= level of advantage). Units A, G, and H all participate in different markets so the assessments of profitability and competitive advantage were done separately for each.

Where a business unit falls on this type of chart gives you an overall gauge of its current strengths or weaknesses:

- **Top right** (such as Unit A) means the unit is in a good competitive position in a good market

- **Bottom left** (such as Unit G) means the unit is in a poor competitive position in a poor market

- **Bottom right** (such as Unit H) means the unit is an advantaged player in an unprofitable market

- **Top left** means the market is profitable but the unit is disadvantaged

What can you do with this information? In the first two cases, the appropriate course of action is relatively certain:

- **Top right** means you have a star that is highly profitable and should be strongly supported and defended. You need to look for information that will tell you what the drivers are of the advantage for that unit and how you can capitalize on it. For example, can you continue to differentiate with well-picked brand extensions? Can you reduce the cost and improve the flexibility of delivering this highly valued complexity and hence allow for more complexity? Does a competitive threat exist?

- Being in the **bottom left** quadrant means the unit is disadvantaged in a bad market. You need to either exit or find ways to make a major and sustained improvement in your competitive position. The latter usually requires a radical reduction in cost (and since complexity is often the largest creator of high cost, look towards simplification). If your offerings are high in cost *and* poorly regarded in a bad industry, management talent and capital may be better applied to other opportunities.

Business units in the other two quadrants occupy ambiguous territory:

- **Bottom right:** You *can* be profitable in a bad market (such as Southwest) but there are generally fewer winners than losers here. With lower overall market profitability, cost control is critical. In Figure 6.3, Unit H is in the lower right, and therefore a prime target for further complexity analysis. It is a high-volume unit in an industry with bad economics, but its products are components in a well-known brand name consumer product, so it has an advantaged position. But they need to reduce cost. Unit H has great potential for value creation, *if* the company can reduce complexity costs and free up operations to focus on process improvements and on customers where the company can be advantaged.

- **Top left:** The market is profitable overall but companies may nonetheless fail to differentiate themselves significantly or they may pick a poor strategy and so struggle. **High overall market profitability is no guarantee of individual corporate success.** If one of your business units falls into this area, your focus needs to be on improving competitive position, which means understanding the sources of advantage in that particular segment. This may mean developing or improving offering features or significantly reducing cost (reducing complexity costs will be a key factor either way), and establishing closer connections with customers.

Mining Market Profitability and Competitive Position Data

Your ability to generate positive EP reflects the costs in the current level of complexity, pricing decisions, and level of differentiation. To gain a rigorous understanding of Competitive Position requires examining levels of differentiation, exploring factors such as performance levels (in quality, speed, product or service features/price), benchmarking your economic costs at each stage of the value chain, and comparing these numbers, as best you can, to your competitors. The goal is to understand the reasons *why* a unit will be less or more profitable over time.

You can start down this analytical path by going back to the market profitability figures you've already gathered and plot EP as a percent of invested capital for you and your major competitors (*see* example in Figure 6.4, next page.)

The question is what accounts for your business being where it is relative to competitors. Your profitability (or lack thereof) can be the result of a number of forces: customer pressures, the intensity of competition (both direct and indirect), supplier pressures, regulatory issues that change the playing field, the threat of future entry by other firms, etc.

Figure 6.4: Simulated Market Profitability Comparison

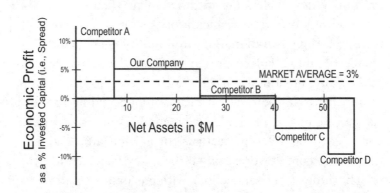

Comparing EP and assets between you and your competitors can be as illuminating as looking at EP of your internal business units. As you might expect, however, the data are somewhat harder to get and you have to decide how you will define exactly what you're comparing. For the purposes of illustration, we've simulated a situation in which the companies each get 100% of their business from the same customer segments. In real life, you and your competitors probably compete only in several of your segments, so you'll have to "disaggregate" financial data to make sure you're comparing EP figures for the segment you're interested in. Data for the analysis of competitors' profitability (and the segments they participate in) often resides inside the company or can be augmented with interviews of suppliers, customers, business managers, or third party sources.

The only downside of the Strategic Position and Market Profitability Comparison charts is that they represent only a snapshot, a moment in time. It will tell you how the market is *currently* rewarding your offering and, by extension, the level of complexity in it. As we have discussed, customer tastes change, competitors enter the market, and market EP diminishes over time as differentiation is eroded. In response, firms will introduce new goods and services, often extending the original line.

So you can add depth to your analysis by looking at **how the market is rewarding (or punishing) complexity over time.** You'll need to either track market performance over time or at least make grounded estimates about future trends, then create a new Strategic Position chart that represents at least two moments in time ("past+now" or "now+future" projections), as shown in Figure 6.5 (next page).

Figure 6.5: Time-oriented Strategic Position Chart

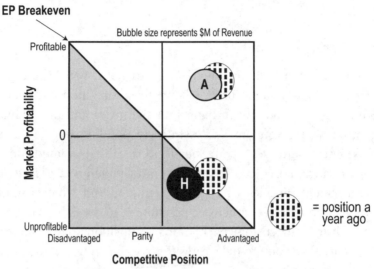

This figure shows the same business units A and H from Figure 6.3 but with the addition of historical data. It is evident that A has generally held advantage over the rest of the market, but its closest competitor has gained substantially in terms of EP advantage and overall growth rates. Hence its "bubble" has shifted to the left. The new bubble for A is also smaller, showing it has contracted in volume. Business Unit H has seen a bigger decline in its fortunes, and its competitors are not thriving either. That's why its bubble has shifted both to the left (a loss of competitive position) and down (less profitability in the market).

From these snapshots come clues: Unit A is at risk to its close competitor; immediate strategic response is required. The company will want to see if it can lower costs, maintain price, and use extra margins to capture back market growth. Can we extend the brand line to grow EP? What is happening in the market Unit H competes within? This may be a quickly commoditizing marketplace. Does the market value any complexity? If not, where are the opportunities for eliminating these costs?

To go beyond speculation in explaining the patterns in all the charts you've created, do a little more digging to find information about industry benchmarks on costs, price, and differentiation, in particular, as those are the most important elements in the design of proactive strategies to gain competitive advantage.

As you examine your own internal figures and market information, explore areas such as:

1) Offering decisions

Is your portfolio differentiated? You can tell if you have differentiated offerings by looking at price relative to competition and market share. Simply put, if you have a higher relative price and are maintaining or gaining share, you are successfully responding to the Voice of the Customer—and yes, your portfolio is differentiated on features, performance, speed of delivery or brand preference. (The market, not management, decides what is differentiated and what is not.) If your units are in a poor competitive position, it may be that you're not close enough to your customers. Looking at positions over time can be the first clue that you are delivering the wrong things or too many things (high complexity).

2) Cost position and configuration decisions

What are your economic costs versus your competitors' costs? If you can achieve lower relative costs at the same price, you are advantaged with higher EP. To estimate differences in cost configurations, a Financial Driver Tree such as Figure 6.6 (next page) can be used to identify "where the dollars live" in order to focus research on the important drivers. Subsequent benchmarking could be built from a number of different sources, such as sales forces, industry publications and research, as well as analysis of goods or services by cost component.

3) Price decisions

What price do you charge relative to the market average (for same product/service and features)? If a higher price, do customers still choose your product or service? The major challenge that companies face is admitting that a feature that costs extra money in fact commands no additional price in the market. One of our clients, a construction equipment producer, was proud of its ability to provide outstanding documentation with its equipment. But in a bid situation, the company could gain no price advantage from its documentation. The market had

Figure 6.6: Financial Driver Tree

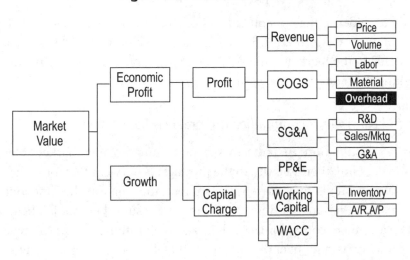

A Financial Driver Tree focuses resources on identifying key cost metrics and benchmarks for use in the Strategic Profile analysis. In the example above, the dominant cost driver is overhead, which became the focus for understanding comparative cost advantage.

changed. Instead of owner/operators, the business was moving to large leasing companies to whom such documentation was less valuable. Assessing competitor pricing can be done a number of different ways, depending on data availability and industry type. Client interviews, analyst reports, as well as research and benchmarking companies, are all potential sources for information.

4) *Speed and direction of competition*

We tend to view our own businesses and offerings as being uniquely differentiated and inimitable. However, tracking the movements of competition over a period of time illustrates just how fast competitors enter profitable markets and steal away advantage *unless a sustainable differentiation exists.* (*See* sidebar, p. 105) As we saw in Chapter 2, Dell was expert at quickly replicating advances made by Compaq and extracting more gross profit and growth with less technical risk and investment, often beating Compaq at its own game by delivering the innovation to customers at nearly the same time.

5) *Trends in market response to complexity*

Is there evidence that customers will pay higher prices for more variety or options? Are formerly premium features or options now taken for granted? Is the market commoditizing, with more and more customers making decisions on price alone?

6) *Indicators of a commoditizing marketplace*

Pay close attention to indicators of a commoditizing market. Many companies link their identity to the products or services they produce or the business units they currently operate, rather than to the functionality or value they are offering customers. As a result, they can fall behind when a segment commoditizes. The Strategic Position analysis can reveal in stark terms how overall market profitability is eroding and put the spotlight on the need to act decisively: redifferentiate, commit to being the low-cost player, or switch segments. Services tend to commoditize less swiftly than do products. Recall that it took Capital One's competitors nearly five years to close the profit gap that their strategy of deliberate complexity proliferation had created. Remember the statement of the CEO of Cisco that "products commoditize so swiftly, that in the end, the only competitive advantage you can sustain is speed, talent, and brand."

Outcome of Strategic Analysis

By the end of this analysis, you should know the relative profitability of your business units and the driving forces behind those Economic Profit figures. If you've been able to diagram two or more points in time, you will also have a trajectory of your business units, as well as a basic understanding of your competitors' strategies.

Even more important than the various charts is the "why" discussions you have presumably held among your top management. You may discover that the underlying cause of the position of a particular "strategic bubble" is not complexity and therefore requires a separate stream of actions. Or you may discover that too much or too little complexity is an underlying driver of poor competitive position or poor market position for a particular business unit.

Should you exit a commodity market?

If you find you're in a commodity market, does that mean you should exit? In letters to shareholders, Warren Buffett describes a commodity marketplace as one which is "certain to cause subnormal profitability in all circumstances but one: a shortage of usable capacity." However, we prefer the definition that one of our clients put forth: a commodity is a product or service that has **yet** to be differentiated.

The second definition is less bleak than Buffett's view, partly because it provides management with the possibility of taking action. (If you adopted Buffett's view, management's only option in a commodity market would be to create a capacity shortage!)

Naturally, there are instances in which the only prudent course of action is to exit a marketplace or segment. But the capability of providing differentiation via speed, pricing, quality or brand can lead to significant competitive advantage. Chapter 1 introduced the United Technologies Automotive story. That division was a producer of coupled hoses—certainly a commodity. Their primary customer, Ford, was troubled by line shutdowns due to lack of availability from their sources. By achieving a 3-day lead time, the UT division became differentiated from other suppliers. They met the customer's needs, became a preferred supplier to Ford, and doubled sales.

So perhaps you *don't* need to exit a commodity market; but it will be difficult to succeed without a cost advantage or a sphere of differentiation and focus that is valued by the customer. There is only room for one "lowest cost" producer in any segment, but there are an unlimited number of slots for differentiated offerings.

This knowledge will help drive your selection of complexity targets. Having focused on units that were at the extremes in the Waterfall chart, and now, based on the discussions of why those units are in a particular competitive/market position, you should be able to focus further on those you have reason to believe are suffering from the impact of complexity. For example, likely business units to target would be:

- Those that offer a very broad range of products or services and generate less EP than competitors

- Those in markets where overall market profitability is declining (complexity tactics may help you reduce costs or find value-added differentiators)

- Those that are performing very well in good markets (you may be able to exploit complexity for further competitive advantage)

It is in units with these kinds of patterns where you should perform a Complexity Profile analysis.

Step 3: Develop a Complexity Profile of selected business units

Step 1 allowed you to identify business units with a lot of value-at-stake, and Step 2 should have allowed you to focus on the reasons for that performance. Here in Step 3, you will compare some of the key drivers of complexity to yield initial insights and provide direction as to where to focus Complexity Value Stream Mapping analysis. This approach will highlight:

- Competitive complexity benchmarks that will help expose your best path for further complexity analysis

- Unique complexity effects, which may warrant special attention

Data You'll Need for a Complexity Profile

The data you'll need for a Complexity Profile consists of measures related to the specific types of complexity there may be in the products or services in the business units you're investigating. The specific metrics will vary by industry and according to availability. They are used in business unit profiles to compare key symptoms of complexity relative to competition, to prioritize and select targets for the rest of the analysis.

Product-oriented companies and manufacturers will likely want to look at metrics such as:

# of different supplier parts	customer lead times
# of unique routings	# different internal parts
# promotional SKUs	% industry standard parts
% revenues from brand extensions	growth or decay rates
% offerings representing 80% of sales	inventory turns
% reuse of components and processes	

Service-oriented companies may be more interested in:

Number of process steps

Number or service options

% shared processes (or commonality) between services

Number of decisions/steps your customers have to navigate to purchase a service, lodge a complaint, etc.

or % of customers that represent 80% of sales

% offerings and services that represent 80% of sales

Identify a handful of metrics that are relevant to the offerings in the business units you've targeted, and collect the needed data both internally and, if you can, externally. Then compare your numbers to other business units and estimates of competitors. While much of this type of data is not publicly available, we've found it possible to build up reasonable profiles based on interviews with sector experts, industry sources, and grounded assumptions.

Charting and Interpreting a Complexity Profile

Once you've gathered the necessary data, it can help to display the results visually as shown in a Complexity Profile chart. Figure 6.7 is an example of a Complexity Profile for Business Unit H from our earlier analysis; Figure 6.8 shows a comparable chart for Unit A. (Since these charts present many different kinds of data, we've made value judgments about whether the raw figures are low or high in order to determine their placement on the chart.)

Figure 6.7: Complexity Profile, Business Unit H

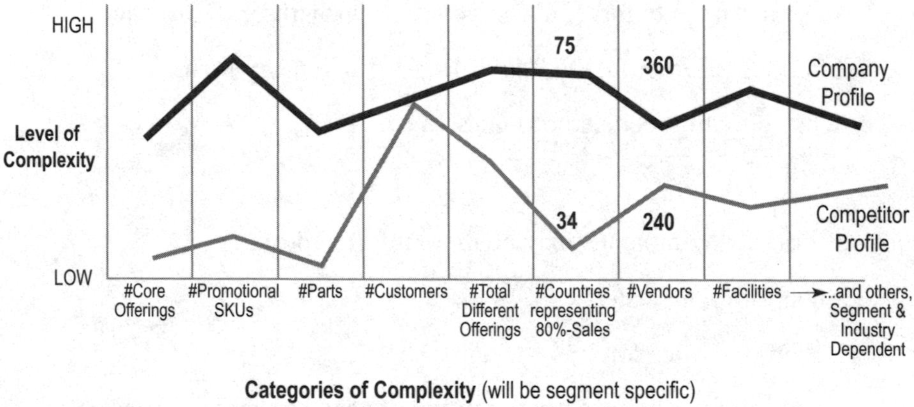

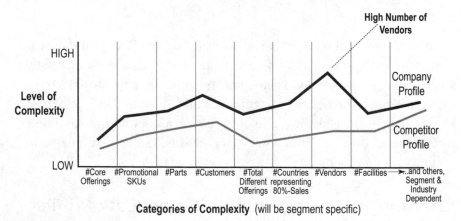

In the profile above, Unit H has higher complexity levels in nearly all categories relative to its chief competitor.

Figure 6.8: Complexity Profile, Business Unit A

Business Unit A shows a close resemblance to its nearest competitor, except for in the number of vendors.

This company conducted further financial analysis for Business Unit A and discovered that it had relatively large procurement costs (likely related to the high number of vendors), and commissioned a quick-win improvement project to tackle the issue. Though they may find opportunities for further cost reduction in Unit A, the bigger opportunities likely reside with Unit H.

Had SKF, a bearing manufacturer, performed this type of analysis, they would have seen they were at a major complexity disadvantage versus Japanese competitors because they had many more parts per plant. That kind of large asymmetry is exactly what you'll find if complexity is an underlying cause of high cost in your organization. However, the % reuse metric allows you to benchmark your present state and may trigger ideas simplifying product design (*see* Chapter 11). If all external factors are equal, then competitive advantage must be obtained by superior offerings, superior (simplified) designs , superior processes, or all three. In any case, delivering an offering with a lower cost of complexity can be a decisive cost advantage.

What You Can Learn From a Complexity Profile

Seeing actual numbers related to complexity metrics or examining a Complexity Profile chart may be the first time management takes a comparative look at complexity. Seeing the chart can trigger useful discussions. For instance, suppose you have extremely high levels of promotional offerings and variations relative to competition and low EP. The natural questions are, "Is the reliance on promotional offerings driving costs through the roof in return for an inadequate level of additional EP? What are the trade-offs? How can our competitors deliver the same product at much lower complexity—what is their business design?" Similar questions will arise for each of the different metrics you decide to chart.

Such charts also make complexity personal: It is one thing to discuss the importance of complexity, quite another to look at your company's complexity metrics vis-à-vis the competition.

Summarizing Phase 1 Lessons: Sources of exploitable advantage

It's a trap that is easy to fall into: a product or service is different, therefore it is differentiated. But this is wrong. Different just means your product or service is not identical to that of your competitors. Differentiation means your product or service has a **unique and tangible** aspect or component that the competition doesn't have and that the customer **recognizes and values** (and therefore would pay for).

For example, you may offer a product in five colors while the competition offers it in only two; or you may let customers pay in four installments while the competition requires full payment. Certainly these are differences. But are they truly differentiation? Only if your customers are willing to pay the cost of the complexity required to produce five color variants or track installment payments.

Understanding what the customer values is dynamic; customer preference can change over time. Incomplete or "once a year" intelligence on competitors can leave you with a false sense of security. We all understand the intrinsic value of our offerings and services, but are they *truly* unique and valuable, relative to competitors? In dynamic markets, it doesn't take long for competitors to catch up.

The power of differentiation, then, is best used offensively ("how can we be uniquely valuable to the customer?" or "how can we act to bolster our key products and services that are unique and differentiated?"), rather than defensively ("we're already differentiated, so we don't need to respond"). And measures for differentiation are best when externally validated, rather than when they are dependent on our own, sometimes biased, judgment.

But once you've identified where you are differentiated in the market through value-add complexity, the journey is not over. Those differentiated features, products, or services all represent sources of exploitable advantage: You may not even be aware of some of the capabilities that are inherent to your company. **But when you can beat the market and are economically profitable, it indicates a source of differentiation that can be exploited in other markets.**

Differentiation, like quality, is whatever the customer says it is. You can be differentiated on cost, quality, delivery, reliability, features, value—all of which create a superior reputation in your market. Warren Buffett comments on See's Candy:

> *It was not the fair market value of inventories, receivable, or fixed assets that produced the premium rates of return, rather it was a combination of intangible assets, particularly a pervasive favorable reputation with consumers based on countless pleasant experiences they have had with both product and personnel. Such a reputation creates a franchise that allows the value of the product to the purchaser, rather than the production cost, to be the major determinant of selling price.*

> *—Berkshire Hathaway Annual Report, 1983*

Economic Profit is usually better for an advantaged player in an industry with low overall economic profitability than it is for a disadvantaged player in a high-margin business. Dell, for instance, estimates that its costs are half that of its competitors. This has catapulted Dell to enormous advantage. It is an advantaged player, generating 34% ROIC over the past five years whereas its principal competitors barely earn their cost of capital. Starbucks demonstrated that commodity products can warrant premium pricing, given the right combination of innovation, service, and quality. Coffee consumption tumbled 50% over four decades until Starbucks reinvented it. Tyson Foods and Perdue Farms pioneered the way with differentiated products, transforming the commodity poultry business with consumer-focused branding of its meat products during the 1990s.

And what about the differentiation of H_2O? A decade ago, the bottled water market barely registered in the U.S. beverage industry. Today it is upwards of a $3.5 billion market. How? By conferring great branding. One such marketer, Peter Carnell, discussed the process of developing the branding.

"We've got to take the asset called water, and move it to an unexpected place," he told *The Wall Street Journal*. "The moment you treat it like water, you're dead."

The strategic tenets driving exploitable advantage

Identifying the key strategic tenets of your company and your competition can yield many insights. For one, how unique is your strategy? If you share all the same strategic tenets with your competition, how will you differentiate your goods and services? What can you observe about your competitors' profiles and their relative differentiation in terms of price and share? (Always include indirect as well as direct competition. You grow comfortable with a set of competitors and tend to draw a strategic frame around them and remove—for purposes of ease of comparison—other emerging trends. These frameworks can become blinders and make us vulnerable.) Check out your competitors' letters to shareholders, public conferences with financial analysts, trade show conversations. This can provide valuable information on strategic direction that can be confirmed by actual sales and marketing efforts.

In fact, you may find you share many of the same strategic tenets with your competition. So how can you differentiate? Remember: differentiate doesn't mean simply *be different*. Why is Dell still growing profitably at the expense of its competitors? Dell differentiated by price, based on an advantaged low-complexity process and a marketing and sales strategy that reinforced ever-lower levels of complexity. One way to summarize the lessons from the various charts and discussions is to build a Strategic Comparison chart, like that shown in Figure 6.9.

Figure 6.9: Strategic Comparison Summary

	Low Price	Quick Delivery	Friendly Service	Global Reach	Differentiated Features	More
Your Company	X	X		X	X	
Company A	X	X				
Company B		X	X		X	
Alternative providers	X	X	X	X		

This figure shows how to summarize insights on competitive differences or similarities. This type of summary is usually done with just a few strategic tenets listed (e.g., low price, quick delivery), which will vary by company and industry.

A simple exercise in identifying the key strategic tenets in your company, and then repeating the exercise, may drive you to see that, from a customer's perspective, there is little difference between competitors, or that the difference is at the margins. Competitors can be quick to copy external strategic moves, but are slow to copy process excellence. This understanding—and the elimination of non-value-add complexity from your processes—can lead to a strategic advantage.

Conclusion

The analytical tools in this chapter help you understand how the market is rewarding complexity in a particular market segment, guiding your strategic actions and approach to complexity over the long term, and guiding you to the highest value targets for further complexity analysis in the short term. The strategic analysis is therefore both the means for facilitating a long-term strategic vision and a way of surfacing the need to conquer complexity. Finally, the analysis will help focus resources on the highest value targets for immediate improvements in profits. Indeed, working on these "value" targets first will accelerate the improvement in Economic Profit. This form of analysis does not replace management judgment or insights that propelled Southwest, ALDI, Capital One, IPM, Henry Ford, Alfred Sloan, and Dell. Rather, it establishes a data foundation that will provide inspiration and suggest opportunities that may be hidden, and at the minimum validate a "hunch."

The three analyses in this chapter are designed to help you identify and prioritize strategic complexity targets based on an understanding of their current and future ability to generate value. Targets will be defined by:

- How various business units are performing compared with each other—which are the biggest creators of value and which are the biggest destroyers of value

- The market and competitive positions of the big creators and big destroyers

- Comparative complexity metrics for your offerings

It is those big creators and destroyers of value that will be the ripest targets and the focus of further complexity analysis.

Endnotes

1 James Works is President of George Group. Over the last 12 years, Mr. Works has gained a reputation for marketing and strategy expertise, including market segmentation, competitor analysis, new product development, business plan development, channel planning, and product line management. Mr. Works is especially skilled in applying the tools of Value Based Management and Market Opportunity Analysis to drive product rationalization, a key component of complexity reduction. Today, his client work is focused on leading senior executives through the planning and deployment of Lean Six Sigma and Complexity Reduction initiatives in Global 500 companies.

2 ROIC = Net Operating Profit After Tax/ Invested Capital where Invested Capital = Total Assets – Current Liabilities.

3 For a discussion of bubble charts, see McTaggert et al., *The Value Imperative* (see chp. 4, n. 13).

CHAPTER 7

Map & Quantify
the Impact of Complexity

(Complexity Analysis Phase 2)

With Lars Maaseidvaag[1]

The strategic analysis in the previous chapter reveals how your business units are doing in terms of Economic Profit (EP), competitive position, and market advantage. The next goal of Complexity Analysis is to identify and quantify the specific drivers of the costs in the targeted business units, to identify the cost-related and/or growth-related opportunities.

The purpose of the next phase of analysis is to expose the true costs of producing and supporting the full variety of offerings in the selected business units—as reflected in the impact they have on your processes. Recall from Chapter 2 that processes with low Process Cycle Efficiency (PCE) have high cost, and that PCE is inversely proportional to several process factors, such as the number of different offerings (the more "things" you have going through a process, the lower your PCE even if you have otherwise well-running processes).

The path to rooting out what is driving low PCE in the business units you've targeted has two elements: (1) visually displaying the work flow and process metrics for the core value stream(s) in the business unit, and (2) analyzing the process data.

This chapter walks through the visual element first, reviewing the steps for gathering relevant process data and generating a map of the complexity in a selected business unit. Such visual maps can be very powerful tools in helping people grasp where and how complexity affects their business, and why it is so necessary to control it. Then we pick up the quantitative analysis piece, showing how to establish baseline PCE measures for the value stream. (Chapter 8 will then complete the picture by providing tools and techniques to identify specific projects related to the targets exposed by the maps and other analyses.)

Overview of Mapping Complexity & Quantifying Impact

You may be familiar with the concept of value stream mapping, originated by Toyota and documented in the book *Learning to See*. A value stream map records all the steps in a process, and labels each activity as being either value-add or non-value-add (from the perspective of the customer). Besides the value-add/non-value-add determination, value stream maps differ from basic flowcharts in that they include process data, such as the time needed to change from one task or product to another (referred to as setup time), processing time per unit, error rates, amount of work- or things-in-process, etc.

Value stream maps are perfectly suited to their primary use in identifying problems such as bottlenecks, waste, rework loops, etc.—all of which can be fixed with traditional quality and process improvement methods, such as Lean Six Sigma. But they have one flaw from the perspective of analyzing complexity: they follow only a *single* offering or family through a process, typically chosen to represent the majority of the volume that flows through the process. The assumption is that by examining the flow of this single offering you will be able to capture data on the biggest drivers of waste in the whole process. This is generally true in high-volume manufacturing, where the total number of part numbers processed at a given activity is less than a dozen and all the flows are nearly identical. But in the majority of other manufacturing and nearly all service processes, neither of these two conditions exist. There are dozens or sometimes hundreds of different products or tasks, and all that can be said about the flows is that they are on the same plane.

Thus by focusing on a single offering or family, traditional value stream maps are blind to complexity—blind to the disproportionate

costs that can be generated by what may be a large number of offerings that collectively contribute little in terms of EP, blind to the disproportionate impact of low-volume offerings. They cannot tell us the true costs of supporting the *full variety* of your offerings—i.e., the costs of supporting your current level of complexity. Hence the need for a *Complexity Value Stream Map* (CVSM), which looks at all of the different activities required for all offerings at each step in a process (*see* Figure 7.1).

Figure 7.1 CVSM Schematic

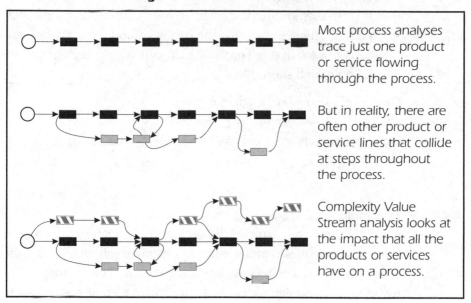

Most process analyses trace just one product or service flowing through the process.

But in reality, there are often other product or service lines that collide at steps throughout the process.

Complexity Value Stream analysis looks at the impact that all the products or services have on a process.

Making a CVSM would be impractical if we had to take data on *all* the services/products at *all* the activities in *all* the processes of *all* our business units. Fortunately we don't have to. Just as we don't need to know the position and velocity of every atom in a gas to predict its pressure and temperature, a sample of process data is adequate for determining PCE and the impact of complexity. You've already narrowed the field by focusing on just a few business units, and now will focus even further: getting a statistical sample of data on a few key activities within a few processes in the business unit. By following this method, you'll be able to create a CVSM that is both manageable and representative of the "full variety" of tasks in the targeted business unit.

Here's a quick look at next three steps in Complexity Analysis, which build from the first three steps in the previous chapter:

4. **Identify the strategic value of your core processes**: You will classify processes by importance and by capability gap in order to identify which processes should be mapped first. (The type of process—marketing, sales, product development, production, delivery, customer support, etc.—doesn't matter because they are all mapped the same way.) The goals are simple: a) to identify which processes are fundamental to your strategy and represent key areas of differentiation for the business, and b) to assess your capability in each of these processes (in which do you excel and in which do you fall short?).

   Graphical summary used: Core Process Grid for summarizing the importance of a process and current level of capability

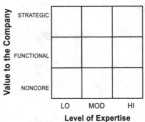

5. **Determine family groupings**: Sort your offerings into families based on the similarity of process flow—the activities that are common to many offerings—and on other factors such as processing time per unit. This sorting activity allows you to determine where to focus limited resources on data collection and observation in order to form the most complete CVSM with the least amount of expenditure. This step narrows the scope of the data collection task—without compromising the integrity of the CVSM by excluding low-volume offerings (which often happens in traditional value stream maps). The full complexity of the offering will be represented here.

   Graphical summary used: Product/ Service Family Grid for sorting offerings in similar groups

	PROCESS STEPS			
Offering	1	2	3	Family Class
1	X		X	A
2	X		X	A
3		X	X	B
4		X	X	B
5	X	X	X	C

6. **Create a Complexity Value Stream Map (CVSM):** Select one representative from each family, and walk the process as if you were that product or service, gathering key process data, and creating a visual map of the results.

Graphical summary used: Complexity Value Stream Map that shows the flow, feedback, transportation, and key metrics for a process

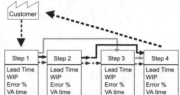

7. **Compute PCE baselines:** You'll use the data collected for the CVSM to calculate baseline Process Cycle Efficiency for the value streams you're analyzing.

Now let's look at the details of these steps.

Step 4: Identify the strategic value of your core processes

Start with a list of all the main processes in the business unit you've targeted for analysis, then classify each according to its strategic value:

- **Strategic Core Process:** Processes you must excel at in order to fulfill your strategic goals, that you must be good at in order to become the best in your business. Most customer-facing processes fall into this category. From a financial point of view, the strategic core processes are the areas of the Value Chain that have a big impact on whether EP is positive or negative. These are the differentiators in your business; the things you do that no one else does, or that no one else can do as well as you.

- **Functional Core Process:** Work you need to do well to create value but that goes largely unnoticed by customers (if you do them well, you simply meet expectations). Functional processes are the entry price for competing in a given market; there is simply no way to effectively compete in the market without executing these processes well.

- **Noncore Process**: Supporting processes or ones required by law. These processes are in some way supporting what your customers see and value, but otherwise are not critical to strategic goals. Some of these processes are required by regulations; others are basic business processes (hiring, accounting, payroll, etc.).

Having classified the processes, evaluate the respective levels of **process expertise or competency**, how good you are at doing that particular kind of work. You only need relative labels for this analysis (low, medium, high), not numerical scores because in this step, it's more important to be directionally correct than to be numerically precise. That's partly because the success or failure of processes is usually evident within an organization. People know when things are going badly—because *someone* has to deal with the consequences (disgruntled customers, lost documentation, stock piling up, and so on). A lack of such problems is an indicator that all is well. We can recognize our internal process capabilities because we live with them.

That's why it is usually fairly easy to determine process competency or expertise. You have two options:

1. **Objective evaluation**, based on preset criteria (benchmarked speeds, error rates, etc.) for a particular type of operation compared to your competitors' processes or the processes of other business units

2. **Subjective evaluation**, based on judgment and experience

Typically, companies will use a combination of both types of evaluation to complete this stage of the analysis, though some may stick with subjective evaluation (e.g., a company's management can decide it is very good at shipping, okay at production, and terrible at marketing). While setting and monitoring metrics can be the most accurate way to determine process advantage, in many cases the use of judgment is sufficient and far easier to achieve. The goal is to help you prioritize your mapping efforts by determining which processes are either most in need of complexity reduction or will provide the biggest growth opportunities.

Once you have identified and evaluated the processes, you now effectively have a set of coordinates for each process that you can enter onto a grid that looks like Figure 7.2:

Figure 7.2: Core Process Grid

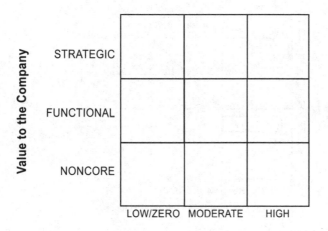

Level of Internal Expertise/Competency

To show how this analysis works, let's start with a simple four process value-stream:

Figure 7.3: Simple 4-step Value Stream

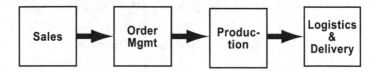

This company decided that...

- Sales was strategic but low to moderately advantaged

- Order management was strategic and moderately advantaged

- Production was functional and moderately to highly advantaged

- Logistics and Delivery were noncore and had poor performance (they are identified as value-destroying processes)

So they end up with a chart like that shown in Figure 7.4.

Figure 7.4: Sample Core Process Analysis—As Is

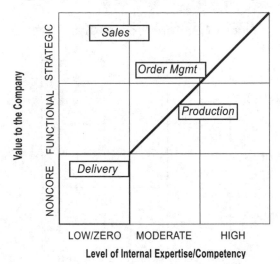

What you do with this information depends on where the processes fall on the chart, as shown in Figure 7.5. The goal is to have processes aligned along the diagonal—meaning you are good at processes that are strategic, and not overinvested in those that are not. More specifically, processes that fall into the strategic zones at the top of the chart or into the Low/Functional or Moderate/Functional zones are prime candidates for CVSM analysis. These are the processes that you must excel at (in the case of the strategic zones), or must improve your capabilities to the average industry expectations (in the case of functional zones).

Figure 7.5: Zones of the Core Process Grid

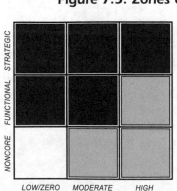

BLACK: Prioritize the CVSM of proccesses that fall in this zone. All strategic processes should be mapped, along with the functional processes at which we do not excel.

GRAY: We have good capability in theses processes. Map only the high-cost processes in this area. Otherwise they are a lower priority for CVSM.

WHITE: We are bad at these processes and they are non-core to our strategy. These may be processes we will eventually outsource. Map only if high cost.

If a process is classified as functional or noncore, but you have a high level of capability, then it should be low on your list of priorities for further analysis: You are doing fine as is. Moreover, it may indicate an opportunity to redeploy resources to areas of higher need.

Once you have the processes laid out in this matrix, review your strategy for this business unit then ask yourself whether the processes you have listed are necessary and sufficient to fulfill that strategy. Where do you need to have a high process advantage to succeed? Are processes missing? Are you overachieving in some areas and underachieving in others? Annotate the chart accordingly (*see* Figure 7.6).

Figure 7.6: Sample Core Process—Where we want to be

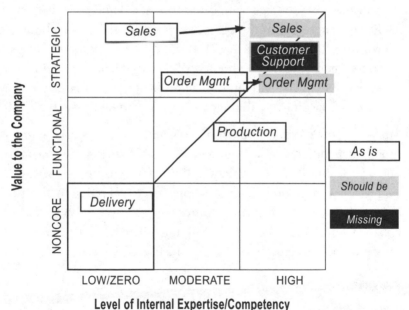

- Disconnect #1: *Sales is strategic to the company, but not done very well yet. They need to strengthen their competency in this process.*
- Disconnect #2: *The company has no customer support process, also deemed important to its future.*
- Disconnect #3: *They are not too bad at order management, but should improve it since that, too, is a strategic process.*

You can use this type of information to help you...

1) **Decide if you have the correct processes in place to support your strategic goals**—are there disconnects? Do you have all the right processes in place? Other questions that can be raised:

   - How do the competitors compare on these core processes?

   - Are there any significant risks (e.g., technological) on the horizon that may dramatically change the nature and competitive position of the core processes?

   - Are the core processes mature, new, aging? As industries age and mature, processes can move from being strategic to functional as the industry stabilizes and consolidates. At this point, other processes may emerge from being functional and become strategic. For instance, within the personal computer market, technological wizardry was once the key strategic differentiator, and still is for some smaller market segments. Within the major segments, price, speed of delivery, and simplification of the ordering process have become key strategic differentiators for companies such as Dell.

2) **Surface "Quick Wins,"** opportunities where a little focused effort will rapidly generate tangible and/or measurable benefits. For instance, if you are "losing PCE" to noncore, disadvantaged processes, you may eventually want to outsource these processes and redeploy the associated capital so you can focus resources on what you do well and what creates value. Often the problem is not intrinsic to the process but rather to the execution of it, in which case external options can

---

Quick Win

The process of clarifying the alignment of your processes to your strategy can yield a number of outcomes:

- It can confirm the alignment and focus of your core processes to your strategy

- It can surface some operational issues that need to be resolved in order to meet your strategy

- It can expose the lack of process support for your strategy, warranting a refocus on process design or a refocus on strategy

improve overall performance. Identifying these opportunities early allows you to set in motion the outsourcing evaluation process. (*See* discussion of process and offering options in Chapter 8.) Consider also how much cost is consumed by the noncore processes. If they represent areas of high cost, it is worthwhile mapping these as well, as there could be significant initial cost savings at stake.

Developing new processes to deal with gaps identified through this analysis is a topic beyond the scope of this book. (*See* Chapter 15 in *Lean Six Sigma* or Chapter 14 in *Lean Six Sigma for Service*.) But deciding on most other actions—improving, repositioning, simplifying processes— will come through the rest of the analysis.

EGI Case Study, Part 1: Core Process Analysis

Electric Generator, Inc.—"We power the world one house at a time"— is a $210M manufacturer of portable, gas-powered generators for the outdoor recreation, residential, and small contractor markets. Currently an industry leader in both quality and durability of its products, the company maintains a solid customer base (approximately 30% market share in each segment) and has historically seen strong revenue growth (7% CAGR).

Within the North American market, EGI already enjoys a strong reputation as a premium brand with engineering leadership as a hallmark. But unfortunately EGI has seen receding margins in the past few years as new players have started to intensify the competition. The CEO is concerned that the crowded offering will diminish their capacity to respond to this competition and new emerging opportunities.

By entering developing markets overseas with strongly engineered products that are reliable and rugged, EGI hopes that the premium product reputation can be spread worldwide, and in time they can begin selling the higher-margin recreational and residential units in the developing markets as they begin to mature.

Thus the two major thrusts of their strategy are to target the premium residential and recreational markets in North America (a current strength and growing market), and to target the extremely high growth markets in developing countries around the world. EGI's generic process map is shown in Figure 7.7.

Figure 7.7: Big Picture of EGI Value Stream

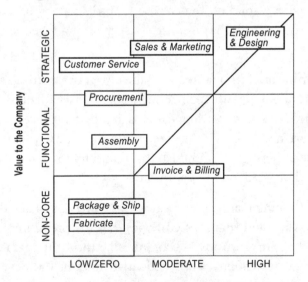

The value stream is currently operating at less than 5% PCE and approximately 30% of their products generate negative EP. The most strategic and value-creating process inside EGI is Engineering, which is the world leader in rapid, customer-responsive design. Manufacturing and, to a lesser extent, marketing are being carried by Engineering. These core processes are displayed in the matrix shown in Figure 7.8.

Figure 7.8: EGI Core Process Matrix, "As-is" View

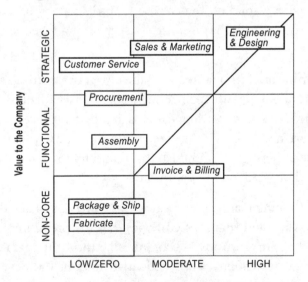

EGI identified eight processes. At the extremes they found they were bad at executing two of the noncore processes (Packaging/Shipping and Fabrication), but very good at a strategic process (Engineering and

Design). They did well at Invoicing and Billing, though they weren't sure whether that process provided key functional capability or was noncore (which is why that box straddles the line). They judged themselves as poor to moderate in the remaining four processes, all of which were either Strategic or Functional.

The goal is to have processes aligned along the diagonal: good at the ones that are strategically important, and not overinvested in those that are not. So the good news is that EGI is not currently overinvesting in noncore processes and is doing very well with a few of their key strategic processes. But there is some bad news. EGI is not where it needs to be competitively. And worse, there are a few processes they've identified as key to their future that are currently not in place. The needed changes are summarized in Figure 7.9.

Figure 7.9: EGI Desired Core Process Status

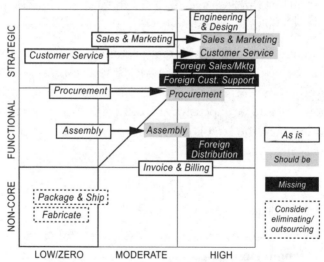

This diagram shows the changes that EGI wants to make in its capabilities. It may eliminate (through outsourcing) the noncore processes at which it performs poorly (lower left corner) and will probably leave alone or outsource Invoice & Billing—investing more in these capabilities would be very low priority. The biggest performance gap is in Customer Service (a Strategic process at which it has low capability), as shown by the long arrow. Lesser gaps exist with Sales & Marketing, Procurement, and Assembly. EGI also needs to develop three new capabilities (two Strategic and one Functional process).

Key observations on the EGI core process matrix:

- Customer service must be dramatically improved for revenue growth opportunities.

- Procurement is a strategic issue but has been handled at the tactical level.

- They should definitely create CVSMs for all the strategic processes, and may want to do procurement as well. This will help them attain world-class cycle efficiencies and sales effectiveness levels.

- Fabrication of metal parts, packaging, and shipping are noncore and the company is not particularly good at them. These are major consumers of capital. They should be evaluated for outsourcing as it is almost certainly quicker and cheaper to have other companies who specialize in these activities perform them. The quality of the delivery of these services will also likely be higher than EGI could achieve by implementing these on their own.

- Foreign sales and marketing, customer support and distribution will be key to the fulfillment of its strategy. But they are missing from EGI's current processes. Developing these capabilities in-house would be expensive and difficult. This is a clear opportunity to leverage the strengths of a service provider that specializes in these areas.

What EGI needs to analyze and execute:

- Elevate customer service into a single global service organization allowing them to improve and gain foreign presence

- Explore partnering for foreign distribution and billing

- Investigate outsourcing of fabrication, packaging, and shipping

- Decide whether to invest any additional effort in assembly or outsource this process

Step 5: Determine family groupings

As mentioned at the start of this chapter, doing a Complexity Value Stream Map (CVSM) that truly includes *all* of your products/services can be impractical unless you have a limited number of offerings. You can make the task manageable by grouping offerings into families and selecting one representative from each family to include in the CVSM. One easy way to start is to create a *Product/Service Family Grid*, which shows what process steps different products or services have in common. An example from a home loan division of a financial institution is shown in Figure 7.10.

Figure 7.10: Service Family Grid

Extended Volume (thousands)	Margin	Service	PROCESS STEPS						Family Class
			Applica-tion	Process-ing	Credit Check	Appraisal	Inspection	Close	
$1,040	2.0%	Refinance ARM	X	X	X	X		X	A
$5,200	2.5%	Refinance Fixed	X	X	X	X		X	A
$1,560	1.8%	New Home ARM	X	X	X	X	X	X	B
$2,600	2.2%	New Home Fixed	X	X	X	X	X	X	B
$520	1.5%	Home Equity	X	X	X	X		X	C
$780	1.4%	Line Of Credit	X	X	X			X	D

This financial services company identified four separate families of services. In theory, they could have clustered "Home Equity" loans (Family C) with the two Refinance options that comprise Family A. But they decided to keep the equity loans as a separate family because the volume is so much lower than either Family A offering. Family B options are distinguished because they require Inspections; Family D is the only offering that does not require an Appraisal.

As you work on a matrix for your own business units, remember that the ultimate goal is to select one representative from each family of offerings to include on the CVSM. One reminder: Chapter 2 discussed the fact that complexity added by low-volume offerings can have a disproportionate impact on a process. Do not automatically cluster low-volume offerings into families with much higher-volume offerings. Rather, pay attention to how much time each offering uses in a process (low-volume offerings often use a higher percentage of time).

You can also build family clusters based on similarity of impact on the resources at each step in terms of time, talent, capacity, reliability, etc. For instance, two parts may follow the same path through a machine shop, but one part may be very intensive in terms of lathe work, while another is very intensive in mill work. It is not enough that they share exactly the same routing (process steps); to be considered as part of the same family, they should also be similar in terms of the total processing time.

EGI Case Study, Part 2: Identifying product families

EGI's electrical generators all have five major subcomponents :

Frame: provides the structure to mount all other components, typically made from simple steel tubes that have been bent, fastened, or welded together

Engine: gasoline, diesel, natural gas, or propane lawnmower-style engine

Fuel tank: typically a plastic molded tank designed to hold between 1 and 5 gallons of fuel

Generator/alternator: typically a self-contained unit that includes the bearings, coils, magnets, and electronic regulation required to deliver power when the unit is rotated by the engine

Distribution Panel: a simple panel that provides the output plugs to deliver power into various types of extension cords

To determine product families, they looked at these five components, commonality of process steps, and processing time per unit. (Target markets did not enter the classification, nor did technologies because the latter are shared across all product lines.) They ended up with three basic families that are similar in their engineering design, production process, and distribution. The result is shown in Figure 7.11.

Figure 7.11: Product Families for EGI

% of each activity total consumed by each product line

	Family	Percent of Co. Volume	Market Share in Area	Gross Margin	Sales & Mktg	Engineering	Fabrication	Assembly	Shipping	Customer Service	Alignment With Corp. Strategy
Small Contractor 5-7 kW	A	5%	2%	2%	5%	6%	3%	3%	5%	2%	L
Small Contractor 8-10 kW	B	2%	1%	9%	5%	12%	8%	1%	2%	1%	M
Residential 5-7 kW	A	20%	9%	6%	20%	20%	12%	16%	20%	26%	M
Recreational 5-7 kW	C	45%	41%	14%	25%	22%	44%	51%	45%	36%	M
Residential 8-10 kW	A	10%	5%	11%	10%	21%	8%	9%	10%	15%	M
Recreational 8-10 kW	B	18%	28%	21%	25%	19%	25%	20%	18%	20%	M
TOTALS		100%			100%	100%	100%	100%	100%	100%	100%

The percentage values entered in the columns for each process are not based on detailed numerical studies, but are quick estimates from readily available financial reports and interviews with key personnel. This method has proven reliable in determining family groupings at a high level.

Family A: The first family consists of the small contractor 5–7 kw range, the residential 5–7 kw range, and the residential 8-10 kw range. These products share the same process steps (no welding or injection molded trim pieces, bolt together frames), are designed for a similar amount of ruggedness and use, consume resources similarly (again, no welding, similar assembly tasks, etc.). They are characterized by moderate-duty frames of traditional steel tube design, smaller fuel capacities, minimal sound attenuation, minimal cosmetic cladding and covers, and relatively few output options in terms of plug types and voltage variants.

Family B: The second family consists of the small contractor 8-10 kw range and the recreational 8-10 kw range. These products share the same process as Family A, with the notable addition of welding. These frames are welded for strength and durability needed for the larger size, higher output, and rugged handling associated with contractor job sites and regular loading and unloading at recreational activities such as camping, etc. The products are characterized by heavy-duty frames of traditional tube design, with a focus on welded rather than bolted joints, large fuel capacities, minimal sound attenuation, minimal cosmetic features, and greater variety of output options in terms of plug types and voltage ranges. The recreational version also includes some plastic trim panels, but they are relatively minor on this version

Family C: The final family consists of the recreational 5-7 kw range. This product is unique. It has a lightweight, single-piece stamped steel uniframe; no assembly or welding is required. The design provides a greater degree of ruggedness, ease of handling, and creative use of space to attain moderately large fuel capacities, very good sound attenuation, completely enclosed cosmetic packaging that also serves to isolate sound and vibration, and user-friendly output options that consolidate all operating information and output plugs in a single panel. This unit is specifically optimized for camping and is very different from the other models. It follows some similar process steps as the other families, but it consumes those resources very differently and has some unique steps.

Step 6: Create a Complexity Value Stream Map

Creating a Complexity Value Stream Map begins the same way as any other process mapping exercise: you need to create a diagram showing the overall flow of work through the processes that comprise the value stream.

For each process step, you'll want to collect the following data (including calculations of the average and standard deviation):

1. **Estimated Cost per Activity:** This is the total cost, not the cost-per-offering

2. **Process Time (P/T):** Total amount of time spent, broken out into value-add and non-value-add time per unit for each type of service or product

3. **Changeover time**: Any time that lapses between changing from one service or product to another, including the time it takes someone to get up to full speed after switching tasks (a learning curve cost)

4. **Queue Time**: The time things spend waiting to be processed

5. **Defects and rework**: Raw counts (and or percentages) of the time and cost needed to "fix" defective services or products at each activity

6. **Demand Rate** (also called **takt time**): The demand rate of customers for each type of service or product

7. **Number of Offerings**: Number of different services or products processed at the activity

8. **Uptime**: Time worked per day minus breaks and interruptions

9. **Things-in-Process or Work-in-Process**: How many items (physical, paper, or electronic) are at each step of the process

> **Involving teams in process mapping**
>
> As in basic flowcharting, it is essential to have both experienced and novice employees physically follow the work as it flows from activity to activity. Those who are familiar with the process can provide a jump start to the mapping process. However, experienced people sometimes "miss the obvious" because they are too familiar with the process. It is the team members who are not familiar with the process and have to learn it from scratch who will most likely ask the simple questions that lead to great discoveries such as hidden steps that are implicitly assumed but undocumented and non-value-add.

10. **Strategic, Functional, or Noncore classification**: The overall process may fall into one category, while steps within the process may fall into another

As you look at each activity in the process, you will classify the activity as **value-add** or **non-value-add**. For example, a call center that is spending half its time with irate customers is 50% non-value-add; the upstream process must be fixed. A warehouse is all non-value-add; something upstream is causing this cost.

With the proper data in hand, the CVSM gives you a clear indication of the process cycle time through the entire process, as well as in subcomponents of the process. Adding this data to the basic flow map results in a diagram like that shown in Figure 7.12 (below).

Figure 7.12: Example CVSM

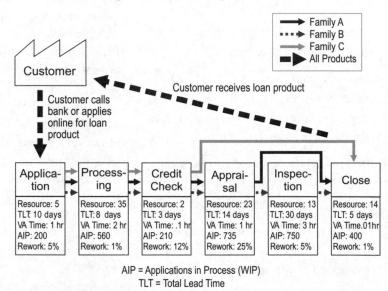

AIP = Applications in Process (WIP)
TLT = Total Lead Time

A Complexity Value Stream Map shows the flow of all product or service families and captures key process data needed to diagnose complexity and quality improvement problems. Overlaying individual value streams onto a single CVSM shows the multiple paths that different offerings follow through the organization, and shows how a single process step is affected by multiple offerings.

It is important to note that the generic examples given here and the EGI case study example are much simplified to fit into the framework of this book. In practice, a CVSM often takes up an entire wall of a room and consists of self-stick notes, spreadsheets, photographs, diagrams, etc., taped to the wall. The CVSM is not intended to be a permanent documentation of the various processes, but a dynamic analysis tool that lives only for the duration of the Complexity Analysis. If you want, you can go into the next level of detail as well, creating a CVSM for each box represented in the original chart, thus drilling down into each area of the organization.

Figure 7.13: EGI Complexity Value Stream Map

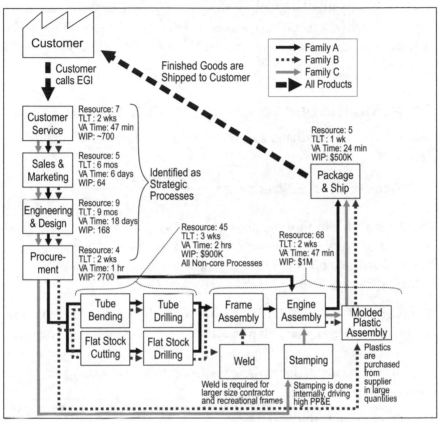

EGI's CVSM shows the flow of all three product families they identified. The products vary in which production steps they use.

EGI Case Study, Part 3: CVSM

Recall that EGI had identified three product families based on their process similarities. They followed a representative product from each family, and blended the results into a single CVSM (Figure 7.13).

Step 7: Compute PCE baselines

(application of the Complexity Equation)

A CVSM visually reinforces the impact of complexity; the other side of the coin is putting numbers to that impact. Quantitative analysis using the Complexity Equation is the key that will help you assess how much work or how many things are in process, and, by extension, the effect those factors have on current levels of PCE. Setting these baselines is the step that will allow you to later explore the impact of changes you might consider.

Data You'll Need to Compute PCE Baselines

You may recall from Chapter 2 that we began with the following definition of PCE:

$$\text{Process Cycle Efficiency} = \frac{\text{Value-add Time}}{\text{Total Lead Time}}$$

Calculating PCE in this way is very easy (*see* sidebar, next page), and works great as way to monitor general outcomes or overall process health. But it is no help at all in identifying the causes of low PCE or telling us how we could go about *improving* PCE.

To understand what it will take to improve PCE, you'll need data on its drivers—the factors that determine how much time is value-add time, how much time is spent in queues or delays, and so on. As you may recall from Chapter 2, that's where the (simplified) Complexity Equation comes in, repeated here.

Simplified Complexity Equation

$$PCE = \frac{2V(1-X-PD)}{N(2A+1)S}$$

V = Total value-add time in the process
P = Processing time per unit
D = Total demand of products or services
X = Percent of products or services with quality defects
N = Number of different tasks performed at an activity
A = Number of activities or steps in the process
S = Longest setup time in the process

Just to illustrate the calculation, here are some sample data:

V = .03	X = 5%	P = .01 hrs/pc	D = 10 pc per hour
N = 4	S = 2 hours	A = 3	

$$PCE = \frac{2V(1-X-PD)}{N(2A+1)S} = \frac{(2*.03)\,[1-.05-(.01*10)]}{4\,[(2*3)+1]\,2}$$

$$= .0009\%$$

Easy calculation of PCE

To use the basic PCE equation, PCE = Value-Add Time / Total Lead Time, start by determining how long it takes any work item to make it all the way through the process (= total lead time). You can get a sample of actual lead times by tracking individual work items through the process (attaching tags onto materials or paperwork that people will stamp at each work station, for example) or looking at email dates on service items. Or you can get an overall estimate of the average lead time using Little's Law by counting up all the Things-in-Process and dividing by the average completion rate:

$$\text{Total Lead Time} = \frac{\text{Number of Things in Process}}{\text{Average Completion Rate}}$$

You might think that measuring actual items would be better than getting an estimate from Little's Law. But in some ways the estimate is actually better. Why? Because the time it takes individual work items to traverse your process may vary considerably—and you won't know whether the item you choose is faster or slower than "normal." In contrast, with Little's Law, you compute an overall average, which may be more representative of the process as a whole.

Once you have either measurements or calculated estimates of total lead time, you need to generate a figure for value-add time. This is relatively easy to do in manufacturing activities: it is the direct labor cost per unit that has often been tabulated by cost accountants. In service activities it usually must be captured by observation.

One tip: Don't worry too much about getting precise measures of value-add time. Even in the best of companies, value-add time will be 20 times or so *smaller* than total lead time. And whenever you're dividing a very small number by a very large number, the outcome won't be much affected by slight changes in the small number. Having figures that are in the right ballpark is sufficient for this phase of the analysis.

Working with the Complexity Equation takes some expertise up front to program a spreadsheet appropriately (Excel™,[2] for example, has been upgraded to include "solvers" that you can use to compute PCE in a few seconds), but once the prep work is done, it's relatively easy to plug in the data you've gathered. Depending on the circumstances, you may be able to simplify the task further by clustering the offerings into perhaps two groups. For example, you could combine all high-volume offerings (those that constitute, say, 80% of revenue) into one "family" and all low-volume offerings (the remaining 20% of revenue) into another—and therefore compare figures between the two families. You lose some discriminatory power with this approach—i.e., you can't point to any single low-volume offering as the source of trouble—but you will be able to tell what would happen if you got rid of all or part of the low-volume offerings, or reduced their *average* setup time, etc. Going for a finer partitioning (looking at individual offerings, or dividing them up into three or more groups) is certainly possible, but in many cases may not tell you much more about the impact of complexity, process flow, or quality on PCE than the simpler two-family approach.

For the purposes of the discussion in this chapter, it's not important for you to understand the details of the equation, but you should know that in practice you'll need both the original PCE equation (value-add time divided by total lead time) and the full Complexity Equation to complete the analysis and quantify the process impact of complexity.

Reflecting reality with the full Complexity Equation

The simplified Complexity Equation assumes that the process is very uniform, each offering having the same demand, taking the same amount of processing time per unit, etc. But we all know that such consistency isn't reality: demands for a given product or service vary through time, demand for one offering will be higher than that for another, different offerings may have tasks that take different times to perform, change-over time from one task to another may differ, etc.

We won't go through all the math here (*see* the Appendix instead), but as you can see, the full Complexity Equation (next page) is a lot more sophisticated than the simplified version we've been using. What it does is account for the impact of *all* the products or services flowing through a value stream—and that's what's missing in traditional analyses where people look at a single product or service.

The complete Complexity Equation[3]

$$(TIP_1\ TIP_2\ ...TIP_N) = 2\left(\sum_{i=1}^{N} S_i\right)(2A+1)(D_1\ D_2\ ...D_N)\begin{pmatrix}(1-X_1-D_1P_1) & -D_2P_1........ & -D_NP_1 \\ -D_1P_2 & (1-X_2-D_2P_2).. & -D_NP_2 \\ . & & \\ -D_1P_N & -D_2P_N.... & (1-X_N-D_NP_N)\end{pmatrix}^{-1}$$

If you're not a math-phile, and few of us are, the complete Complexity Equation looks intimidating. But as Mark Twain said about a Wagner opera: "It's not as bad as it sounds."

Accounting for variation

While the approach of clustering high- and low-volume offerings simplifies the process greatly and gives management some quick insights, it doesn't account for an important factor: the *variation* in the offerings. And this variation will in fact cause lower PCE.

As we mentioned in Chapter 2, low-volume offerings often have a much higher variation in demand than high-volume offerings (*see* p. 35). We can use the Six Sigma metric Coefficient of Variation to quantify demand variability:

$$\text{Coefficient of Variation} = \frac{\sigma_{demand}}{\text{Mean}_{demand}}$$

where σ_{demand} = one standard deviation of demand

We usually find that high-volume offerings have a Coefficient of Variation of about 25%, but that low-volume offerings may have a variability on the order of 100%.

In instances where you think this effect is substantial, you can add the coefficients of variation into the PCE calculations, though it will require simulation applications to do so. (We have developed a library of these curves for clients to use so that they do not need to perform simulations.[4])

> **The accidental value of GAAP figures**
>
> Value-add time is one case where typical cost accounting provides data that (accidentally) is of process value. Most manufacturing cost accounting systems capture a figure called *direct labor cost* which does not include rework, overhead cost (the non-value-add costs). Thus direct labor cost can be used as a rough first-order estimate for value-add cost before the complexity value stream mapping process is executed. If you look for this number in your accounting systems, you'll likely find that most processes are running below 5% PCE—providing a powerful motivation to find the non-value-add costs.

Calculating PCE Baselines: EGI example

The Complexity Equation confirms a fact that is, for many of us, intuitive: that each element of a process—steps, options, offerings—eats away or destroys PCE, adding time, increasing delays, increasing the chance of errors.

The CVSM for the Electric Generators, Inc. (EGI) was shown in Figure 7.13. Here are some basic data from their fabrication area:

- It takes about 20 minutes to package each engine. $V = 0.32$ **hrs/engine**

- No scrap is generated so $X = 0$

- $P = .107$ **hrs/pc**

- EGI sends out replacement engines on a regular basis of about 0.5 engines / hour in any given day. $D = 0.5 / \text{hr}$

- There are 8 different engines that are sent as replacements. $N = 8$

- There are 3 activities involved in the process: picking the engine, packing the engine, and labeling the packaging. $A = 3$

- It takes on average 0.5 hrs to setup for each different type of engine that is going to be packaged for shipping. $S = 0.5$ **hr**

$$PCE = \frac{2V(1-X-PD)}{N(2A+1)S} = \frac{(2*.32)[1-0-(.107*.5)]}{8[(2*3)+1](.5)}$$

$$= 2.16\%$$

This is a fair PCE for EGI, but poor against benchmarking standards.

You will perform this same kind of analysis for the value streams in the core processes you've targeted for analysis. One note: At this point in the analysis, you'll just be collecting data to help you calculate *current* PCE. In the next phase, you'll be using the equation to play out "what if" or "what will it take" scenarios. For example, if a process currently has a PCE of 5% and a company wants to triple that to 15% because it will allow them to cut out half of their non-value-add costs, they'd start from

Revisiting your Core Process Analysis

From Figure 7.13 EGI can see that relatively few of their processes are actually "strategic." The majority of their resources and effort are deployed in the functional and noncore areas. Another way to represent that insight is to create bar charts that show the total time, resources, etc., spent in the three process strata (Strategic, Functional, Noncore), as shown in Figure 7.14.

Figure 7.14: Bar charts Resource deployment by Core Strata

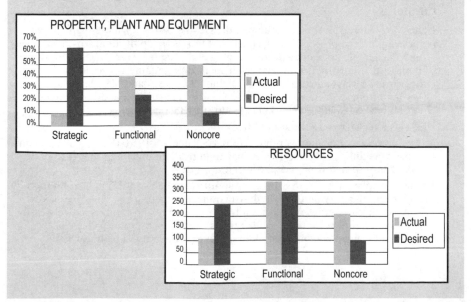

the baseline measures then make adjustments to see how much improve-ment is needed in *which* factors to achieve the 15% PCE: By how much would they have to reduce N (getting rid of variants on products or serv-ice, for example)? How many tasks or steps would they need to cut out? Which activities in the process do they need to improve (e.g., by reduc-ing setup time, improving quality)? And so on.

Conclusion

A Complexity Value Stream Map provides the first visual indications of how a company can be consumed with non-strategic processes—and moreover, what can be done to improve your processes and your portfo-lio of products or services. The data gathered is also used to quantita-tively evaluate baseline PCE. In the next phase of the analysis, you investigate *why* PCE levels are high or low, which will allow you to define specific projects to help you improve PCE and Economic Profit.

Endnotes

1 Lars Maaseidvaag has been working at the George Group for more than six years focusing on lean process improvement and process simplification. His focus areas include: complexity value stream mapping and complexity analysis, queuing theo-ry, discrete event simulation, and mathematical programming. Mr. Maaseidvaag has earned several advanced degrees including an MBA and MSE in Operations Research from the University of Texas. He is also currently pursuing a PhD in Operations Research at The Illinois Institute of Technology.

2 Excel is a registered trademark of Microsoft

3 The Complexity Equation is protected by US Patents 5,195,041 and 5,351,195 and patents pending. Interested parties may inquire about obtaining the equation in spreadsheet format from www.georgegroup.com

4 In practice, we have had to bring several different analysis tools to bear on the problem of quantifying the PCE destruction within a process. The Complexity Equation itself requires no special solvers or software and can be relatively easily modeled in an Excel spreadsheet. At times, specific sub-problems have been addressed using a combination of mixed-integer-programming, linear program, and discrete event simulation.

CHAPTER 8

Build a
Complexity Value Agenda

(Complexity Analysis Phase 3)

Having discovered that a certain core process within a value stream has a certain Process Cycle Efficiency (PCE) level is a good first step but it doesn't really tell what, if anything, you can or should do about it. Numbers seen in isolation mean nothing. The ultimate goal is to help you make data-based decisions about the best way for your business to improve Economic Profit (EP) and realize all the associated benefits, such as lower cost and higher shareholder value.

That's why in this chapter we'll look at transforming the data used to generate the Complexity Value Steam Map to understand the drivers of PCE *for the specific value streams you're studying*. That kind of thinking will help you identify:

- Exactly where EP is being destroyed.

- How big the opportunities are (as measured in terms of EP improvement).

- What it will take to improve EP. Is low PCE caused by how work is being done in the process activities (i.e., because of low quality or poor process flow) or is it because there are too many tasks flowing through the process (a high level of complexity)? Will improvement require complexity strategies, Lean methods, Six Sigma, or some combination?

The goal of this entire methodology is developing a Complexity Value Agenda, a plan that describes what projects will be implemented in what sequence, and for what specific benefit in terms of **value-creation-at-stake** (expressed in predicted gains in Economic Profit). The top priorities are often represented in a value agenda chart like that shown in Figure 8.1. They are called "agendas" because they show the sequence in which specific projects or efforts will be implemented. The size of the estimated value creation and prioritized sequence of initiatives will vary from company to company.

Figure 8.1: Format of a Complexity Value Agenda

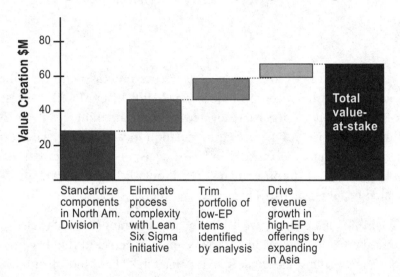

A Complexity Value Agenda depicts predicted gains from specific process- and offering-related improvements as measured through likely impact on EP. The improvement efforts are shown in order from the biggest to smallest gains—which is often the order in which they will be implemented—with the total "value-at-stake" in a final bar. These graphical representations of Complexity Value Agendas are good communication tools that help launch first-wave complexity and process improvement projects.

Overview of Developing a Complexity Value Agenda

The four steps in this chapter add more depth to your understanding the offerings and value streams you studied in Phase 2, using the combined information to identify specific complexity-related projects.

Step 8. Calculate EP% for offerings: In the first phase of this analysis, you calculated EP for each of your business units. Now it's time to do the same thing for the offerings within the units that you've selected for the analysis.

Step 9. Perform a Substructure Analysis: A substructure analysis looks at how much similarity there is in the components of the offerings that use the value stream you have just mapped. This type of analysis will be simpler for manufacturing operations that have documentation on part numbers used in various end products, but can be applied in services as well. The purpose is to expose duplicate or near-duplicate efforts that could be combined in order to reduce the complexity of the product/service design and delivery.

Graphical summary used: Varies depending on context.

Step 10. Calculate PCE Destruction and complete a Complexity Matrix: This kind of matrix uses data from a Complexity Value Stream Map to pinpoint which process activities and/or offerings suffer the most from quality, speed, or complexity problems—and, vice versa, which suffer the fewest problems (and therefore are ripe for exploitation).

Graphical summary used: Complexity Matrix showing how much PCE each offering family consumes at each process step.

Product or Service Family	Step 1	Step 2	Step 3	Total	EP$
A					
B					
C					

Step 11. Evaluate potential impact of process or offering changes: Once you've pinpointed specific process or offering problems/opportunities, you need to decide what to do in response. There are various ways to build on process or offering opportunities, and multiple strategies for dealing with problem areas (ranging from process improvement to repricing). Starting from the PCE destruction baselines, you can play with the factors

in the Complexity Equation to evaluate what would happen if you selected one or two of the options.

Step 12. Select options and build business cases for selected opportunities: In order to make sound decisions about which particular initiatives to implement, it helps to review and compare specifically what resources and timing would be required to achieve the defined level of return.

Step 13. Create a Complexity Value Agenda (and Execute!): Once you've selected the initiatives you will attack first, summarize the decisions in a Complexity Value Agenda that shows the specific initiatives and expected contribution to your company's value.

Graphical summary used: Complexity Value Agenda Chart that depicts the projects selected for implementation, their projected gain in EP, and the combined gain.

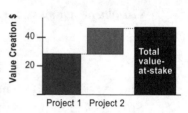

Step 8: Calculate EP% for offerings
(with an adjustment for the Cost of Complexity)

Complexity analysis is concerned with determining what is destroying the most PCE or consuming the least amount of PCE in an area that matters. To figure out "what matters" you will revisit the Waterfall chart and associated financial analysis, this time examining products or services instead of entire business units as you did in Phase 1. In other words, perform EP analysis to understand not only whether an offering is potentially destroying PCE but also whether an offering is destroying (or creating) value for shareholders.

Data You'll Need to Calculate EP% by Offering

Calculating EP is done the same way we described in Chapter 6. The base data will likely require two adjustments to accounting-calculated profitability figures:

- The first is in overhead. Use the Complexity Value Stream Map to apportion overhead expense, by activity, to a particular offering.

- The second is the application of capital charges. As we know, the omission of capital charges (also highlighted in the mapping process) can skew profitability figures to actions that destroy shareholder value.

EP assessment by product or service yields both an indication of the areas of profitability in your organization, as well as eye-opening insights into which offerings are winners or losers (often contrary to expectations). Particularly with offering assessments, it is the correct application of capital charges that can generate the most insight. Many low-capital products or services are overlooked as sources of profitability *because* they are low-capital. Sometimes the internal capital allocation process tends to view asset-intensive businesses as more important simply because they are in the habit of seeking more capital.

Part of the task in getting to "true" EP numbers means adjusting GAAP figures to account for the cost of complexity. To understand the rationale, consider a "perfect process" in which work flows directly from value-add activity to value-add activity and then directly to the customer. It has a PCE of 100%: no *time* wasted in errors, rework, delays, setup time; no *costs* spent on stockrooms, customer returns, supervision, etc.

But as we all know, reality is not so clean. And to the extent that a product or service destroys PCE, it should bear an adjusted percentage of non-value-add cost. Therefore, we should assign non-value-add costs, discovered in the Complexity Value Stream Map (which will happen when you calculate PCE Destruction later in this method). Going through this calculation gives us better information on which to base decisions about where to apply finite resources.

For the purposes of illustration look at the data in Figure 8.2 (next page).

Assume that the manufacturing overhead cost is completely and exclusively non-value-add cost. Managerial Accounting would spread overhead costs based on a percentage of revenue volume basis, or "earned hours" or some other volume-related parameter. Since in this example there is an 80/20 split in volume, overhead (row 4) is similarly split, and thus both high- and low-volume products end up with a 20% Gross Profit Margin percent (row 6).

Figure 8.2: Complexity Adjustments to Managerial Accounting

	Managerial Accounting (all figures in $ millions or %)			
		HIGH VOL	LOW VOL	TOTAL
1	Revenue	80	20	100
2	Material	32	8	40
3	Labor	8	2	10
4	Mfg Overhead	24	6	30
5	Gross Profit Margin	16	4	20
6	GPM% (Managerial Acctg)	20%	20%	20%
7	SG&A	12%	12%	
8	Operating Profit	8%	8%	
9	After-Tax Profit	5%	5%	
		CORRECTION FOR COST OF COMPLEXITY		
10	Mfg Overhead			30
11	% PCE Destruction	70%	30%	100%
12	Mfg Ohd Distribution	21	9	30
13	Gross Profit Margin	19	1	20
14	GPM% (Corr for Complexity)	23.8%	5.0%	20.0%
15	SG&A	12%	12%	
16	Operating Profit	11.8%	-7.0%	
17	After-Tax Profit %	7.3%	-4.4%	
18	After-Tax Dollars	5.9	-0.9	
19	Invested Capital	12	5	
20	Capital Charge (7%)	0.84	0.35	
21	Economic Profit	5.0	-1.2	

Based on a Complexity Value Stream analysis, however, the company learns that PCE destruction is more like a 70/30 split (row 11)—the high-volume products receive less allocation due to the smaller amount of PCE destruction per unit volume, and vice versa for the low-volume products. Applying that correction to overhead leads to an actual GPM% closer to 24% for the high-volume products and only 5% for the low-volume products (row 14). The low-volume products don't look quite so attractive anymore, do they? Note that in practice we would employ PCE Destruction to assign to a number of different cost pools; the above example is for purposes of illustration.

Finally, we calculate the Economic Profit of each segment of the product line as shown on rows 19 to 21. Managerial Accounting makes no such calculation, yet it is vital from a value creation and project selection viewpoint.

Though this example describes complexity adjustments to manufacturing overhead cost, the same approach can be applied to marketing, engineering, administration… any process. Also, this example uses a simple 80/20 Pareto split between volume levels, but the method works for far finer partitions. Using corrected accounting figures, a sample EP analysis of offerings is shown in Figure 8.3.

Figure 8.3: Analysis of a Portfolio by EP%

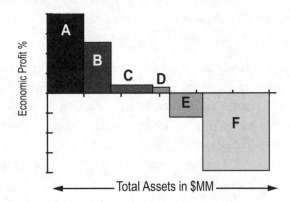

This analysis proceeds exactly like the original Waterfall chart shown in Chapter 6 except here we're comparing offerings within business units. Once EP is calculated for each offering, arrange them in order from biggest positive to biggest negative. The width of the bars shows assets consumed by that offering.

Step 9: Perform a substructure analysis

"A little digging for Quick Wins"

One of the things you'll likely discover when you investigate complexity is that multiple products or services use separate processes, parts, steps, etc., when in fact they could be using the *same* processes, parts, steps, etc. This principle of having multiple offerings share how they are created is called **commonality**. In banking, for example, it may be that the only thing separating two different loan processes is one or two forms; the rest could be identical. But if the two types of loans are handled by different work units, you'll have a lot of duplicated effort. Similarly, two products or product families may share many parts or components or process steps, but be handled separately.

A problem arises because often times similar products or services in your business may appear through this analysis to be destroying value because you're doing all the work separately. But they could be made economically profitable if you make adjustments so that the different offerings share process steps, components, tasks, forms, etc. (this reduces the number of activities, "A," in the Complexity Equation, and other factors that affect PCE).

A **substructure analysis** can help you identify whether such underlying separateness is causing low EP figures, and therefore identify offerings that are salvageable even though they may have performed poorly in all of the other analyses.

Data You'll Need to Perform a Substructure Analysis

The principle of substructure analysis is a little easier to understand in manufacturing than in services, so we'll start by looking at how this applies to products. In manufacturing, the parts and components needed for a given item are usually captured in a bill-of-material (BOM), *see* Figure 8.4. The steps used to produce that product are defined in Routing plans. These two pieces of information can help you uncover logical family groupings and determine how much of each product truly is unique.

Figure 8.4: Looking for Commonalities Between Bills-of-Material

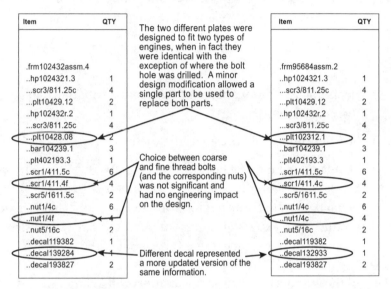

Segments of two Bill-of-Materials from Electric Generator Inc.
for two frames that differ in only four parts

EGI compared the bills-of-material for two frames that were treated as entirely separate assemblies. They discovered the two frames shared all but four parts in common, and three of the four "different" parts added no form, function, or feature to the frame. By comparing the bills-of-material for different products, EGI was able to find areas of commonality that could potentially be exploited to simplify product design and manufacture (which reduces non-value-add work and will translate into improved PCE).

This kind of information is not as easy to come by in services, so you'll have to do more digging. Try comparing the types of paperwork used in different processes, commonality in the software applications, common process steps (perhaps revealed in the value stream map), and so on.

Interpreting a Substructure Analysis

How can the information gained from the substructure analysis impact process PCE? Recall that N, the number of products in the process, and A, the number of activities in the process, are both prime drivers of PCE destruction according to the Complexity Equation. If you can use fewer components and reduce the number of unique steps in the process, you can lower both N and A, minimizing the number of Things-in-Process.

The output of substructure analysis is therefore a list of similar process tasks or product/service components from multiple offerings. The goal is to combine these similar elements. Here are a few examples:

- Replacing three different bolts that are within 1/16th-inch in length with a single bolt

- Replacing two mortgage application forms with one that combines the needed information

- Sharing subassemblies between more products

- Standardizing the sequence of process steps (e.g., some items may be painted first, then assembled, others assembled and then painted, which creates extra complexity in the management of product flow, extra work in maintaining information systems, and probably inconsistency in the final product the customer sees).

Many of the outputs of substructure analysis will fall into the category of "quick wins," meaning that projects can be formed and executed rather quickly to address the identified problem. This allows the client to begin demonstrating benefits early in the process, building momentum for change. The case study of International Power Machines introduced in Chapter 1 was completely the result of substructure analysis; building on commonality made the difference between mediocre and meteoric performance. (For more on commonality in both products and service, see Chapters 11 and 12.)

Step 10: Calculate PCE Destruction and complete a Complexity Matrix

To get to a list of projects that will improve PCE, we need a way to quantitatively identify offering and process issues that are destroying PCE. The best tool for the job is called the Complexity Matrix, depicted schematically in Figure 8.5.

Figure 8.5: Format of a Complexity Matrix

Product or Service Family	Process Step 1	Process Step 2	Process Step 3	Process Step 4	Total for Each Family	EP$ (million)	% Commonality
A							
B		PCE destruction figures go here					
C							
D							

The aim of a Complexity Matrix is to analyze your business or business unit to understand where opportunities for improvement and value creation exist. The Matrix also illustrates Economic Profit (dollars) by product, after adjusting for the costs of complexity, and % commonality, which indicates how well you leverage common parts and subcomponents across families.

The heart of the Complexity Matrix is populated by a figure called PCE Destruction (PCED).

$$PCED = \frac{\left(\dfrac{(\text{PCE of all steps except Target}) - (\text{PCE Baseline})}{\text{PCE Baseline}}\right) * 100}{\text{Demand}}$$

There are three important aspects of the PCED equation:

1) You're comparing the process *with* and *without* the particular step for each family of offerings (that's the "baseline minus target" part of the equation). It's like asking "what would PCE be if we removed this step for this offering?"

2) The impact is being expressed as a ratio or percentage of the "with and without" figure compared to the baseline. That means you may get numbers bigger than 1 (equivalent to 100%). For instance, if PCE rose from 1% to 4% when an offering was eliminated, then that offering was destroying 3% of PCE or *three times* the amount of the baseline PCE.

3) The ratio is adjusted for demand so the final PCED number is a "per unit" figure. We've made the point multiple times that low-volume offerings have a proportionately greater impact on PCE than high-volume offerings. Suppose you got the numbers used in item 2 (an increase from 1% to 4% PCE) for both a low-volume

(say, 10 unit) offering and a high-volume (say, 100 unit) offering. The PCEDs would be 30 for the low-volume vs. 3 for the high volume.

In interpreting PCE Destruction, higher numbers are always worse than low numbers. What's "high" and what's "low" will depend on your situation—but higher numbers mean that that combination of offering and process task is consuming more PCE than those with lower numbers.

For example, suppose you're calculating PCED for the third step in an order entry process for two services and got the following numbers:

PCED for Step 3 in Service #1 (low volume):

PCE baseline for order entry process = 5.4%

PCE for the process without Step 3 = 6.0%

Demand = 10 orders/hr

PCED for Step 3 = { [(6% − 5.4%) / 5.4%] * 100}/ 10 = 11.11/10 = 1.11

> *Interpretation: PCE would increase by a factor of 1.11 if this low-volume service no longer went through Step 3*

PCED for Step 3 in Service #2 (high volume)

Baseline = 5.4%

PCE w/o Step 3 = 6.0%

Demand = 80 orders/hr

PCED = (same as above except divide by 80) = 11.11/80 = 0.139

> *Interpretation: PCE would increase by a factor of .139 if this high-volume service no longer went through Step 3*

These calculations bear out our logic: that the low-volume service destroys more PCE than the high-volume service (PCED of 1.11 vs. PCED of 0.139). Looked at from the opposite viewpoint, you will gain more PCE if you get rid of one low-volume service than if you get rid of one high-volume service.

Data You'll Need for PCE Destruction and the Complexity Matrix

The three pieces of information you need for a Complexity Matrix are:

1) **PCE destruction** calculated as described above. This will tell you how much of the PCE is being destroyed or consumed by each product or service, at each workstation or process step.

2) **Economic Profit** (positive or negative) for each of the offerings (or offering families) included in your Complexity Value Stream Map (calculated as described in Chapter 6).

3) **Percent commonality**, the number of components and/or tasks shared by products or services within a family (this is an outcome of substructure analysis, *see* p. 150). Percent commonality metrics indicate the opportunities to reduce complexity by eliminating duplication of components/tasks.

Cautions on using EP wisely

We've been using a current measure of EP as our metric for shareholder perspective and performance measurement. However, using current EP as the *sole* criterion for project selection can lead you astray since it is a snapshot in time. The right measure is to look at the value creation (EP over time) and judge the value of your business *with* and *without* a particular product/service. In the main, a high negative EP is often a destroyer of value over time, and vice versa. But there are exceptions and cautions:

- If offering performance is cyclical, EP may be positive at the peak of the cycle (and result in underinvestment) or negative at the trough of the cycle (and appear a likely candidate for rationalization). For instance, looking at athletic wear sales in November is probably going to unfairly rank the swimsuit products as being low volume/EP.

- If offerings are at the beginning of their life cycle, you expect EP to be low but the future value of the product or service could be high.

- Be aware of potential obsolescence: A high EP now doesn't mean much if the product or service is obsolete in a year or two.

One other caution: If there is any danger in the use of EP, it is due to an excessive focus on the value destroyers rather than the value creators. If an offering has a high EP, the company may assume it has a unique advantage. It may then underinvest in the high EP business leaving the offerings vulnerable to attack.

For example, Iomega dominated the market for magnetic mass storage (the "Bernoulli Box") and became strongly profitable in the early 1990s. Management decided to enter the mature tape memory business to increase growth rates. This was a high-investment, low-return business that drained engineering resources from the lucrative Bernoulli box business and opened up a window for a competitor.

The only valid measure of investment decisions and project selection is the discounted value of EP over a 3 to 5 year horizon. If you have some doubts as to growth rates, perform the calculation for a range of reasonable values. One example is shown in Figure 8.6.

Figure 8.6: Projecting EP Gains Over Time

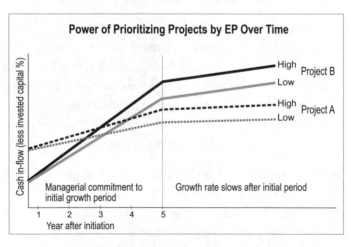

In evaluating whether to invest in various projects, it helps to use metrics that evaluate not only current Economic Profit (EP), but the discounted value of EP over time. In year 1, Project A looks superior, but from a 5-year perspective, Project B is the clear winner.

This is another reason for regularly returning to the Strategic Profile analysis (bubble chart analysis) to guard against complacency.

Completing and Interpreting a Complexity Matrix

Figure 8.7 shows PCE and other data translated into a Complexity Matrix.

Figure 8.7: Complexity Matrix

Service Family	Process Step 1	Process Step 2	Process Step 3	Process Step 4	Total for Each Family	EP$ (million)	% Commonality
A	1.9%	2.3%	1.4%	5.9%	11.5%	30.9	10%
B	4.3%	2.8%	6.0%	6.0%	19.1%	10.2	14%
C	12.8%	12.7%	14.4%	31.0%	70.9%	5.3	4%
D	38.2%	47.6%	18.3%	17.5%	121.6%	(21.3)	7%

This Complexity Matrix is for a company with four-step value stream through which four main service families travel. Service Families A and B are both high volume; Families C and D are low volume. (* = elements common to all services in this family)

The fundamental purpose of a Complexity Matrix is to determine whether PCE is being destroyed by a *process* activity (look *down* the matrix columns, as shown in Figure 8.8) or by a *product or service* (look *across* the matrix rows, as shown in Figure 8.9).

The penalty for overlooking future Economic Profit

At Texas Instruments in the 1990s, the Economic Profit of Germanium transistors was very positive but that of Integrated Circuits was negative (the latter was still its the infancy of its life cycle). A competent but internally focused Operations VP proposed, and received approval for, a large capex budget request for Germanium production. Integrated Circuits, meanwhile, was starved pending its becoming profitable. The VP of Marketing, having perceived the change in market trends, was furious but unable to alter the decision, saying: "This guy will make his plan but we will miss the market!"

TI's lack of early investment in Integrated Circuits opened up a gap for Bob Noyce (then of Fairchild Semiconductor, later of Intel fame) to dominate industrial Integrated Circuits for about three years before TI counterattacked with powerful new products.

Figure 8.8: Complexity Matrix Displaying a Process Problem

Service Family	Process Step 1	Process Step 2	Process Step 3	⬇ Process Step 4	Total for Each Family	EP$ (million)	% Commonality
A	1.9%	2.3%	1.4%	5.9%	11.5%	30.9	10%
B	4.3%	2.8%	6.0%	6.0%	19.1%	10.2	14%
C	12.8%	12.7%	14.4%	31.0%	70.9%	5.3	4%
D	38.2%	47.6%	18.3%	17.5%	121.6%	(21.3)	7%

Here, Process Step 4 has high PCE Destruction levels relative to the other steps in the process, which would indicate an improvement opportunity. It is not the worst offender in Service D, but it is still very high (and Family D has high PCE destruction across all steps, indicating a potential service problem). Based on this data, we would investigate and target improvements on this process activity.

Figure 8.9: Complexity Matrix Displaying a "Family" Problem

Service Family	Process Step 1	Process Step 2	Process Step 3	Process Step 4	Total for Each Family	EP$ (million)	% Commonality
A	1.9%	2.3%	1.4%	5.9%	11.5%	30.9	10%
B	4.3%	2.8%	6.0%	6.0%	19.1%	10.2	14%
⬇ C	12.8%	12.7%	14.4%	31.0%	70.9%	5.3	4%
⬇ D	38.2%	47.6%	18.3%	17.5%	121.6%	(21.3)	7%

We also know from looking at the matrix that Families C and D represent areas for potential improvement (high numbers go across the bottom two rows). We would investigate the potential for strategies such as outsourcing for Family C (as it is still generating EP). Product Family D is hurting our processes and our value creation, so we would turn to some of the strategies described in Chapter 10.

Step 11: Evaluate potential impact of process or offering changes

The best path to value creation for your business will depend on which pattern you find in the Complexity Matrix. Here's a quick overview of the options; more details follow.

A. **Process interventions:** If you patterns of very high or very low numbers in the matrix columns), the problem or opportunity lies in changing the process. The options are...

> **Option #1: Capitalize on high PCEs and capabilities**—recognize the key processes that represent areas of exploitable advantage and leverage those to new profit opportunities in adjacent business areas or new business areas.

> **Option #2: Improve/redesign the process**—eliminate non-value-add work and/or improve quality such that all products/services traversing the process will have improved EP)

> **Option #3: Outsource the process**—make the decision to **stop** doing what you cannot do better than somebody else, and redeploy the assets, management focus, and attention on areas of strategic importance.

B. **Offering interventions:** If the matrix patterns are across rows, you have individual or families of products or service that need attention:

> **Option #4: Grow/extend the offering or portfolio**—increase EP of the offering by exploiting high PCE processes and carefully adding product complexity to broaden customer options and features (possibly diverting demand from low PCE products to the variants of the high PCE product).

> **Option #5: Improve the offering design/configuration**—reduce cost by simplifying design.

> **Option #6: Reprice or stratify the offering**—change the value equation for the offering by generating more revenue from or reducing costs for the particular customer segments served.

> **Option #7: Retarget the offering or family**—while your processes may be efficient, you may have lost customer contact and seen your EP slip as a result. Focus on capturing Voice of the Customer and redirecting your offering to a slightly different segment, customer set, delivery channel, or branding.

> **Option #8: Remove (outsource or eliminate) the offering or family**

We'll walk through each of these options in more depth, then show you how to add numbers to them.

Path A: Value creation from process improvement

If you find when looking at your Complexity Matrix that there are consistently high or consistently low values in any particular column, that means you have a process opportunity (= high PCE values) or problem (= low PCE values).

Option #1: Capitalize on high PCEs and capabilities

If you find that you are really good at doing something, by all means consider ways to exploit that advantage. Minimally, make sure that the systems used in the business units you're studying are copied to all other business units that use those systems. You might also look for ways to build on that capability. Though we can't say the following example arose because of a complexity analysis, it does illustrate this option: First Data, an $8 billion company that leads the market in processing credit card transactions, recently extended into the new market of healthcare data processing. The reason: it recognized that its processes for managing and processing data were globally competitive and could be leveraged to great advantage in multiple contexts, not just banking. First Data essentially provides back-office support for credit card issuers, for whom this type of processing would be highly inefficient. First Data is another example of a concept that is critical to Conquering Complexity: That one company's value-destroying process is another company's value creator.

Option #2: Improve/redesign the process

If you find that a given process activity consistently consumes PCE across all product/service families, then your best option is to use tried-and-true process improvement tools associated with disciplines such as Lean Six Sigma. Almost any of the tools—Pull Systems and visual controls, setup reduction, mistake proofing, defect reduction, etc.—can help you reduce lead time and decrease the number of errors, all of which would contribute to a higher PCE. We cover some of the basics of simplifying processes in Chapter 12; there are many other resources on Lean and Six Sigma that can point you in other directions as well.

You may also find that the process is poor because it is ill-designed and needs to be either outsourced (*see* next option) or rebuilt (if it's of strategic value). If the latter, then Design for Lean Six Sigma (DFLSS) provides numerous tools and a robust methodology (*see* sidebar).

Importance of Design for Lean Six Sigma (DFLSS)

DFLSS provides a methodology and set of tools for new product and service development. It's about designing in quality and speed rather than improving them. The essence of DFLSS is to ensure design quality and predictability during the early design phases, a much more effective and less expensive way to get to Six Sigma quality. Design for Lean Six Sigma also accelerates the development of new products to consistently be the first to market with innovative products. At the same time, it helps drive the cost of new product development down and improve new product design and quality. DFLSS employs a structured integrated product development methodology and a comprehensive set of robust tools to drive product quality, innovation, faster time-to-market, and lower product costs. Methods include: Quality Function Deployment, Robust Engineering, and Theory of Inventive Problem Solving (also known as TRIZ).

Option #3: Outsource the process

Another option for processes that are destroying PCE across all products/services is to outsource the *entire process*. This option may also arise much earlier in the analysis process, if, as in our EGI case study, you find processes that you do poorly and that are noncore—they end up on the bottom left corner of the Core Process Grid.

Sometimes people will come to this decision through yet another route—when they are considering outsourcing a particular product or service. That kind of move will lower the volume of "stuff" going through a process but do little to reduce the overhead.

Path B: Value creation from offering improvement

If the *way* in which your organization does work (its processes) is not the principal destroyer of Process Cycle Efficiency, the driver of complexity has to lie within your products or services themselves. We'll start with with a discussion of what to do if you find offerings with low PCED values (= growth opportunities) then cover how to mitigate or eliminate offerings that are destroying value.

Option #4: Grow/extend the offering or portfolio

Complexity analysis isn't just concerned with troublespots. You may also uncover innate strengths and areas of high profitability that you can grow intelligently. The methodology preserves the link of process and strategy explicitly for this reason.

You may, in fact, find some true jewels with high EP that consume little PCE. These offerings should be placed on a special watch list to detect competitive action. Your insights can be leveraged to increase volumes and revenues of those jewels, or extend such offerings. Again, use the Complexity Equation to play "what if" games and calculate the impact of making portfolio changes.

For example, if you're considering brand line extensions or acquisitions, ask: "If we double the number of products, what will happen to PCE and lead time?" Or ask questions of even greater importance, such as: "How much will non-value-add costs increase if we take this course of action?"

Obviously, these decisions can spur your sales but also have a vital strategic impact on your business. To that end, complexity analysis performed during acquisition due diligence can complement the strategic analysis and help you understand the potential impact *before acquisition*, and realize the value *during integration*.

Option #5: Improve the offering design/configuration

Many products/services that are identified as chief PCE destroyers and that have marginal or negative EP are allowed to remain in a corporate

How to grow an offering

In the early nineties, Texas Instrument's new CEO, Tom Engibous, moved decisively to divest the memory business (as Intel had already done) and strengthen TI's high performers. The firm had developed an early lead in Digital Signal Processing (DSP) chips used in cell phones, fax machines, etc., and was being threatened by all the usual suspects and by the likes of mighty Intel. The company focused internal resources on the DSP, and also made a score of related acquisitions that created a constellation of strength in DSP. This could not have occurred if management energies and corporate resources had been drained in the wasteland that the memory market had become. What was it worth? Judge for yourself (*see* Figure 8.10).

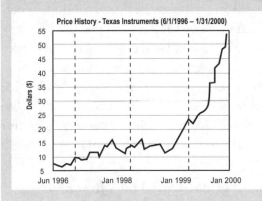

Price History - Texas Instruments (6/1/1996 – 1/31/2000)

Figure 8.10

The company was immeasurably stronger and better able to weather the future debacle in the telecommunications industry than any of its competitors.

portfolio in the belief that they could be improved to a point of profitability. As you'll see later in this chapter, the Complexity Equation allows you to test this suspicion by seeing just how much you have to improve the various components of PCE to reach a point where EP becomes positive.

The basic approach to simplifying product or service designs or configurations is known as commonality, where you look for ways to reduce the number of internal parts, components, tasks, etc., while still offering a full variety of offerings to customers.

A low % commonality score is another indication that there is potential for improving EP by looking for increasing crossover in product or service components.

Option #6: Reprice or stratify the offering

Changing the design of a product or service (Option 4) changes the cost component of EP. Of course the opposite side of the coin is to generate more revenue *relative to cost*. There are a number of variations on this idea, but you need to receive more for the product/service by charging more or by redirecting customers to lower-cost channels. Some companies will first evaluate the potential impact of design changes, then pursue repricing or rechanneling for offerings that will never be economically profitable.

Option #7: Retarget the offering or family

You may discover you have excellent processes, but your offerings generate only moderate to low or even negative EP. How can this be? The only explanations are that you may be competing in a commodity segment or that you have chosen efficiency at the expense of effectiveness and have lost the Voice of the Customer. If you have great process capabilities, see the previous discussion about how to capitalize on that advantage. But you should also identify ways to add differentiation to your products/services or reapply your expertise to a new market area.

Option #8: Remove (eliminate or outsource) the offering or family

It is likely that after all this analysis, you'll have to acknowledge that some offerings have such low (or even negative) EP *and* poor PCE (i.e., a lot of non-value-add cost) that it's unlikely you can ever deliver them profitably. Or you may find, for example, a clear Pareto effect in volume or revenue (e.g., 20% of the volume is responsible for 80% of the PCE destruction). These are situations when you have to seriously consider removing the offering from your value streams. Removal could be achieved through outsourcing, by clever use of marketing to redirect customers to your more profitable offerings (*see* the Dell example in Chapter 3, p 49), or through outright deletion.

A common objection to the removal or outsourcing of a particular product or service is the claim that it's a loss-leader of critical strategic importance. If it truly is, then it should be evaluated in conjunction with its partner products/services to understand overall PCE and profits.

For example, if we are judging one product as a loss-leader for another, is the pair of products in combination profitable? Why is it so strategically important? Why not simply outsource the unprofitable portion? (Pick your value segments.) Some customers may demand a full array of products/services, but are those the best customers for your business? Whenever action is taken on such items, the business case should fully enunciate the plan in terms of the "connected" family. (*See* Chapter 9 for more on changing product/service portfolios.)

This also prompts discussion of another potential line of action. If the loss-leaders must be retained—but they are the cause of low PCE—then the only option left is to apply process-improvement tools to the entire process. By incrementally applying cost-reduction methodologies, the loss can be minimized.

> **For more guidance on how to act on these options see the following chapters:**
>
> Option 4: Grow/extend offering—Chapter 10 or Chapter 16
>
> Option 5: Improve product design—Chapter 11
>
> Option 5: Improve service/process design—Chapter 12
>
> Option 6: Reprice or stratify offering—Chapter 9 and Chapter 10
>
> Option 7: Redirect—Chapter 6 and Chapter 10
>
> Option 8: Removal—Chapter 9

Generating "the list"

As you review your matrix and select appropriate options, start generating a list of potential projects to address troublespots or take advantage of opportunities. The next step will be formalizing the project ideas by building a business case for one, including estimates of expected gains, resources required, and timelines. This information will enable you to complete the final step, prioritization of opportunities.

Adding Numbers to the Options: What-If analyses with the Complexity Equation

As you review the Complexity Matrix for your own business and consider the various options for the opportunities you discover, you're going to start asking yourself questions such as "What would happen if we removed this offering?" or "If we could eliminate setup in this operation, what would that do to PCE?" The Complexity Equation gives you a way to answer those questions. We'll walk through several EGI examples to show you how this works.

What-If #1: The impact of removing a process step

EGI's first test of PCE destruction is the impact of removing stamping from the operations by outsourcing it to more efficient producers. Their original CVSM showed that this was one of their noncore operations.

Using their CVSM data, they can see what would happen *if stamping was removed but everything else stayed the same…*

> Steps in process = 9 (down from 10)
> Setup Time = 0.8 hr (down from 1 hr)
> Processing Time = 0.0009 hr / pc (down from .001)

From the full Complexity Equation, we get…

> New expected level of WIP = 40,366 pc
>> (note: WIP has been adjusted to account for obsolete inventory in the process)
> The new TLT would be 40,366 / 467 = 86.4 hrs
> TLT is reduced from 120 hours to 86.4 hrs
> WIP is reduced from 56,000 to 40,366

The overall impact? We can do calculations quickly by going back to the basic version of the PCE equation:

> PCE = Value-add time(VA) divided by Total Lead Time (TLT)
> VA remains constant (still producing the same number of the same parts)

TLT is now 86.4 hours

PCE_{new} = 2 hrs / 86.4 hrs = 2.3%

PCE_{new} − PCE_{old} = 2.3% - 1.6% = 0.7% improvement in PCE

The change in PCE shows that stamping "destroyed" 0.7% of PCE. This represents an improvement of over 40% in the PCE of the process. However, even with this improvement, the fact that stamping is a noncore process for EGI may still motivate the need to outsource the stamping process completely.

What-If #2: *The impact of removing an offering family*

When EGI created its CVSM, one family they identified consisted of only two products for their small contractor customer base. Now EGI wants to investigate the impact of simply stopping production of that family (in our terms, they'd be simplifying their product portfolio).

Here are the relevant data for the entire manufacturing process, fabrication through shipping, *before* changes are made...

Total Lead Time is 6 weeks (240 hrs)

Total VA = 192 minutes

PCE = VA/TLT = 192 min / 240 hr * 60 min/hr = 1.3%

WIP = $2.4M or 4800 equivalent finished generators (average cost of $500, sales price of $626, GPM of 20%)

Exit rate = 4800/240 = 20 Generators per hour output

Aggregate demand = 20 pc / hr

Steps in process = 25

Parts in process = 6

Cumulative Setup Times = 3 hr

Processing Time = 0.008 hr / pc (each unit takes more than 0.008 hrs, but this is scaled by the number of parallel assembly stations)

If the two small contractor products were dropped but everything else remained the same (again calculated from the full Complexity Equation)...

Aggregate demand = 18.6 pc / hr
  (*down from 20; volume decreased by 7%*)
Parts in process = 4 (*down from 6; removed two products*)

New expected WIP is ~2480 equivalent pieces
New TLT = 2480 / 18.6 = 133 hrs (*from 240 hours*)
WIP value is down from $2.4M to $2.14M, a $260,000 reduction in WIP

To gauge overall impact, they go back to the basic PCE equation again:

New PCE = VA / TLT = 192 min / (130 hrs * 60 min/hr) = 2.4%
PCE consumed by the small contractor products
  = 2.4% − 1.3% = 1.1%

Since the cost of capital is about 10%, such a reduction is worth about $26,000 per year. However, this product family is chewing up about one percent of PCE… what is that worth? An analysis of PCE gain vs. gross profit suggests that at a sales volume of $210 million, that level of reduction would cost about $1.2 million in gross profit—which may drive it into negative EP territory.

However, by either eliminating the product or driving PCE upward through design simplification or process improvement, the family may be robustly profitable. (This example illustrates why Lean, a discipline focused on process speed, was often helpless in justifying efforts based on inventory reductions… the real money was in non-value-add cost. It also explains why Lean was not applied as much in service applications where inventory often did not exist except as data.)

EGI has other figures that will help simplify their decision: The two small contractor products account for only $1.5M of $21.6M in sales. Profits from both lines are only $59K. Also, extra capacity freed by the removal of these products will allow additional capital expenditures to be avoided or postponed, etc.

Given these figures, what would you advise EGI?

Step 12: Select options and build business cases for selected opportunities

As in our EGI case study, once you start crunching some numbers, it will become clearer what specific actions you want to take to address the complexity problems or opportunities you've identified. We've pointed out before that the stakes are high, so before taking action it helps to subject your proposals to a formal business analysis.

If you're like most businesses, you probably already have a proposals approval process in place that involves a number of stakeholders and decision makers. In most ways, the business case for a complexity-driven project will be the same as for any other project, but keep in mind that the concept of complexity as a business issue and the kind of language we're using in this book will be entirely new for most people in your organization, so you may want to pay close attention to:

1. Connections between this project and the strategic/business direction

2. Project scope: which issues are going to be resolved, which aren't

3. Baseline metrics

4. Communication and credibility

5. Coordination with other projects and other teams

6. Plans for risk/contingencies

Here's more details on why...

1. **Connections between this project and the strategic business direction.** All agenda items should support the corporate strategy and business needs. Indeed, the methodology drives us to focus on areas of strategic importance. However, as implementation begins (with consequences for many stakeholders), it is important to *clearly* lay out the impact because not everyone was privy to how you reached the decision to work on a particular project. This will also provide a final

opportunity for course correction should something have been inadvertently missed. It also helps to include some description of the future state, i.e., what your business will look like in three to five years if the project is successful.

2. **Project scope.** By their very nature, many complexity-related projects will be more strategic and cut across more groups and functions than typical business projects. That requires an even crisper enunciation of what is *in* and what is *out of* scope. Discuss the project with all the process owners and stakeholders in advance. Phrase your statements as what value is at stake (e.g., a product is unprofitable on a value basis and is a high PCE-consumer, impacting your ability to compete, and driving up costs across the product line, etc.) so as to gain their insights and enthusiastic support, or to detect possible resistance.

3. **Baseline metrics.** Before you can agree on where you are going, all the decision makers in your organization have to agree on where you are today. In completing the various analyses spelled out in the previous chapters, you will have already established baseline metrics for EP and PCE destruction level (and a number of submeasures such as processing time, yield, value-add time, etc). Since many people may be unfamiliar with the metrics associated with value stream mapping and value creation, be sure to include enough detail so that others will appreciate the impact of the figures you're presenting.

4. **Communication and credibility**. Many of the cultural issues surrounding complexity can be either mitigated or inflamed by the level and quality of communication. The questions are predictable: Why are we doing this? What do the data say? What will it mean for me (and my group)? What does it mean for us as a company? (These concerns will be especially apparent the more radical the changes proposed.) Your business case documentation becomes the starting point for many discussions, between marketing and manufacturing, between R&D and sales, etc. It should cover many of the questions that will be asked regarding complexity-related projects. But think broader than the business case to make sure that all stakeholders are informed, if not actually involved in the planning and implementation of selected projects.

From Baseline to Trend: Tracking the dollar impact from complexity projects

In the course of performing a Complexity Analysis, you will document the current PCE. If you track PCE for the affected processes over time, you can create a graph of PCE vs. cost like the one in Chapter 2.

Figure 2.1—repeated from Chapter 2

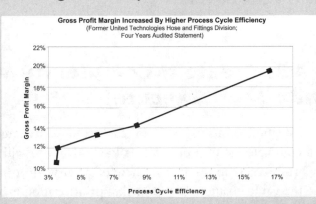

In this case, every percentage point of PCE% gain translated into an increase in gross profit of about 0.6%.

5. **Coordination with other projects and other teams**. Most businesses have some sort of existing system for identifying and executing projects (such as a Six Sigma infrastructure). Complexity Analysis should be largely conducted at the executive levels, though projects may be implemented at many different levels. In addition, a Complexity Value Agenda often includes several projects that are related (e.g., a reduction in the offering may be paired with a subsequent closure of production capacity). Identify interrelationships between your Complexity Agenda projects and projects arising through other pathways. Make sure efforts are coordinated between the groups—including clear accountabilities and responsibilities, resource requirements, timelines—so you can maintain your priorities and avoid any contradictory efforts.

6. **Plans for risks and contingencies**. What—and who—are potential roadblocks for success in this action? Stakeholder issues can be significant. Identify the risks, classify their severity, likelihood and the abil-

ity to detect them, and formulate an action plan for the highest priority risks. A key (and usual) outcome of risk analysis is the requirement for a stakeholder analysis. In the event of a product deletion, or a change in the business or site closure, further planning around this is required. Another major source of risk is disruption to customers, requiring a Business Continuity Plan, i.e., a detailed plan for migrating processes, customers, etc.

Step 13: Create a Complexity Value Agenda (and Execute!)

Once you have built a business case for each complexity target, you can compile a complete list of projects. It is likely that you will have more value opportunities than resources. Therefore you want to prioritize to accelerate the value creation. The principal prioritization is by value-at-stake. However, a secondary prioritization is the consideration of the nature of the project: Is it highly customer-focused, and hence more urgent? What is the risk profile for the project (and moreover, what risks exist that cannot be managed away through select investments)?

Once you've made the selection, compile the list of projects and their expected contribution to value creation, and identify the priority sequence. Summarize the results in a bar chart like that shown in Figure 8.1 (another example is shown later).

The EGI Case Study: Prioritizing and Building a Value Agenda

Obviously space does not permit us to walk you through a complete case study of a business, but we will give you a flavor for how these tools are used by returning to the EGI company we've been following. Part of the picture we did not address in earlier chapters was the Strategic Position analysis, depicted in Figure 8.11.

Figure 8.11: EGI Strategic Position Chart (One year ago and today)

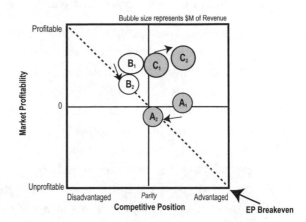

- Family A has slipped in competitive position over the last year in what is only a moderately profitable market. This indicates an area of concern unless action is taken.

- Family B has not lost ground against competitors in terms of relative EP, although it did see a drop in some volume. It still has a weak competitive position. However the overall market profitability seems to be eroding.

- Family C represents the only good news. The market profitability is high and EGI is continuing to improve its relative competitive position. However, there has been no revenue growth over the past year. A focus on growing the high-EP Family C would drive up shareholder returns.

They have now also completed a Complexity Matrix (*see* Figure 8.12).

Figure 8.12: Complexity Matrix for EGI

Product Family	Procure-ment	Fabrica-tion	Assembly	Pack & Ship	Total for Each Family	EP$ (million)	% Commonality
Family A- Contractor 5-7, Residential	10.4%	38.2%	10.5%	6.3%	64.5%	5.0	5%
Family B- Contractor 8-10, Recreational 8-10	13.4%	45.2%	23.4%	4.8%	86.0%	0.5	4%
Family C- Recreational 5-7	4.2%	10.4%	0.9%	3.2%	18.8%	21.3	1%

Fabrication is the biggest PCE-destroying step, and Family B is the worst product family. Family C is extremely profitable with very good processes, and therefore represents a potential area of growth.

As a result of these analyses, EGI reached the following conclusions:

Family C is the main profitable family representing the small recreational generators. Recall that these are the generators that use the advanced unibody frame design. Looking at the Complexity Matrix it is clear that Family C has good, low PCE destruction numbers with the exception of the Fabrication step. EGI had invested in a large, inefficient stamping press to support the fabrication of the unibody components. If the stamped unibody construction technique can be extended to other product lines, there is an opportunity to either optimize EGI's own stamping process through process improvements, or outsource the stamping work to a partner that specializes in metal stamping. The strategic position chart shows that this family is competitively advantaged in an economically profitable market. Thus any improvements in this family are likely to be doubly rewarded.

Family B is barely profitable, mainly due to the contribution of the recreational 8-10 kw model. However, it is clear that the fabrication and assembly steps of this product are much less efficient. Procurement is also somewhat impacted due to the higher part count. Family B is competitively disadvantaged in a market with moderate (but decreasing) total EP. Given EGI's relatively weak standing in the contractor market, there is an opportunity here to eliminate (outsource or delete) the contractor machine completely and redesign the large recreational machine to be more common with the unibody small recreational machine, creating a coherent family platform strategy for that market. This would dramatically relieve load on the inefficient fabrication and assembly processes.

Family A is somewhat profitable, due primarily to the residential models. Again, all models are suffering from high PCE destruction in the fabrication and assembly. The small contractor model is particularly unattractive due to its reliance on poor fabrication and assembly processes. Recall that there is tremendous growth in the foreign markets at this time. An opportunity to redesign models focused on the foreign residential markets will allow EGI to capture some of the tremendous growth in those markets, while providing a more cost-effective residential model for the domestic market.

After discussing all their information, EGI developed the following list of initiatives:

1. **Develop platform models in Family A to focus on the foreign residential markets** that will allow EGI to capture some of the tremendous growth in those markets, while providing a more cost effective residential model for the domestic market.

2. **Outsource fabrication.** This is a value-destroying activity for EGI, consuming high levels of PCE. There is no strategic advantage to invest in improving this process. The customers really don't care who does the fabrication, and it is a capital-intensive activity for which many adequate sources exist.

3. **Eliminate the contractor machine in Family B and redesign the large recreational machine** to be more common with the unibody small recreational machine, creating a coherent family platform strategy for that market. This would dramatically relieve load on the inefficient fabrication and assembly processes.

4. **Attack Procurement with Lean Six Sigma.** Independent of the impact of Families A and B, Procurement reveals opportunity for improvement in PCE. Focused use of Lean Six Sigma tools is recommended to drive improvement.

EGI also identified some other ideas for consideration: The Complexity Value Stream Map shows that the majority of plant space is devoted to holding finished goods inventory, which does not even appear as an "activity" in the PCE equations though it does show up as a non-value-add cost on the map. The destruction of PCE by the fabrication activities is really due to their long setup times, which led to batch processing (a deadly sin when you're trying to maximize PCE). By outsourcing fabrication, most of the remaining setup times can be easily reduced to near zero by a focused implementation of Lean improvement methods. This will allow lead times to be cut by 75%, reducing invested capital and freeing space for growth in economically profitable products. EGI cannot count this as a reduction in overhead cost yet, because the space is currently owned. However, as capacity is increased, or if the space is sublet, EGI could include the elimination of warehouse space as a true cost reduction.

After completing the formal business cases, and with a prioritized order for execution, EGI now has a Complexity Value Agenda, as shown in Figure 8.13.

Figure 8.13: EGI Complexity Value Agenda

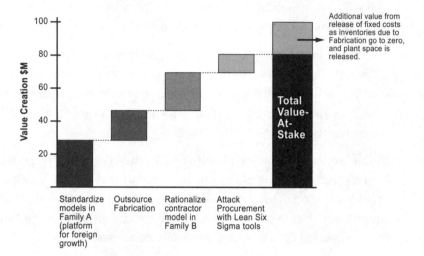

Total Value-at-Stake from initial wave of Complexity projects (excluding step-change benefits from fixed costs) = $80M. This initial agenda launches EGI on a commitment to conquering complexity, and preventing the re-emergence of non-value-add complexity.

You'll note that the chart shows the goals, the sequence of projects, and expected total value-at-stake for the portfolio of projects. The goal of implementing these projects can be displayed in a "future state" Strategic Position chart as shown in Figure 8.14 (next page).

Based on the financial impact of the Complexity Value Agenda, EGI's future vision is plotted on a Strategic Position chart. EGI's initiatives are unlikely to generate an immediate competitive response, as its strategies do not require disclosure and are internal moves. When competitors finally respond on cost—which they will—EGI will be in a good position to counter though differentiation since they will have taken the lead in tackling the cost of complexity.

Figure 8.14: EGI Strategic Position Chart—"Future Vision"

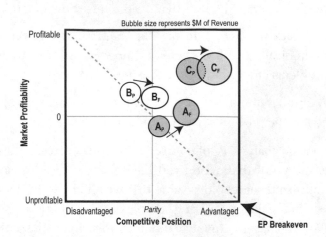

In the next year, EGI will invest in improving Business Unit A (moving it's bubble to the right), and start competing in foreign markets which makes the overall market profitability picture brighter (hence the bubble also moves up on the chart). It will also be improving B's competitive position, but expects the market to be in worse shape (so its bubble moves right and down). Its investments in Unit C should improve its competitive position and expected revenue, though the market should remain the same (so it's bubble moves to the right and gets bigger, but does not change position vertically).

Conclusion

The process described in this and the previous two chapters will leave you with a lot of insights into your company that range well beyond the impact of complexity. The logic, documentation, and calculations provide the "rigor" behind complexity decisions that we've been promising to deliver to you throughout this book. If anyone asks you to explain why a particular project was chosen or what you hoped to accomplish, you'll be able to track the decision-making process with documentation such as:

- Strategic position charts that reflect the overall competitive position of your business units

- Waterfall charts of both business units and individual product/service families that capture just how much EP is at stake

- Complexity Value Stream Maps and their associated data that dramatically display where and how complexity, quality, or Lean problems are affecting your business

- A number of matrices that link broad thinking to projects targeted at specific process steps or product/service families

Acting on the analysis is, of course, up to you. The case studies in Part I provide the proof that action can have the kinds of impact on overall profitability and shareholder value that we all crave. To do so, however, you'll need to make conquering complexity part of the strategic vision of your P&L managers. Involve them in this analysis so they become conversant with the costs of complexity, so that they can drive the vision to shareholder value. The remaining parts of this book provide more details on how to take action on the options you've chosen (*see* Part III) and how to truly leverage the effort you're investing in this effort (*see* Part IV).

PART III

Implementing Complexity Agendas

CHAPTER 9

Simplifying Product and Service Lines
Going for Big Gains in Economic Profit

Exploiting complexity to grow premium markets and brands is a proven strategy to create higher margins and shareholder value. It requires the orchestration of product development, R&D, and marketing focused on common goals for new product and service introductions. But proliferation *for its own sake* (without a view to value) will create only complexity costs and reap none of the benefits, and potentially curb the growth it was designed to stimulate. It is an easy trap to fall into, and to defeat it often requires the shattering of mental models and the reshaping of corporate identities.

It sometimes takes great acts of creative destruction to overcome this institutionalization. As we will discuss below, many consumer goods companies in the late 1990s, for whom proliferation had become a way of doing business, reorganized with a focus on value and made tough decisions on eliminating products that were destroying value. In so doing, they lived up to the spirit of the economist Joseph Schumpeter, who in the 1930s wrote:

> This process of Creative Destruction is the essential fact about capitalism. It is what capitalism consists in and what every capitalist concern has got to live in.[1]

No wonder, then, that one of the more common initial decisions resulting from complexity analysis is to simplify a portfolio of products and services and remove those that *can never* attain positive Economic Profit (EP). At the heart of the decision is the need to reach positive Economic Profitability, a factor that hinges on your business's answers to the following questions:

- Can we, through process improvement (Lean Six Sigma, internal standardization, etc.), attain positive Economic Profit?

- Can we improve the profitability by changing the cost component? (by outsourcing or reducing capital requirements, for example)

- Can we improve the profitability by increasing prices?

- Can we improve profitability through greater volume?

- Can we change the game? (e.g., change the offering strategy)

When the answer to all these questions is no, and your portfolio is cluttered with value-destroying offerings, then simplification of your product or service lines (sometimes called **rationalization**) is the only appropriate course of action.

The need for "portfolio simplification" can arise for a number of reasons. Earlier in the book we discussed a former United Technologies (UT) automotive division that went from near collapse to strong financial performance based in large part on their improvements in Process Cycle Efficiency and cost reduction. Here's a part of the story that needs some emphasis: *Their first step was recognizing that the Toyota and International Truck businesses were perpetually destroying value and even the rosiest projections in cost reduction could not make them earn more than the cost of capital.* The decision was made to withdraw from these products.

To many people, any course of action that advocates getting rid of products, services, or customers will sound ill-advised. Won't eliminating offerings reduce sales, no matter the impact on costs? The flaw in this conventional wisdom is the emphasis on maximizing revenue, even if that action destroys shareholder value.

In reality, eliminating low Economic Profit (low EP) products and services can free up resources to provide better services to the customers and offerings you keep. At the former UT division, for example, eliminating the Toyota and International Truck business took away 30% to 40% of the work that had previously consumed the time and attention of management, engineering, marketing, etc.! That allowed them much greater focus on the remaining (profitable) core business, and stimulated incredible gains in productivity as well as responsiveness and growth.

When they learned that their largest remaining customer, Ford, was having assembly line shortages because of long lead times from an internal supplier who could not cope with mix fluctuations, this division was in a position to steal that business because they were able to supply any of 168 different part numbers with a 3-day lead time. Ford nearly doubled its orders within a year. Figure 9.1 shows the revenue growth in this company.

Figure 9.1: Revenue Growth *After* Product Line Simplification

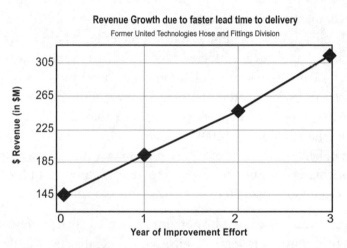

No one predicted this kind of growth as a result of trimming this company's product line. But the ability to focus their efforts improved delivery time so greatly that they started to win new business. In short, this was the unexpected result of targeting a large opportunity and solving a problem of great value to the customer.

This phenomenon has long been observed by others, such as George Stalk, who has studied the impact of faster lead times:

> *When a... competitor can open up a response advantage with turn-around times three to four times faster than its competitors, it will almost always grow three times faster than the average for the industry and will be twice as profitable as the average for all competitors. Moreover, these estimates are floors.*[2]

In this case, Ford was an exceptionally demanding customer—but according to George Stalk, these are often the most profitable[3]:

> The most attractive customers are often the most difficult to satisfy. These customers are demanding—wanting exactly what meets their needs. If you can satisfy them they will be reluctant to take their business elsewhere. They become dependent, and dependency can be profitable.

But even so, a potential revenue loss is a significant event. So what's it like for companies that have taken the plunge and simplified their offerings? Here's another example: When Procter & Gamble set about conquering complexity, it focused on reducing complexity-causing behaviors such as packaging variations and discounting, and also on simplifying its portfolio. Results were dramatic. For example, Head & Shoulders shampoo variants were cut by more than 50%,[4] but sales per item more than doubled. Overall, volumes grew two to three times faster after simplification than before. And even taking into account the new value pricing (a means to avoid the discounting complexity), its revenues rose more than 20%.

These were great results, but by not unprecedented. True, rationalization without the appropriate rigor of analysis is generally unwise. But without a doubt, inaction over complexity due to fears of revenue loss will only sustain the pattern of value destruction. And we've seen through this book how complexity can dilute your management focus and time, can weaken your marketing and advertising focus by spreading the budget too thin—in essence, can weaken your levers for growth.

Moreover, there is a strategic advantage in simplifying your portfolio. Before such a move, a company may believe that its product and service lines represent significant diversification and stability of revenues; that it is somehow insulated from market gyrations by the breadth of its portfolio. But the prosperity, or even survival, of a company usually depends on just a small percentage of those offerings. Emerging from that illusion can be a strategically transformative process. Reducing the breadth of your portfolio should not be viewed as a permanent reduction in revenue. Rather it should viewed as the precondition for focusing resources in areas that will generate both revenue growth and positive Economic Profitability. In Buffett's trenchant style:

> *A good managerial record (measured by Economic returns) is more a function of which boat you get into rather than how effectively you row. If you find yourself on a chronically leaking boat, energy devoted to changing boats is likely to be more productive than energy devoted to patching leaks.*

> —*Berkshire Hathaway Annual Report, 1985*

There are many ways to simplify your offerings and reduce your value-destroying levels of complexity, including:

- Adjusting pricing
- Simplifying configurations in products or services
- Dropping some customers ("adjusting your customer portfolio")
- Deleting product/services lines

We'll discuss each of these options and consider how to overcome some of the most common roadblocks to simplification.

The Pricing Lever

Raising the prices of unprofitable low-volume offerings (service options, SKUs, etc.) increases the value of these items and encourages customers to switch to higher-performance offerings within the same product family. This is accelerated by promoting the "old" offering alongside the new, which improves customers' ability to compare and increases the likelihood of a switch.

Pricing is one of the most powerful tools for building a high-value portfolio. It has tremendous leverage, as shown in Figure 9.2.

Figure 9.2: Leverage in Price Changes

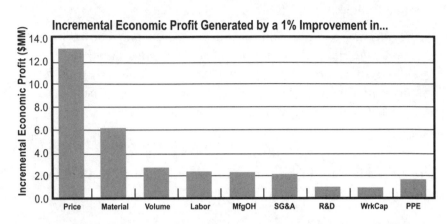

This chart compares how much EP is gained by making a 1% gain in various levers in one particular company (though this pattern is common in many business sectors). As you can see, increasing price has more than twice the impact of any other lever. Of course, market pressures will determine how customers will react to a price increase, but it is an alternative to eliminating offerings that are not currently economically profitable.

Unfortunately, many managers in flat markets are reluctant to tackle pricing initiatives for fear of alienating customers, and tend to err towards the other end of the spectrum: price discounting. As a lever on value creation, as you might guess, price discounting can have a disastrous effect. The normal argument for doing this is to drive sales. But the evidence shows that the benefits of price discounting are only temporary:

> Price promotions tend to have little long-term effect on sales volume... They quickly snap back to baseline.[5]

Furthermore, maintaining low pricing for a product or service that is *not* economically profitable is effectively subsidizing a set of customers or offerings. In those cases, adjusting your pricing is a very effective way of improving profitability or redirecting customers elsewhere.

That doesn't necessarily mean altering the list price of your product or services; it may simply mean fortifying your internal controls on pricing. In most situations, the list price and final *settled* price are very different. Individual rebates, allowances, incentives, etc., all are part of the pricing equation—and they all add to the complexity of administrating a service or product line. Excessive price discounting *as a strategy* has the net effect of creating whole new categories of overhead, and creating potential pricing pitfalls. Each discounted price level essentially creates a separate offering that needs to be handled by your systems and staff. Consider the following:

> In the 1990s, as manufacturers discounted prices, many grocery chains purchased additional warehouses for storage of the surplus inventory. Inventories soared and, on average, a grocery product took 104 days to reach the checkout counter. With the huge inventories, grocers were driven to create centers where manufacturers would come to pick up damaged or out-of-date merchandise. Total inventories in the grocery industry supply chain grew to $90 billion.
>
> With deal offers and discounts becoming so complex, the invoicing process became hopelessly complicated. A working group estimated that for a typical 100 store grocery chain, a total of 25,000 annual invoices would be received in the dry grocery category during a typical year. And, due to the complexity, 70% of these (or 18,000) would be rejected from routine payment and require manual handling.
>
> The chain of non-value-add costs was extensive. New functions emerged: Invoice Audit Specialists who would attempt to reclaim additional deductions from manufacturers, and Grocery Arbitrageurs, who would attempt to exploit unequal discounting by manufacturers around the country. But perhaps the biggest cost of all was the distraction from the customer: management became embroiled in this combat, instead of focusing on developing efficient supply chains and meeting the needs of the customer.[6]

Pricing complexity affects many industries, perhaps none more so than airlines, which have historically tried to manage multiple price points. British Airways, however, identified its "yield management policies"— using complex price discrimination systems as a means to fill flights, which in their case meant nearly everyone on the plane was paying a different price—as one of the areas in which it was at a disadvantage compared to the discount airlines, such as Ryanair and easyJet.

In short, discounting and price promotions can create huge inefficiencies in your administrative functions and supply chain without any net long-term gain in sales, but with permanent increased costs of maintenance. It can also create extra capital and overhead costs, and be off-putting to customers. Examine your pricing policies and analyze the net benefit after taking into account *all* the costs and impacts. Simplifying the price structure may save you from having to cut the product or service line entirely.

Promotional offerings and brand extensions

Promotional offerings and brand extensions have been at the center of proliferation over the last 20 years. Promotional offerings are known to increase the total number of offering variations in a company by 25% to 50%. The driving logic has been the desire to respond to competitor moves, absorb excess capacity, and claim a share of customers' spending.

But, as we've said repeatedly in this book, the costs of such complexity are rarely exposed in full. Promotional offerings can clog the supply chain and can impose additional overhead costs. What few benefits there are—help to support a brand, or help to launch a new product—are typically short lived. Further, by definition, promotional items or offerings are low-volume.

Line extensions can extract value from a particularly rich segment and steal market share from competitors. But equally as often, their impact can be negative: weakening the line logic; losing control of retailers' display (as product lines grow, retailers are forced to choose which products they shelve); and increasing costs. In fact, studies of product line extensions have shown that[7]:

- Line extensions do not increase demand
- Unit costs for multi-item lines can be 25% to 45% higher than producing only the most popular item in the line
- The incremental approach to line extensions and promotions, and subsequent increases in cost, mask the fact that companies are moving towards whole new cost structures

We're not arguing that promotional offerings or line extensions are necessarily a bad idea—clearly in many cases they have generated value—just that you should consider the full costs before taking that route.

Simplifying Product or Service Configurations: Exploiting naturally occurring configurations

Portfolio simplification decisions usually mean that a company needs to weed through its portfolio to cut back costs. The inherent assumption is normally that simplification decisions are the last resort to cost-management because customers prefer *more* to *less*.

But in fact simplification can often be a value-add step for the customers—it takes out much of the offering complexity that impedes the customer experience. Secondly, good simplification strategies are often more about growth than about cost, as we will discuss in examples to follow. And finally, simplification can be the centerpiece of an ongoing *offensive* strategy that focuses on capturing value for the customer.

Market-leading companies such as Dell and Toyota have mastered the art of using these principles proactively and integrating them into the way they do business. As we discussed in Chapter 3, Dell has developed a very strong brand as a made-to-order company, advertising custom-built PCs. However, Dell quickly exploited the fact that most people bought in what they called *naturally occurring configurations*—just two of the many configurations they produced accounted for 80% of sales. Dell then heavily promoted and marketed those configurations and drove demand upwards of 95% of sales even while it retained its brand leadership as the build-to-order company.

As Dell showed, savvy marketing can help you simplify a product or service line. This strategy depends on a strong understanding of the customer and your costs to deliver the product or service. But the institutionalized capability to look for natural market patterns, then capturing and marketing them to steal market share, can significantly benefit the customer and the company.

Another technique for managing configuration or options complexity is a stratification approach that breaks your portfolio into three categories based on how much they already have in common:

- options or configurations that already share a lot in common

- options or configurations with a moderate level of "commonality" that could be made available on a build-to-order basis (appropriately priced)

- options or configurations that are so unique that they may never be profitable and therefore should be considered for deletion

Figure 9.3 illustrates how this type of analysis works.

Figure 9.3: Evaluating the Commonality in Options

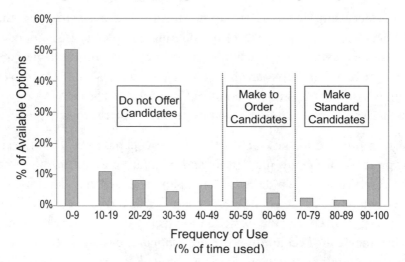

This "Option Usage" distribution for an equipment manufacturer shows how often different options are actually used. For example, the first bar shows that 50% of available options are used only 0–9% of the time. To simplify the portfolio and maximize value, options were stratified based on volume. High usage options were candidates for "commonization" (creating platforms for use across products), medium-usage options were offered as Make-to-Orders, and low-usage options were deleted entirely from the portfolio.[8]

Adjusting Your Customer Portfolio

Simplifying a product or service portfolio is one way to maximize value; simplifying your customer portfolio is another. Many times, an unprofitable customer is one who simply buys an unprofitable product. But it is not always as simple as that: different customers who buy the same product can still differ in the cost to serve them or the value they place on your products. Unprofitable customers may be expensive because they rarely make a purchase, pay slowly (if at all), demand an extra level of service, consume a disproportionate amount of your resources—or any combination of these factors. Or they may be unprofitable because they inherently see less value in your offerings compared with your profitable customer set, and so will be more price sensitive. (It was this concept that led FedEx to classify its business customers into three types based on profitability: the good, the bad, and the ugly.[9])

Customers represent another dimension of profitability, and a company may not want to keep all its current customers. In many industries, such as consumer products manufacturing, banking, and telecom, this new attitude has replaced the old adage of *the customer is always right*—a philosophy that could lead to a situation where your "good" customers were cross-subsidizing "bad" and "ugly" ones. Consider the following excerpt from a recent *Fortune* article[10]:

> *Who are your unprofitable customers? We recently asked that question of top executives at one of America's biggest retailers. They responded defiantly that they had no unprofitable customers. Understand that this company was in trouble—it wasn't even earning enough to cover its cost of capital, Wall Street analysts were beating it up, and its stock was performing worse than the shares of most competitors. Yet its leaders insisted that through some dark financial voodoo, millions of profitable customers somehow added up to an unprofitable company.*

Of course the truth, which shocked this top retailer, was that certain customers were destroying shareholder value—and yet the firm was continuing to spend money pursuing them. Who is an unprofitable customer? The same *Fortune* article went on:

> *Imagine a company that launches a big push for new customers and acquires 5,000 of them at a cost of $1,000 each. That amount is what the company spends on advertising, promotion, sales calls, and so forth to get those customers in the door. To keep things simple we'll assume that the new*

customers don't produce any business in the year in which they're acquired, so the company's operating profit is $5 million lower than it otherwise would have been. That is, it has invested $5 million in the hope of realizing much more than $5 million in future profits....

This company looks like a star. Investors are frantic to buy the stock. The directors are paying management zillions. Yet every new customer is unprofitable. The more customers the company adds, the more value it destroys.

Does this scenario sound familiar? Leaving aside the simplified numbers, does it suggest Gap's recent experience as it furiously acquired new customers by opening new stores on every corner, then saw its stock collapse? Or WorldCom's spectacular run-up as it offered cash incentives to attract new customers, then crashed and burned? Or cellular phone companies nationwide that did the same thing?

What scares so many managers we talk to is that they have no idea whether they're facing this disaster, because they don't know how to look across their firm's products, regions, and sales channels to understand customer profitability. They don't know what it costs them to acquire customers or how long they hold customers or what it costs to maintain them, so they have no idea how much money they make (or lose) on each one.

The Pareto principle applies well to customer profitability (and has been proven in studies[11]), but the 80/20 rule doesn't and shouldn't imply that you need only two types of customer-focused strategies. There are multiple tiers of customer behavior that require different strategies and result in different levels of profitability. For example, in one study, the top 20% of customers, while the most profitable, also appeared to be almost 10 times as responsive to changes in service quality.[12] This information is incredibly powerful as you consider, say, changes in service options or your retention strategy.

The goal is of course to make *all* customers profitable. This sometimes means "firing" customers, but more often means changing the way that you serve them. The need for understanding customer profitability in more detail has sparked a number of different approaches. One uses multi-tiered segmentation[13]:

Platinum tier: most profitable customers; typically heavy users of the product, not overly price sensitive, willing to invest in and try new offerings, and committed to the brand

Gold tier: less profitable than Platinum; may seek discounts and work with multiple vendors

Iron tier: customers that provide volume needed to utilize firm capacity, but whose spending levels, loyalty, and profitability are insufficient to warrant special treatment

Lead tier: value-destroying customers

The Platinum tier clearly moves the company up the PCE curve and the Lead tier sinks the company (as the name implies).

The strategic intent is to move customers in the lower tiers up to the next tier—and to scale the cost to serve to the level of profitability. For instance, often what stops a Gold customer from becoming a Platinum customer is the question of brand loyalty; creating structural relationships with a Gold segment can help them. That strategy doesn't always work with the Lead tier; it is usually harder to move them up to a higher tier because "bad customer" characteristics tend to be limiting and fairly dominating. (Management generally has no more success converting value-destroying customers than did their alchemical counterparts in the Middle Ages who pursued the Philosopher's stone that purportedly would convert lead into gold.[14])

If a customer doesn't adequately value your service, that tends to define their interactions with you. Generally your options are limited to raising prices or reducing the costs to serve those customers. Raising prices is not a vindictive act; it simply reflects the true cost to serve those customers. Higher prices can be dually beneficial: On the one hand, if the customer accepts the new price, you now have a newly minted profitable customer. If the customer rejects the new price, then you've off-loaded an unprofitable customer, also improving profits.

The other avenue is reducing the costs to serve that customer. In many situations, the best scenario is one which combines both, using pricing as a steering mechanism. For example, Fidelity Investments, the world's largest mutual fund company, realized that some customers were unprofitable because of the channels they used. So they instituted an automated phone system that identified unprofitable customers and routed them into longer queues, so that the more profitable customers could be served more quickly. If the unprofitable customers switched to lower-cost channels—such as the internet—they became profitable. If they didn't like the new experience and left, Fidelity became more profitable without them. Fidelity found that 96% of those customers stayed. Bank of America employed the same methodology by capping the number of free teller visits per month, encouraging cheaper online banking; Southwest gives you lower fares when you buy on the internet; American Airlines sells upgrades cheaper on the internet, and so on.

The decision to rationalize your customer base—and reduce the non-value-add complexity—while counterintuitive in many industries, is often best handled in this fashion: by moving customers to lower-cost channels and hence making them profitable. Again, ability to understand true economic costs is crucial.

Options for Deletion of a Product or Service

Brand-killing has remained an unwritten chapter in the marketer's handbook and an underused tool in the marketer's arsenal.

—Nirmalya Kumar, author of a 10-year study on rationalization programs in the U.S. and Europe.[15]

Despite your best efforts at changing prices, reducing internal support costs, or other steps, it may be impossible to turn around an economically unprofitable product or service. That will leave you with a range of options for off-loading the offering:

- **Merge with another offering:** In corporate mergers the management team often must quickly decide which portfolio items remain and which are to go. However, when two brands are equally strong and neither generates positive EP, it may make sense to gradually merge the two brands together over time, in terms of features, attributes, channels, etc. The "may" in the previous sentence is conditioned on the projection that the reduction in the cost of complexity will make the surviving brand generate positive EP. Strong marketing messages can help transition the customer in the same way it can be used to drive naturally occurring configurations.

- **Sell the offering:** It may be economically unprofitable for your company, but in the hands of another company with different channels, process capabilities, and customers, the product or service may have strong value. Selling happens frequently in industries such as consumer goods. Of course, there is always a caveat, particularly when thinning a crowded portfolio. You do not want your divested products to reappear as competitors to your residual offerings; and you will want to assess the reputation risk: consumers may not be aware that a brand has changed hands—if they have a bad experience, they may associate it with your name. Experience shows that customers are not at all displeased by your withdrawal from a product line so long as an adequate alternative source exists or can be developed. Without question, withdrawal of an offering causes some "loss of face" to marketing...whose budget does not include the impact of negative EP. As former Intel CEO Andy Grove and others have pointed out, this impediment to withdrawal is greatly exaggerated (more on this later).

- **Gradual extinction:** What to do with the cash-generating brands that are still popular but outside your strategic focus? One option: slash support costs for the product or service at the expense of growth. One level of fixed cost is the management time and "standard" allocation for support and management. By slashing these costs, moving personnel to other offerings, stopping marketing and advertising support, otherwise unprofitable offerings can be made profitable. This can be viewed as transforming the product or service into a "cash cow" to use Bruce Henderson's colorful term. As volume contracts, prices may be increased to support fixed costs. Texas Instruments' production of Germanium transistors continued five years beyond projected life, and earned handsome profits and ROIC until the end...when the last product sold was the best deal ever done. Stopping spending on non-strategic products can generate quick improvements in cost and allow cash to be redeployed into higher growth and Economic Profit opportunities.

- **Limit the offering:** Restricting distribution to areas that purchase higher volumes and are more profitable can accomplish a partial deletion. However, while this will eliminate many of the variable costs of the offering, it will leave untouched many of the fixed costs—the quantum-leap opportunity—built-in to the offering.

- Kill outright: Many firms are wary of killing a product outright. But remember: far less than 100% of your products and services generates the bulk of your Economic Profits. (Recall again that EP is *operating profit* minus capital costs. Just because operating profit > 0 does not mean that EP is >0.) A significant percentage of your products and services may generate negative EPs—which means customers see little value in them and so would not care if they were yanked off the shelves, dropped from the website, pulled from a brochure tomorrow. (The key is distinguishing the good from the bad, which is the reason for doing a Complexity Analysis.)

Managing Deletions

Most new introductions are analyzed on an incremental basis, ignoring the fixed costs they also lock in—so many are viewed as more attractive than they should be. In the same way, many product deletions are viewed as less attractive than they should be, i.e., ignoring entire categories of fixed costs that can be removed. To manage a delete, you need to:

1) **Assess the costs and financial impact of deletion:** Evaluate costs such as disposal of inventories (product or materials in manufacturing; marketing or support materials in services), which may have to be marked down or written off. Other financial impacts include:

- **The need to reapply overhead costs.** The volume of the unprofitable product or service may have absorbed overhead allocation and the deletion will result in the need to reapply the overhead cost to other products or services.

- **Reevaluation of EP based on improved PCE.** At a minimum, use the simplified Complexity Equation of Chapter 2 to recompute PCE You can then use the data from the Complexity Value Stream Map to estimate the beneficial cost impact that is not available from managerial accounting. For offerings in which demand is not uniform, you may need to use the full Complexity Equation in the Appendix.

- **Use or removal of newly freed-up assets or capacity.** To avoid turning the new capacity into an unused asset, designate a plan for using it (e.g., a new product or service introduction) or removing it (e.g., the closure of a plant; shifting personnel to other jobs).

2) **Address customer needs:** No one wants to cause customer trauma. There are a variety of ways to mitigate the impact of product or service loss, including pricing mechanisms and marketing-led inducements to switch from the product/service to be deleted. Consider also outsourcing: finding third-parties to continue producing the good or delivering the service and hence provide seamless coverage for your customers.

3) **Analyze the opportunity to remove fixed costs:** Deleting products and services yields savings in variable costs, but cut too shallowly and you risk leaving money on the table. In manufacturing in particular, look for pivot points (disclosed by the Complexity Value Stream Map) that yield the opportunity to close a warehouse, a factory, or discontinue a brand. It is generally brands, rather than products, that consume marketing resources. Consumer goods companies have demonstrated the impact of concentrating marketing budgets around core power brands. In service companies, many of the unique skills needed to deal with difficult customers can be redirected to more profitable customers or eliminated.

4) **Understand the institutional forces:** Bear in mind that institutional forces tend towards inertia and preservation of the status quo, many of which we'll talk about next.

Roadblocks to Simplification

Announce that you are eliminating product or service lines, and you're likely to hear a number of objections:

"This product/service is strategically important"

"It's a loss-leader"

"This product or service defines who we are" ("It's our core competence")

"Customers will react negatively"

"It's early in the life cycle; profitability will come"

"It's all Marketing's fault"… or… "Manufacturing has no idea about customers"

Overcoming these objections is partly a matter of having ready replies, partly an issue of listening to your internal constituents and establishing a two-way conversation about what is best for the business. Here are some suggestions for dealing with these roadblocks.

"Retaining the product is strategically important"… "It's a loss-leader"… "This product defines who we are"

Any strategy that makes an "inward look" the first priority is dangerous and possibly destructive of shareholder value. Some of the most powerful counterarguments to statements like these reside in the recent experiences of high-profile companies. For example…

For a time, Intel *meant* computer memory just like Xerox *means* copiers. But as well-publicized accounts of Intel point out, the company stumbled into the development of microprocessors as a way to produce a dozen custom circuits with one chip for a specific customer. The microprocessor took off, just as the memory market was becoming more capital intensive with tighter margins.

In fact, there came a point when the market no longer valued memory expertise at a price that would allow Intel to survive—that ground had been taken by the Japanese. Had Intel stuck to what the industry would call its "core competency," they would have ended up in bankruptcy.

The decision seemed clear: get out of the memory business. But Intel *meant* memory. That was the "core competence" of its managers. When then-CEO Andy Grove broached the issue of scuttling memory and focusing on microprocessors, Gordon Moore (of Moore's Law fame) observed that programming would become a key competency, and that the majority of Intel managers and executives would not, could not, make the transition. The human capital had become obsolete and obstructive, and its own internal competency represented Intel's greatest barrier to taking the necessary action for survival.

Another impediment was concern over what Intel's customers would think. Grove made the plunge and learned programming, but much of Intel's management was replaced. The response of the customers was "we've been wondering why you were waiting" and became good customers for microprocessors.

Companies like Mostek, Texas Instruments (whose CEO decided to "stand and fight"), and others either went out of business or took huge write-offs in shutdown of memory operations.

The success at Intel represents a new era in strategic thinking. Most companies are stuck in a paradigm where strategic decisions are based on *what the company does well* (its core competencies, in modern lingo) instead of *what customers value.*

The reverse needs to be true if you want to conquer complexity and achieve maximum Economic Profit. Value creation will come from...

1) recognition and responsiveness to customer and market demands

2) recognition of technological opportunities and peril

3) competitive realities of Economic Profit

4) corporate capabilities and "core competencies"

...*in that order.* The first three criteria test whether you are in a first-class business, and if not, how you can redeploy out of value-destroying complexity. If you pass the first three criteria on *all of your products and services*, then certainly the fourth, core competencies, should properly be the initial focus of intellectual capital and financial investment. Having conducted many analyses of Economic Profit, we always find some products or services that generate negative EP and should be addressed by the methods described below. Then, and only then, is a focus on core competencies entirely appropriate.

The unspoken objection

You'll hear a lot of different rationales about why your company needs to keep the status quo—some legitimate, others less so. In major changes, the hidden agenda is one of legitimate fear: "If we get out of a business that I run, and get into an entirely different business, I may lose my job." This is a hidden agenda that does not serve the interests of shareholders for whom we are all stewards of value. It simply cannot be a consideration in the long-term strategy of the business—but it *is* a delicate political situation that can harm or build internal trust depending on how it's handled.

You can avoid some of the internal turmoil by remembering that most managers (and staff) will be unaware of the existence of the PCE metric, of the true impact of low-volume offerings, of the difference between operating profit and Economic Profit. So they will not understand complexity-based arguments for deleting a product or service unless they are first educated in those basic concepts. Education is key. We therefore recommend holding a one-day "Cost of Complexity" workshop for all executive and key managers before your company starts discussing whether to keep or delete offerings.

History, in fact, rebuts a core competency viewpoint. As you approach Grand Central Station in New York City from the south on Park Avenue, you see a statue of Commodore Vanderbilt. Why was he a Commodore? Because his first fortune was made in operating steamboats on inland lakes. Nobody knew steamboats better. That was his "core competency." But Criterion 2, technological change, intervened. He quickly saw the future of trains, sold his steamship line, and created the New York Central Railroad, well known to players of Monopoly. He remained a Commodore in name only. Had he stayed in his core competency comfort zone, he would certainly have gone bankrupt.

Viewed through the lens of the value creation criteria, what can we say about the example of Henry Ford? He clearly ran afoul of Criterion 1 (responsiveness to customers), and did not respond to the changing demands of the market. Rather, he focused on Criterion 4, investing in his manufacturing core competency and achieving the most cost-efficient production of a car ever attained…a car that nobody wanted.

Warren Buffett started his current business by purchasing a failing textile company, Berkshire Hathaway. Despite his backing of competent management and great patience, Buffett finally saw that Criterion 3 made it impossible to earn even the cost of capital in the textile business. Overcapacity and foreign competition was not going to go away.

> *We had the option of making a large capital expenditure that would have reduced variable cost. Each(capex) proposal looked like an immediate winner but the promised benefits were illusory. Our competitors were stepping up to the same expenditures, and the reduced costs became the baseline for reduced prices throughout the industry: viewed collectively; the decisions neutralized each other and were irrational…as Dr. Sam Johnson has said: "A horse that can count to ten is a remarkable horse, not a remarkable mathematician."*
> *Likewise, a company that allocates capital brilliantly within its industry is a remarkable textile company, not a remarkable business.*

> —*Berkshire Hathaway Annual Report, 1985*

201

Buffett sold the textile business and redeployed the cash into the purchase of National Indemnity Life—the foundation for one of the most spectacular success stories in history. Buffett could have stayed with his "core competence." The result would have mimicked his far stronger rival, Burlington Industries, which chose that path. Burlington invested nearly $3 billion in the textile business between 1964 and 1985, which amounted to about $200/share. The stock traded for $60/share in 1964 and advanced to $64 by 1985, while the Consumer Price Index tripled; hence each share has lost two-thirds of its purchasing power and the $200 per share with it.

> *We look for first class businesses accompanied by first class managements. Good jockeys will do well on good horses, but not on broken down nags. Our textile company had good management, but we were never going to make any progress while running in quicksand.*
>
> —*Berkshire Hathaway Annual Report, 1989*

In these and many other cases, restricting the corporate sphere to existing core competencies would have led to bankruptcy. Any time a core competency constrains you to a market where you *cannot* earn positive EP, it is an obstacle to creating shareholder value. You can, you must, redeploy financial and intellectual capital to products and markets where you can create shareholder value. We value core competencies only to the extent that they are capable of creating shareholder value or being the springboard to a new sphere… and that is all.

If you encounter objections based on a core competency view of the world, here's what to do:

1) Define the strategic importance of the product or service: does it represent a value-rich segment that the company is entering, or anchor a valuable segment?

2) Understand its EP ability: if the argument is that it is a loss-leader for other offerings, what is the direct mapping to these other offerings? (In other words, prove it.) If correlation is high, is that entire segment worth keeping?

3) If management agrees on the retention of a money loser for strategic reasons (profitable customers demand it), then the product or service requires special levels of scrutiny, with high levels of accountability. Everyone should agree on the *explicit* reason for retention. Retention should be done on an exception basis. And a plan for improving profitability is required: *Can we improve the process? Do we have to do all the work ourselves or can we outsource?*

"Customers will react negatively"

The answer to this objection is "not if the deletion is well planned." Some of the mechanisms described in this chapter can reduce the chances of negative customer reaction. A growing body of research indicates that customers respond favorably to clear lines with good integrity and logic. All customers are not all created equal. We want to focus on delivering value to the highest-value customers.

"It's early in the life cycle; profitability will come"

It is a natural instinct to be optimistic about the future. But projections of rapid growth used to justify new offerings should be challenged. It is true that with innovative products or services expenses can be much greater than revenue because of development costs and low adoption rates. And no one has a crystal ball.

But if we are to truly conquer complexity, we have to at least challenge assumptions of profitability. What are they based on? Why do people believe that the product or service will succeed? Do the growth rates reflect introductions of similar products or services? Who is accountable for making this product succeed? What is their strategy? What are our decision criteria and timeline for evaluating these new offerings?

The answers may not alter the decision to retain the product or service, but the answers may alter our strategy going forward and help surface assumptions on which decisions are based—and which can later be checked against performance to provide input for the *next* introduction.

A case study in customer demand

When integrated circuits were first sold commercially, industrial firms were allegedly concerned about "noise sensitivity." Texas Instruments' sales department kept pressuring marketing to force engineering to develop a "noise *insensitive*" product to counteract that effect and meet the market need.

In fact, such a product had been developed by Amelco. It achieved high noise thresholds by using high voltages, which resulted in high power dissipation (i.e., was not power efficient). Engineering at TI felt that this was the wrong answer.

To resolve the issue, TI's marketing department conducted a survey of likely industrial customers who were not yet buying any integrated circuits. The survey of over 100 companies indicated no plans to ever buy the Amelco product. Texas Instruments' Marketing VP, Dick Hanschen, concluded: **"This is a huge *potential* market, but with no demand!"**

In fact, as soon as industrial customers saw that the standard circuits were not noise sensitive, huge industrial demand for the standard circuits took off.

The high-voltage circuits would have generated so much waste power that only very simple circuits were possible. Had TI misdirected engineering effort, it could never have created the complex functions with which it later destroyed Fairchild's lead in the industrial market. Amelco is now only a distant memory, along with other failures like Clevite, Transitron, Philco, Sylvania, Tung-Sol, and on and on.

"It's all Marketing's fault" or "Manufacturing has no idea about customers"

While most companies understand the dynamic of product/service life cycles and the need to introduce new varieties and brands, very few companies have methodologies in place for systematically managing the *end* of a life cycle. So it is not unusual that functional groups in the organization tend to blame each other for the creation of complexity.

In his 1977 *Harvard Business Review* article, "Can Marketing and Manufacturing Coexist,"[16] Benson Shapiro described the paramount "need for cooperation." Over the last 30 years, the speed of the markets, the increased sophistication of customers' buying habits, and the rise in global competition has supercharged that requirement. Only with a cross-functional perspective (and therefore team) can successful offering deletion and management strategies be executed and become a cultural norm. Divert blame-issues and instead set about building cooperation. Achieving consensus in a timely fashion on these issues is intrinsic to small organizations, or to large organizations organized around small units as described above. It can only be achieved in larger, functionally organized units by deliberate mapping and process improvement.

Conclusion: Biting the simplification bullet

In *Only the Paranoid Survive*, Andy Grove, then the CEO of Intel, described the ordeal of withdrawing from the memory market. The forces that impeded this change were monumental and required nothing less than a major turnover of management whose skills were no longer of value to the corporation. On a smaller scale, every company has some products or services that are stars, and other that do not and never will earn their cost of capital.

The desire to protect what we all produce or deliver is strong, even in the most forward-looking of companies. The best counter to those concerns is a complexity analysis based on facts and calculations of EP. It can demonstrate without a doubt whether a product or service is creating or destroying value. That's not to say you should write off any offering that does poorly in the analysis; indeed, much of this book is dedicated to ways you can improve PCE and remove non-value-add costs to make offerings more economically profitable. But even so, don't hesitate to bite the simplification bullet when needed and open up new possibilities for strengthening and growing the strategic core that remains.

In any case, remember this is a top-down effort. If you are in a subordinate position, you must engage P&L managers in the process for it to have any success.

Endnotes

1 Joseph Schumpeter, Business Cycles: *A Theoretical Historical and Statistical Analysis of the Capitalist Process* (London: Porcupine Press, 1989).

2 George Stalk, *Competing Against Time: How Time-Based Competition is Reshaping Global Markets* (New York: Free Press, 1990), p. 4.

3 Ibid., p. 149

4 Steven M. Cristol and Peter Sealey, *Simplicity Marketing: End Brand Complexity, Clutter, and Confusion* (New York: Free Press, 2000).

5 Shuba Srinivasan, Koen Pauwels, Dominique Hanssens, Marnik Dekimpe, "Who Benefits from Price Promotions?" *Harvard Business Review*, September 2002.

6 Cristol and Sealey, *Simplicity Marketing*.

7 Quelch and Kenny, "Extend Profits, not Product Lines" (see chap. 2, n. 1).

8 Taha and Mitchell, "How Complexity Costs" (see chap. 4, n. 15).

9 Valarie Zeithaml, Roland T. Rust and Katherine N. Lemon, "The Customer Pyramid: Creating and Serving Profitable Customers," *California Management Review* 43 (Summer 2001).

10 Larry Selden and Geoffrey Colvin, "Will This Customer Sink Your Stock?" *Fortune*, September 30, 2002.

11 Zeithaml, Rust and Lemon, "The Customer Pyramid."

12 *Ibid.*

13 *Ibid.*

14 Lead was finally transmuted into gold in 1937 by Glenn Seaborg using the Berkeley cyclotron not the Philosophers Stone.

15 Nirmalya Kuma, "Kill a Brand, Keep a Customer," *Harvard Business Review*, December 2003.

16 Benson P. Shapiro, "Can Marketing and Manufacturing Co-exist," *Harvard Business Review*, September 1, 1977.

CHAPTER 10

Finding the Complexity
That Customers Value

With Kimberly Watson-Hemphill[1]

Our whole business is far too complicated, and it makes it difficult for our people to deliver. When I arrived here it was clear to me that the success of easyJet and Ryanair was not just built around lower costs.

—Rod Eddington, CEO, British Airways, 2002

We often talk to customers about 'relevant technology'... We think it's our job to help our customers sort out the technology relevant to today's needs from the bleeding edge.

—Michael Dell, CEO, Dell Computer[2]

What British Airways is discovering, and what CEO Rod Eddington referred to is that complexity in your offerings can be a customer turnoff. In a personally championed war on complexity, Eddington recently attacked the traditional airline pricing model of micro-revenue yield management—and British Airways' pricing model in particular as "massively complex and not at all transparent"—and launched an initiative to copy the simpler and more customer-friendly pricing model of low-cost rivals easyJet and Ryanair. "We had to learn very quickly and we're still learning," he said.

British Airways also launched a number of other complexity initiatives: reducing the supplier base by 75%; moving from a "Noah's Ark" fleet—

with two of everything—to a few standard aircraft types; and outsourcing large tracts of its in-house (and previously treasured) IT system. Eddington's focus on reducing the complexity of the customer experience echoes efforts at other companies, who are asking themselves: "**Am I hard to do business with?**" Here are two other examples:

> *Nissan, for example, reportedly had 87 different varieties of steering wheels, most of which were great engineering feats. But customers did not want many of them and disliked having to choose from so many options.*[3]

> *Sales of cough and cold medicines fell 5 percent… in part because the consumer was confused not only by the large number of products but also by the "appearance of multi-symptom remedies.*[4]

British Airways is only one of many companies that are learning they have to take a close, hard look not just at the breadth of their offerings, but how much their customers *value* those offerings. We'll look at customer choice and value in this chapter.

A Case Study in Choice Explosion

Walk into a supermarket in 1970 and it's unlikely that you would have felt starved for choice. But you would have had only 20% of the choices available today. The average supermarket now carries about 35,000 items, compared to 8,000 a few decades ago. To cope with this explosion of variety, the size of the average store has increased, but not enough to keep pace with the rise of stock keeping units (SKUs) (*see* Figure 10.1, next page)—so shelf space has become more precious.

What drove this relatively recent phenomenon? Many factors. Since World War II, when scarcities deprived people of choice, the compensatory marketing mantra has been *more is better*. Advances in manufacturing have made new products, promotions, and brand extensions far cheaper and quicker to produce. Database marketing and IT have

Figure 10.1: Explosion in Supermarket Offerings

Index of SKUs per store vs. Supermarket size

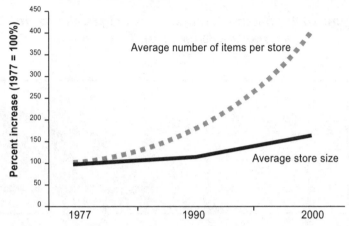

This chart shows how the number of different items (SKUs) carried by grocery stores has far outstripped growth in the physical size of these stores. Hence the increasing competition for prominent shelf space. Sources: Progressive Grocer; Food Marketing Institute; *Simplicity Marketing* (Cristol & Sealey)

increased a company's ability to successfully segment and target specific customer groups. Incomes have risen, making the pot of gold at the end of the rainbow far richer. Television and other media have propelled the age of advertising, which needs new products and services to sell. And extensions and innovations have secured customer loyalty and repeat business, keeping popular brands fresh.

But perhaps the greatest—and most obvious—reason is simply that customers have generally responded. Indeed, companies that haven't correctly captured the Voice of the Customer and then acted decisively have languished.

In premium product markets, such as cereals and cookies, consumers respond well to aggressive advertising and *demand* a certain level of innovation and choice. In these product categories, proliferation can lead to value creation and be a wise investment in spite of the costs. Consider those companies that help stock the supermarket shelves. Consumer goods companies such as Colgate-Palmolive have had great success with the proliferation of products through brand extensions, innovations, and acquisitions (*see* Figure 10.2 for share prices over last 20 years).

Figure 10.2: Shareholder Returns of Colgate-Palmolive (CL) vs. the Dow Jones (DJI) (1980–2003)

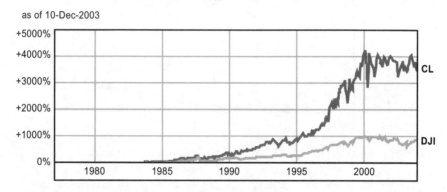

Colgate-Palmolive has seen great shareholder returns over the last 20 years, far outperforming the market.

But is there room for profit improvement? Clearly, yes. According to a P&G Study, 25% of the SKUs stocked in supermarket shelves sell less than one unit per month. One of the reasons for the high number of low-volume products is the trend towards brand extensions. Table 10.A (next page) illustrates how part of the growth explosion has been in the extension of brands with different packaging, promotion, and versioning. With innovation and genuinely new products hard to conjure up, many companies have been using the line extension as one of their chief growth vehicles.

Rapid brand and product/service proliferation and variety are institutionalized in most corporations as the result of a number of factors: the speed of the market, dynamic competition, increased customer buying power, the need to defend shelf space. Just as 3M has dictated that 30% of its revenues will come from new products, many companies set goals for proliferation in advance of market shifts on the premise that it will counteract tendencies to be complacent with current offerings.

Table 10.A: SKU Explosion in Consumer Items

	1970	2000
Crest toothpaste	15 SKUs Mint or original, one formula in tubes only	45 SKUs including tubes and pumps of gel, paste, tartar control, baking soda, glitter for kids, mint or original flavor
Philadelphia Cream Cheese	3 SKUs Three sizes of one flavor in one foil-wrapped block cheese form	30 SKUs Block or soft or whipped; regular or light; 15 flavors, ranging from Roasted Garlic to Apple Cinnamon to Jalapeno
Coca-Cola	6 SKUs just classic Coke in cans or glass bottles	25 SKUs 5 container sizes (some containers plastic, others aluminum); regular, cherry, diet, diet cherry, caffeine-free diet, caffeine-free regular, etc.

Source: Cristol and Sealey, *Simplicity Marketing*, 2000

Is this a good thing? If the proliferation of offerings is creating Economic Profit, yes. But when it is done at the expense of shareholder value, no. This is what author Michael McGrath means when he says that "product proliferation can result from the company being overly customer-focused."[5]

We all know of companies that paid a price by waiting too long to act (underproliferating), but there are also dangers with overproliferation. The following example is illustrative:

> By the mid-1990s, IBM's PC division was struggling with an unmanageable number of different models and huge economic losses. The losses prompted action and over the next three years IBM cut its models from 3,400 to 150, options from 750 to 350, and number of different parts in inventory from 56,000 to 15,000. By 1997, its PC business was growing faster than the industry.[6]

But if, from the customer's perspective, "More is Better" (as is generally believed), is there ever a point at which "More is Too Much"? The answer is increasingly "Yes."

The concept of overchoice as destroyer of value creation has its roots in one of the most fundamental equations of Lean: Little's Law (*see* page 37), which relates the amount of work or "things" in process to lead time (how quickly you can get work done). The lesson of Little's Law is that the single biggest determinant of speed is the number of things we are working on at any given moment.

Surveys frequently cite one of the greatest causes of stress in our lives today as being the lack of time, and that many of us would willingly pay a premium for time-saving features and services. A Datamonitor study found that people were willing to pay an 8.3% premium for simpler positioned brands, and 52% were willing to switch brands for simplicity-positioned products.

Now let's consider Little's Law with a twist. Instead of Work-in-Process, substitute decisions-in-process, or the "decision burden" we place on ourselves and customers.

We have a fixed capacity to make decisions, so the greater the number of decisions required of the customer, the longer the time demands. If we are time-pressed, a value-add feature may be *a reduction in the number of choices required of us*. The customer's worst nightmare is having to weed through your vast number of offerings (such as Nissan's 87 different types of steering wheel) to get to the "good stuff." Customer-attuned companies such as Dell and Toyota have leveraged this principle, guiding customers into precomposed packages, making informed decisions for the customer while enabling customer-specific tailoring.

It is perhaps not surprising that customers would at some point react negatively to the excess complexity of offerings, price points, options, and so on. Consumers are flooded with ever-expanding choice even as their capacity to make decisions, their leisure time, etc., has remained finite. Back in 1970, in his book *Future Shock,* author Alvin Toffler wrote: "Ironically, the people of the future may suffer not from an absence of choice, but from a paralyzing surfeit of it. They may turn out to be the victims of that peculiar super-industrial dilemma: overchoice."

What Customers Want vs. What They Value

Every day, everyone from product designers to service managers is making decisions about what to offer your customers. In many situations, the push to "give customers what they want" has led to uncontrolled proliferation in products/services, options, features, etc. When leaders have little idea about what customers would be excited to buy, they allow, if not openly encourage, this proliferation. The result is an explosion of the costs in your organization and in the number of products or services that are not economically profitable.

The previous chapter discussed several ways to address this problem by changing your price structure to improve profitability or eliminating offerings entirely from your portfolio. But the root of the problem is a failure to understand specifically what it is that your customers value about your products or services and *how much* they value it.

Unfortunately, if you went to a Voice of the Customer seminar or read up on VOC techniques, almost all of the attention would be on the first part of the last sentence—*what* customers value—with very little attention to the *how much* question. In this chapter we'll switch that emphasis, spending most of the time on techniques that will help you understand your customers' priorities and purchasing factors.

Technique #1: Key Buying Factor analysis[7]

One way in which complexity can reduce Economic Profit is simply this: spending money on things that customers don't want and won't pay a premium for (such as features they're not seeking). That's why you should always check whether the features/functions of your service or product match what your customers need.

An example of this analysis is shown in Figure 10.3. This company asked an important customer to identify what they thought was most important in the company's offering, then rate the company versus three competitors. The bars on the chart indicate the customer's importance rating; each line tracks how well the company or one of its competitors did relative to those ratings. The most important takeaway from this chart is that the company did poorly on the customer's top seven attributes; they did well only on the remaining eight attributes. This company (and its competitors) had mistakenly focused on attributes that were lower in importance to the customer. The results showed up in the offering's poor financial performance.

Figure 10.3: Key Buying Factor Analysis

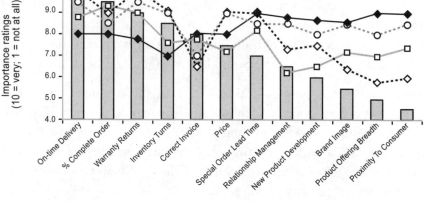

This type of chart helps pinpoint what your customers consider value-add. As you can see, none of the companies performed consistently well relative to the customer's top priorities; most of them performed much better on attributes that weren't nearly as important to the customer. If the company that did this analysis can improve performance across all of the customer's priorities, they could gain an advantage.

There are several additional things to note on this chart: First, the customer was not looking for increased options (= increased complexity of the offering). Second, price is nowhere near top on the list, which means that if the company can deliver on the important service support functions rated highly by the customer (on-time delivery, correct invoices, etc.), they can charge enough to make the offering economically profitable.

For non-commodity goods, this is usually the case. The most powerful defense against pricing pressure is the ability to uniquely capture the Voice of the Customer. In *Trading Up*, authors Michael Silverstein and Neil Fiske describe what they see as a shift in consumer behavior and marketing response: "America's middle-market consumers are trading up... willing, even eager, to pay a premium price for remarkable goods... that possess higher levels of quality, taste and aspiration." The ability to accurately capture the wants and needs of that particular segment has big payoffs for companies, they say—the ability to "shatter the price-volume demand curve."

Technique #2: Kano analysis

Another way of understanding how customers evaluate options or features was developed by Dr. Noriaki Kano, who demonstrated the need to understand the different types of customer needs and wants. He highlighted the risks of:

1. Providing features superfluous to customers' needs—and willingness to pay

2. Delighting them in one area, but failing them in a more fundamental way, and losing their business

3. Focusing on what customers *say*, not what they *think* or *do*

The Kano model, depicted in Figure 10.4 (next page), directs attention to two dimensions and three types of customer requirements. The first dimension is the degree to which the customers' requirements are fulfilled. The second dimension is the customer response to the first dimension. The Kano model predicts that the degree of customer satisfaction depends on the degree of fulfillment, but is different for the three different types of customer expectations.

Figure 10.4: Kano Analysis Model

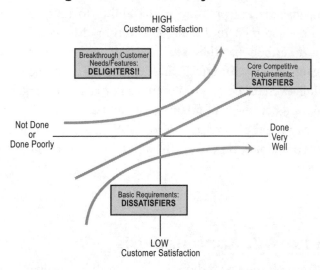

Dissatisfier—these are customer requirements so obvious that they are not explicitly stated as such. When these requirements are met, the customer may say nothing; however, when they are not met, the customer will complain. Example: towels in a hotel room.

Satisfier—requirements that are overtly stated and of which customers are well aware. When more of these are delivered, the customer perceives additional benefit. Examples: a coffeemaker in the hotel room, a large selection of cable TV channels, a nice breakfast buffet.

Delighter—requirements that customers are not aware of (sometimes called "latent" needs). When they are not delivered, customers don't notice. When they are, customers are delighted. Example: high-speed in-room internet access in your hotel room.

Many of you may be shaking your head at the Delighter example; for many business people who travel, high-speed internet access has, over time, gone from being a Delighter to a Dissatisfier—that is, the ability to generate a premium based on this feature has been eroded, as it has become a basic tenet of a good hotel stay. Features tend to follow the reverse Kano curve, a trend present in most products and services because customer demands continue to increase. Last year's exciting feature is this year's status quo.

Delighter characteristics are what enable companies to differentiate themselves from the pack, and depend upon innovation. U.K.-based Virgin Atlantic has a radically different transatlantic flight model, as it challenged a commoditizing industry and broke with convention in offering extra services, such as chauffeur service to and from the airport, on-board massages and a full bar, complete with bar stools.

Said chairman Richard Branson: "My staff were maddened to hear that I met a man on the airport bus who suggested that we offer on-board massages. They tease me, and call it 'Richard's straw poll of one,' but time and again the extra services which Virgin offers have been suggested to us by customers."

How does the Kano model relate to complexity? If the proposed new functionality gets the product or service only to a basic level of performance, then it is required—you have to do it no matter the cost. If you are adding performance needs, then you need to do a cost/benefit analysis. If the functionality would be a Delighter, you need to combine a cost/benefit analysis with strategic analysis of the potential for market differentiation versus the cost of complexity. If Branson is going to put a dedicated masseur on the flight, then the cost/benefit analysis is straightforward. However, if the job is combined with others, it competes for resources and may increase response times, say, for serving food—impacting PCE.

We all know how customer value drifts over time, which may spur new products, services, and proliferation to capture more Delighter needs. But—and this is the insidious effect that complexity can have on retention—when efforts to do this compromise Satisfier and Dissatisfier needs, customers will flee and your competitors will benefit.

Technique #3: Functional analysis

A technique designed to specifically support product and service design processes is known as **functional analysis**, which looks at how the customer will be using the product or service (application analysis) and then understanding the functions that the product needs to perform to meet the customer requirements. This information feeds into the design process to develop high-level concepts that will truly meet the customer needs. By focusing on functionality, the design team is freed up to generate creative concepts that satisfy the customer's needs, avoiding features and options that may be technically interesting, but "in search of a customer."

The first step in defining the functions is to understand how the product or service will be used and in what environments. A child's bike, for instance, might be used for riding around the neighborhood, for off-road riding in parks, or even for amateur racing. It's likely that there will be different types of customers interested in the different uses, and your company will have to decide if you want to serve all of the various markets or target just a few.

Once the applications associated with the target market have been adequately defined, the next step is to define the functions associated with the application(s).

- What does the customer want the product/service to do?
- What does the product/service do for the customer?
- What does the customer believe he/she's paying for?

Teams must look at different levels of functionality:

Primary or **Basic:** Active function of the product/service

Secondary or **Support:** Support the active functions
- Prepare the product for use (installation, setup)
- Make it more reliable (maintenance)
- Make it more fun (styling)

Figure 10.5 (next page) shows an example of a functional analysis for the child's bike example begun above, including both primary and secondary functions. In practice, the analysis would continue further, breaking down each function to specific actions taken by the customer during use. (A comparable example of functional analysis in a service is shown in Figure 10.6.)

Figure 10.5: Functional Analysis of a Product

High-End Children's Bicycle

Purchase Bicycle	Transport Bicycle	Assemble Bicycle	Adjust Bicycle	Ride Bicycle	Maintain Bicycle
• Select Bicycle • Select Options • Buy Bicycle • Buy Extras	• Lift Package • Place in Vehicle • Close Door • Load Crane on Truck • Secure Crane • Move Crane	• Remove Bicycle from Package • Find Instructions • Locate Tools • Read Instructions • Assemble Bicycle	• Adjust Seat • Adjust Handlebars • Tools not required	• Sit on Bicycle • Check for Adjustment • Check Brakes for Function • Place Feet on Pedals • Push Forward	• Clean Bicycle • Inspect Bicycle • Inspect Brakes • Replace Pads • Inspect Shifter

Gray = Bicycle Primary and Secondary Functions
Black = Lower Level Product and Service Functions

As its name implies, a functional analysis identifies each of the key functions a product or service must perform in order to meet customer needs. This analysis of a high-end children's bike identifies six main actions the customer performs over the lifecycle of using the bike including details on associated bike functions.

Figure 10.6: Functional Analysis of a Service

Service: Online Banking
Critical Application:
Day-to-Day Money Mgmt.

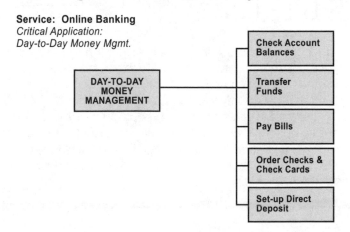

For services, functional analysis is sometimes easier done through a tree diagram such as this. What's important is that the broadest functions that customers are looking for (checking account balances, paying bills) are described in "method-independent" terms. At some banks, checking account balances can be done in person, over the phone, or via the internet.

The kind of information supplied by functional analysis also allows for greater specificity in *financial* analysis to make sure that money is being spent in the right place. If feature #1 provides 25% of the primary functionality, then it would make sense that it be allocated around 25% of the cost. If a large percentage of the product or service cost is taken up with items that provide very little of what the customer is purchasing the product for—these items should be considered for cost reduction. We can invest this savings to improve the functionality that is most important to the customer, as shown in the example in Figure 10.7.

Figure 10.7: Functional Analysis of a Dishwasher

Part #	Part Name	Qty	Cost Each	Total Cost	Compon. Function	Prod Func supported				Cost Allocations		
						Cleans dishes	Looks good	Rinses dishes	Dries dishes	% of Comp Func.	Cost	% of Total Cost
FD2004DX	Door	1	$25.00	$25.00	Seals washer	B	N	B	B	30%	$7.50	4.52%
					Dispenses soap	B	N	N	N	15%	$3.75	2.26%

This is a small portion of a much larger table summarizing the functions that a dishwasher has to perform and how those relate to components and cost. Purchasers of a dishwasher are usually willing to pay for a product that cleans, rinses, and dries dishes and that looks good. These functions are listed in the middle of this table, then different components and their costs are assessed to see how much they contribute to the desired functions. In the full matrix, the team discovered that the rack and air dryer system both cost $10, representing about 6% of the unit cost.

Functional analysis provides an understanding of the functions that are major cost drivers, and functions where cost exceeds what customers would likely be willing to pay (in which case you can explore alternative ways to accomplish the same function with lower cost, *see* Chapters 11 and 12). When you are considering a redesign, you can invest in improving areas that are critical to key product functions, and reduce cost in areas that are not.

Technique #4: Conjoint analysis

As any product or service designer knows, customers rarely base their purchasing decision on just one factor. Almost always they are looking for a specific combination of features, options, price, and so on. The tool that helps you find the most economically profitable combinations is called **conjoint analysis**, a scientific approach used to *simultaneously* analyze multiple factors related to a product, service, or process.

The purpose of conjoint analysis is to understand how purchasing decisions will change based on different "packages" of product/service attributes. The steps are to...

1. Identify key product/service attributes.

2. Identify possible levels you want to test. A "level" is the amount of the feature or attribute you're considering for the product or service. Typically, you select two levels for each key attribute, such as present/absent (including or not including the feature), high/low (including a little or a lot of the attribute), fast/slow, etc.

3. Identify combinations of attributes. The choice is never random— rather, it is based on specific protocols laid out in design of experiments methodology.

4. Have customers rate or rank the combinations.

5. Analyze the resulting data as a designed experiment.

6. Make trade-off decisions.

To illustrate this process, here's a simulation we use in training that incorporates features of actual examples. A pizza restaurant is investigating some changes in their product line. The restaurant management wants to add a high-value product with more pepperoni and more cheese, but are unsure if they will be able to turn the extra cost into extra margin. The team decides to investigate four attributes, and have identified two levels for each factor:

Pepperoni - 100 slices vs. 50 slices   Cheese - 5 oz. vs. 8 oz.
Crust - Thick vs. Thin   Price - $6.99 vs. $8.99

They identified eight specific combinations they wanted to test—one combination was 100 pepperoni slices, 5 oz of cheese, thick crust, and an $8.99 price—and asked customers to rank the combinations in order of preference.

Some aspects of the results you can probably predict yourself, such as that there was a marked preference for having more pepperoni (*see* Figure 10.8).

Figure 10.8: Pizza Conjoint Analysis

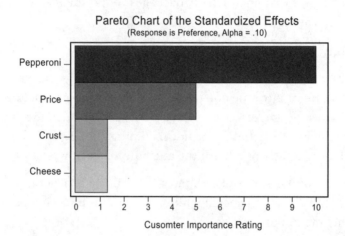

A Pareto chart of standardized responses shows that pepperoni is the most important feature to the customer, and that price is second in importance. Crust type and cheese do not look to be statistically significant.

What you may not have predicted is that crust and amount of cheese were *not* big factors in the customers' decision. What does that mean? A more detailed trade-off analysis of the results allowed the team to state categorically that going for the lower amount of pepperoni would adversely affect customer purchasing *no matter what they did with the other features*. Conversely, if they went for the higher level of pepperoni, they could charge the higher price with minimal effect—and since crust and amount of cheese had little impact either way, these options could simply be set at the most economical levels.

Conjoint Case 1: Hospitality

A major hotel chain was redesigning its frequent guest program. They wanted to understand the value of hotel points and frequent flyer miles. They were also considering offering some free snacks or a free in-room movie. They wanted to understand which of these services customers would prefer, and if the customers would pay more for the amenities. For the conjoint analysis, the team identified two levels for each of five factors:

> Room rate – $80 vs. $100
> Hotel points – 0 points vs. 500 points
> Frequent flyer miles – 0 miles vs. 500 miles
> Free in-room movie – No vs. yes
> Free snacks in room – No vs. yes

They then defined eight different packages with different combinations of these factors and asked customers to compare the packages in sets of two (Package #1 vs. Package #5, for example). The results of these comparisons are shown in Figure 10.9 (next page). What's most impor-

---

Conjoint analysis and design of experiments

Conjoint Analysis is an outgrowth of a branch of applied statistics called design of experiments (DOE). If you haven't encountered DOE before, you're missing out! It is one of the most versatile and powerful tools for data-based decision making.

DOE encompasses a range of experimental techniques used to study multiple factors *at the same time*. That last phrase is especially important: being able to *simultaneously* study a number factors means:

1) We get a lot more information from each experiment

2) We can look for interactions and dependencies between factors

It's the interactions and dependencies that lie at the heart of conjoint analysis because we want to understand how customer reactions to our products or services *depends on* or *affects* the prices they are willing to pay. We've discussed DOE briefly in our previous books (*Lean Six Sigma* and *Lean Six Sigma for Service*), and there are a lot of other resources on the topic. We highly recommend that you look into it.

tant as far as making decisions is the final column, which shows the overall importance rating for each package.

Figure 10.9: Customer Preferences for Hotel Services

Hotel Frequent Guest Program	Package 1	Package 2	Package 3	Package 4	Package 5	Package 6	Package 7	Package 8	Sum of normalized ratings	Relative Score
Package 1	1.00	5.00	0.33	5.00	3.00	5.00	1.00	1.00	1.29	16.2%
Package 2	0.20	1.00	0.20	0.33	0.20	0.33	0.20	0.20	0.22	2.7%
Package 3	3.00	5.00	1.00	5.00	3.00	5.00	3.00	3.00	2.27	26.4%
Package 4	0.20	3.00	0.20	1.00	0.33	0.33	0.20	0.20	0.32	4.0%
Package 5	0.33	5.00	0.33	3.00	1.00	5.00	0.33	5.00	1.13	14.1%
Package 6	0.20	3.00	0.20	3.00	0.20	1.00	0.20	0.20	0.40	5.0%
Package 7	1.00	5.00	0.33	5.00	3.00	5.00	3.00	3.00	1.44	18.0%
Package 8	1.00	5.00	0.33	5.00	0.20	5.00	1.00	1.00	0.93	11.6%

By linking these ratings to what was in each package, the team reached both obvious and non-obvious conclusions:

1) Not surprisingly, price was most important

2) Customers were also interested in hotel points and free snacks, but frequent flyer miles and free in-room movies were not a factor in their decisions

3) Customers would prefer getting a lower room rate of $80 with both of the perks they cared about

4) An option of paying an $85 rate and getting hotel points was preferred to the lower price and no options

Case #2: Crane design

A manufacturer of mobile hydraulic cranes identified a strategic threat in the rough-terrain market. A significant competitor had targeted the 0- to 50-ton segment, growing market share at the manufacturer's expense.

	Mkt Share (2 yrs prior)	Current Mkt Share
Competitor	18.6%	30.7%
Our Company	60.1%	44.2%

Margins were eroding due to the competitor's aggressive pricing and a market shift to lower-margin products. A global survey was launched to understand the Voice of the Customer. The survey included conjoint analysis to identify key marketing requirements for the new crane and statistically establish customer preference data.

As shown in Figure 10.10, the most important feature was, surprisingly, boom length, not price. The medium boom length was almost as desirable as the longest, but the third choice would not have been marketable. Customers would pay significantly more for the stronger load chart.

Figure 10.10: Conjoint Analysis of Cranes

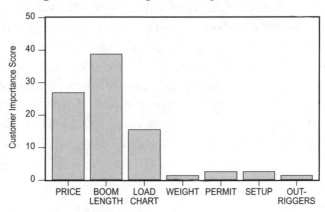

Though the company expected price to be the most important purchasing factor, it turned out that boom length was the priority for customers.

Conclusion: Considering complexity when developing customer-focused strategies

As P&G, Unilever, and many others have found, conquering complexity both reduces costs and spurs growth: the redeployment of resources to other parts of the value chain improves profitability and focus. But a key to unlocking this growth is knowing what your customers want, and *how much* of it they want, and creating a flexible process to deliver it *when* they want it at *lowest* cost. This analysis not only accelerates growth, but also prevents new products or services from coming to market with non-value-add features that impose a cost on your company. You can offset or minimize the costs associated with providing differentiated offerings to desirable market segments if your strategies include:

- Strong segmentation by target markets and customers

- Variety to meet the needs of the target markets

- Focus on the value creators

We need a clear understanding of who our profitable customers are and the variety and breadth of offerings required to capture and retain this target market. Clarity in this helps us avoid proliferation that does not add value and which may clutter the branding. Proliferation usually clusters around the segments of high value, the premium categories where market share *does* equal value; but as we've discussed, value can erode over time as customer expectations change. Consider the cosmetics industry: Japan's Shiseido, the world's fourth-largest cosmetic company, updates its offerings as frequently as every month.[8] Says president Akira Gemma: "We see our customers as our own competitors. We need to move ahead not because other brands are doing so but because our customers' needs are changing."

Endnotes

1 See a brief bio for Kimberly Watson-Hemphill on p. 246, note 1.

2 Dell and Magretta, "The Power of Virtual Integration" (see chap. 3, n. 1).

3 B. Joseph Pine II, Bart Victor and Andrew C. Boynton, "Making Mass Customization Work," in *Markets of One: Creating Customer-Unique Value through Mass Customization*, ed. James H. Gilmore and B. Joseph Pine II (Boston: Harvard Business School Press, 2000).

4 Mass Market Retailer, April 16, 2002, citing an Information Resources Inc. study, quoted in "Do Consumers Have Too Many Choices," *Food Distributor Magazine*, July 2001.

5 Michael McGrath, *Product Strategy for High Technology Companies: Accelerating Your Business to Web Speed* (New York: McGraw-Hill, 2000).

6 Raju Nariseti, "How IBM Turned Around its Ailing PC Division," *The Wall Street Journal*, March 12, 1998.

7 We would like to thank Bruno Ternon for his valuable input on this topic. Mr. Ternon is the Director for the European Office of George Group Consulting. His experience includes more than 18 years of experience in new product development for a number of different industries ranging from consumer goods, to high technology products for the defense industry, to the heavy construction industry. During this period, he personally led numerous projects from a white paper concept to full production. He is an expert in Product Cost Reduction and Complexity Reduction.

8 Kathleen M. Eisenstadt and Shona L. Brown, "Time Pacing: Competing in Markets that Won't Stand Still," *Harvard Business Review*, March 1, 1998.

CHAPTER 11

Avoiding the Big Costs

Using Complexity Principles to Simplify Product Designs

With Kimberly Watson-Hemphill[1]

On Planet Detroit… automakers used to pride themselves on reinventing the wheel with every model. In 1999, when former Chrysler CEO Bob Eaton introduced the Jeep Grand Cherokee, he proudly held up a bag that he said contained all of the carryover parts. His point was that this Jeep was practically a whole new animal.

—Fortune, February 2004, "Detroit Buffs Up"

In Chapter 1, we introduced the case of IPM, a manufacturer of Uninterruptible Power Supplies, devices used primarily to protect mainframe computers. The company started out with just one product (at one power rating), but kept adding products in answer to the "complexity that customers want."

The challenges for IPM didn't stop with having to deliver a wide range of product offerings. Though the company was reasonably good at forecasting total sales, management found it impossible to predict demand for *specific* ratings—and since the product at each rating had a unique design, this made it impossible to forecast component demand. The CEO, coauthor Mike George, became so vexed with this problem that he called a dozen customers and asked them why they had not purchased what they had forecast the month before. Their answers included responses like "we miscalculated our loads" and "we thought we had 208 volt service, but in fact we have 480 volt service, so we needed a different product," or "we needed special relays… alarms… instrumentation" and on and on.

In short, IPM was in a position where it could not cut back on the breadth of its offerings, yet the expense of supporting separate designs and dealing with wild fluctuations in demand was killing the company. What they had to do was find a way to simplify the designs and the processes for delivering those designs without sacrificing the broad offering that was important to their customers. (Later in this chapter we'll provide details on *how* they did this.)

Many businesses find themselves in similar situations. They don't want to cut out offerings because they could lose customers and markets. But supporting low Process Cycle Efficiencies and higher internal costs are causing a slow death.

As most product people know, **the design determines 70% to 80% of the manufacturing and use costs**. (And a substantial proportion of that, typically 20%, is driven by complexity unless you drive it down!) To have any hope of significant changes in the Economic Profit of products, we therefore have to work up front, on the design. The guiding principles for solving this complexity challenge are:

1) An emphasis on **commonality**, which means looking for similar or related functionalities currently provided by *different* parts, processes, components, etc., and building a common way to provide that functionality. (If you remember the Complexity Equation, this step effectively reduces the number of different parts, N, and hence will drive you up the PCE curve.)

2) **Exploiting reuse/recycling**, never design a different part or process when there is an existing one that, with suitable modification, provides the needed functionality. This includes recycling everything from designs to used parts or products. Think of it this way: customers are willing to pay more for new products that bring a true innovation. If a component of your design does not contribute to the new innovation, its cost should be minimized. Reuse is a key method to do this.

3) **Design with the life cycle in mind,** which includes everything from design for manufacture and assembly to design simplicity to leverage Lean principles. Think about how all the elements of a product or service will play out through the entire process from gathering the Voice of the Customer all the way through concept, planning, design, manufacture and assembly, use, maintenance, and reuse or disposal.

In this chapter, we'll look at each of these concepts in more depth and explore their relationship to simplifying product innovation, design, and delivery. (Service design is discussed explicitly in the next chapter, but there are several principles here that apply to all areas.)

> **Before you start "common-izing"...**
>
> The givens in this chapter are that (A) you've done a business-level value analysis to make sure that the investment you're about to make in time and energy is being spent on strategically important product lines (per Chapter 10's advice), and that (B) you've done a value-add analysis to make sure you're trying to preserve things that your customers want and are willing to pay for. You shouldn't be investing a single dollar in simplifying a product line that's destroying value in your organization or that represents something your customers don't want!

Simplicity Principle #1: Emphasize commonality

The principle of commonality appears in many guises when designing products. Two of the most powerful are:

A) **Modularity,** the grouping of like functional elements into logical and separate subassemblies that share common elements

B) **Platforms,** foundational designs (likely composed of standard modules) that serve as the basis for multiple end products

A. Commonality Through Modularization

As you probably guessed from its name, modularization means dividing up a design into units or modules that provide a specific functionality. In a bike, for example, you would have the brake module, the gear module, the frame module, etc. The "module" can be anything from a single part to an assembly of many parts. What's key is that a module provides its functionality on its own, independent of the rest of the product.

Since this isn't a book on design or engineering, we don't have the space to get into the details of how to implement modularity principles (we'll save that for another day), but here's a quick overview of the basic approach we use.

In practice, it's not always easy to make modularity decisions, which require careful consideration of what parts or components can or should be grouped into modules, which should be left as standalone components, what design should be used for the module itself, and so on. Generally, companies have found it works best to…

1) Define specific cost-reduction goals for the complexity reduction effort

2) Work first on products that are considered technically stable and where you have existing products (either yours or a competitor's) to use as examples

3) Create cross-functional teams of designers, engineers, production staff, etc.

4) Have the team identify the factors that will drive modularity decisions (*see* Table 11.A for some examples)

5) Have the team construct a matrix of current component and modular relationships, and evaluate which of them could serve as the basis for the standard module or evaluate new design options for their modularity

Table 11.A: Factors That Drive Commonality Decisions

Commonality among products	Technological stability
Functional independence	Functional upgradability
Cost	Long design life
Ease of manufacturing	Design adaptability
Ease of maintenance	Ease of quality assurance

The decision to combine specific elements of a design is usually made by following a decision tree like that shown in Figure 11.1.

Figure 11.1: Decision Tree for Modularity

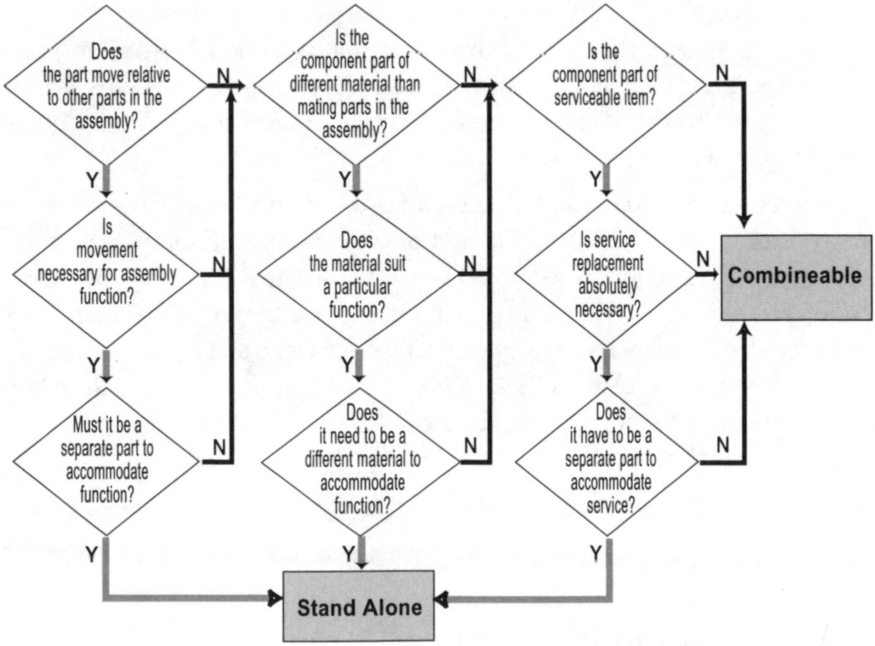

A decision tree like this is used to help teams decide what elements or components of design can be combined and which need to be kept separate.

Modularization at Shiseido

At the end of Chapter 10, we discussed Japanese cosmetics giant Shiseido which, in response to customer demand, refreshes its product line on a monthly basis. How can it do that without seeing the costs of complexity skyrocket? The answer lies in its approach to modularization. Managers separate the development of the products themselves from the packaging. They can therefore "refresh" the product line through changes in the packaging and formatting (color, shape, size, etc). They typically change the packaging far more frequently than the products themselves.

Commonality vs. standardization

Commonality and standardization are both techniques that build off "sameness," but they play very different roles in an organization.

Commonality is a product design and delivery technique that confers *flexibility* or variety. Through commonality, you will end up producing different products that internally share a lot in their materials, designs, components, etc. This can be an incredibly powerful way to expand the offering without breaking the bank.

Standardization is quite the opposite. It fights against flexibility or variety by enforcing the use of a specific part or procedure. Standardization is a variation-reduction technique, used when variability is *harmful*. For example, if you know that steps 1 to 15 of some procedure must be followed in order to reduce the possibility of errors or defects, then you need to standardize on that sequence. Or if you know that material from Supplier C is far superior to those from Supplier D, then you standardize on purchasing from Supplier C.

To reliably produce high-quality, differentiated offerings, you'll need both techniques.

B. Commonality Through Platforms

In its simplest sense, a platform is any unit (module, group of modules, etc.) that serves as a base for multiple end products. The core of the platform consists of **standard components and subsystems** (and the tasks used to handle those components) that are *reusable* in many offerings.

Companies that apply platform thinking generally set a target of having all or some subset of their end products sharing 90% of their components, either in the form of separate parts or standard modules.

Combining standard modules into a few basic platforms will allow you to offer many flavors of your offering and focus design attention on delivering real incremental differentiation on top of the standard platform. Developing platform-based processes and the intellectual capital required to execute those processes will allow you to add these differentiated flavors *quickly* in response to changing customer needs.

Using platform thinking in services

Building foundational elements that can easily be adapted for different end purposes is not an approach restricted to physical product components. You can greatly increase your leverage of resources by applying platform thinking to the processes used to produce and deliver products. This may become obvious once you've developed modules or a platform for the product itself—once IPM, for example, collapsed seven different designs into one, then it could develop a common process for all end products. But even if you don't end up with a single design or single product platform, there still may be portions of your processes that can be shared between multiple offerings. The same approach can be applied to the intellectual capital invested in your products, such as marketing activities, process development/documentation, design knowledge, and so on.

Pushing for unique value-add

At a minimum, applying commonality techniques should be driven by the question, "Do the observed differences in these products or tasks add value?" Remember, "add value" means that the task or component has a unique form, feature, or function for which *the customer* would be willing to pay. If two separate tasks or components do the same thing, we can replace one of them.

You don't have to stop at simply weeding out superfluous components or design elements. Many companies use a drive for commonality to push for innovation: "Can we design a *new* task or component that will incorporate the unique value-add and hence *replace* several offerings?" To go this extra step, you need to understand the costs and benefits to be achieved, because it may require a significant investment of resources.

Case Study: IPM's applications of platform thinking

When IPM first started wrestling with their internal complexity problems, they called together a team of design engineers and a consultant who studied all products in the 10 kw to 80 kw range. They noticed that in the lower half of that range (from 10 kw to 40 kw), many of the differences between ratings were entirely transparent to the customer and had minor cost differences when combined volumes were considered. Here are two quick examples:

- A component called "bus bars" (which conduct electricity) was slightly smaller on 10 kw than on 40 kw products.

- "Heat sinks" used single-side cooling on 10 kw and double-side cooling at 40 kw

These kind of minor differences in design were common, reflecting the unplanned evolution of a historical process. Once the concept of commonization was accepted, designers realized they could condense these into one mechanical design for the higher power rating and still use it for the lower ratings for a negligible increase in material cost. These and other changes—including the addition of a $100 component (a high-power semiconductor switch) to the $12,000 units—means that *every* unit at every power rating could be wired and assembled in identical fashion.

In the new design, some components were, in fact, unused at full power. But the gains made by simplifying the design and manufacture process far offset these investments.

- Because all the products were now mechanically identical, IPM could simplify the manufacturing process. Commonization eliminated a lot of non-value-add work (such as inspection and rework) and the associated cost and delays.

- Work instructions became much simpler, and photographic work instructions meant virtually anybody could do anybody else's job (tribal knowledge was replaced with transferable skills).

- The standardized design meant IPM could place blanket orders for hundreds of cabinets used to house the power supplies. This cut the cost by more than 50%. Not having to develop its own cabinets meant IPM *avoided* the expense of hiring, training, and supporting jobs like metal working, welding, painting, and so on. Cabinet building was simply not a "core competence" process that would make the company great (in Jim Collins' context) and hence was outsourced.

Because fewer of its resources were tied up in design and product, IPM could put more efforts on the high-value-add areas of the business such as new innovation and marketing. The cumulative effects of these changes is reflected in Figure 11.2 (next page).

Quantifying the impact

In the Complexity Equation (*see* p. 32), problems like IPM's would show up in a large "N"—the number of product offerings. Trying to work on other drivers of complexity, such as quality or setup time (which also show up in the Complexity Equation) *before* reducing N would have been a waste of resources.

Ultimately, IPM cut the N down by at least 6 and cut setup time by at least 2 (in the machine shop). Although at that time nobody in America (to our knowledge) was measuring PCE, we can now use the Complexity Equation to verify that IPM's PCE went up 12 fold!

$$\frac{PCE_{AFTER}}{PCE_{BEFORE}} = \frac{\dfrac{2V(1 - X - PD)}{(N_{after})(2A+1)(S_{after})}}{\dfrac{2V(1 - X - PD)}{(N)(2A+1)(S)}} = \frac{(N)(2A+1)(S)}{\left(\dfrac{N}{6}\right)(2A+1)\left(\dfrac{S}{2}\right)} = \frac{1}{\dfrac{1}{12}} = 12$$

Figure 11.2: IPM Gains from Commonization

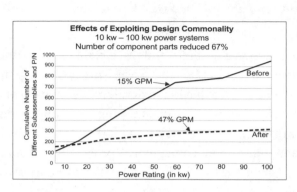

By simplifying the designs of its products without reducing the number or types of products offered, IPM was able to greatly reduce costs and more than double Gross Profit Margin.

Benefits of Commonality

With few exceptions, most products and services today have been developed with little thought given to commonality of any sort. That means many opportunities fall into the "low-hanging fruit" categories. The benefits accrued from commonality include:

- Improved efficiency through elimination of non-value-add cost

- Reduced lead time (improved time-to-market and order-to-delivery)

- Reduced working capital requirements

- Fewer chances for errors or mistakes ("defect reduction")

- Improved flexibility throughout operations

- Better use of resources

… All resulting in higher ROIC and shareholder value.

In addition, once a "chunk" of an offering is common-ized, it can be outsourced to someone who has a lower cost base than you do. This frees you to apply scarce intellectual capital to high ROIC opportunities. So long as you can find a supplier who will deliver quality product at prices that barely would earn your cost of capital, it is rational to outsource.

Commonality allows for innovation and customization

Another benefit of commonality is that it allows manufacturers to devote more resources to the variable elements that customers are willing to pay for, i.e., to customize products. Remember that the purpose of commonality thinking is *not* to end up with a lot of products that are exactly alike, but rather to reduce the costs of providing end-product variety to customers.

For example, platform design created by IPM for its power suppliers left a blank area in the standard cabinet design that could be used for custom meters and relays—provided at extra cost to those customers willing to pay. (Those who weren't willing to pay were convinced that the standard unit would meet their needs.)

Wide use of modularity and platforms allows for what manufacturers call **mass customization** (which is not as much of an oxymoron as it may sound)—adding differentiating features, options, and modules onto a standard platform in "customized" configurations, typically as late in the manufacturing process as possible and in practice after the basic unit is finished. This helps an organization keep its working capital requirement low, while still providing variety to its customers.

The problem with the concept of adding flavor at the end (mass customization) is that late customization inherently limits the amount of variety or flavors you can add. The reason that the customization is traditionally done at the end is that it prevents the need for multiple switching of upstream tasks (captured as setup time in the Complexity Equation). Toyota explicitly *rejects* any such notion, and deliberately introduces the "flavors" as far upstream as possible. They can do this *without* incurring any loss of PCE because they are masters of techniques such as the Four Step Rapid Setup method (*see* p. 254 in Chapter 12) and demand commonization / standardization across engineering.

Simplicity Principle #2: Exploit design reuse/recycling

The aspect of design reuse/recycling most pertinent to a discussion of complexity relates to establishing a standard policy that product designers never use a new or different design when one exists that already meets or nearly meets the functional requirements. For example, imagine that you work for a bike manufacturer and were asked to design a new children's mountain bike. Rather than starting from scratch, you look through the brake assemblies (modules) your company already produces and find one that provides the required functionality. By using an existing module, you've automatically...

- Saved design time, which will get the product to the market quicker.

- Saved purchasing time. There is no need to find and qualify new suppliers, no need to train staff on new procedures or introduce new purchasing procedures—the purchasing staff will just have to order more of what they're already ordering.

- Saved material purchasing and handling costs. There is no need to find new space and systems for receiving, storing, and handling new components.

- Reduced variability in your inventory requirements by driving more volume into fewer part numbers.

- Saved computing time/space. There is no need to enter new component codes into a purchasing database.

- Reduced chances for mistakes and errors that can occur whenever something new is added to a process or procedure.

Do that for all or most of the design components of the new bike, and you can start tallying up all the complexity you *haven't* generated in your company. However, the probability that an existing component or service exactly matches your new need is smaller than the probability that something "close" exists. This then triggers an effort to design a new component, system or service that is "backward compatible" with all existing offerings but also meets the need of the new product. This generic approach may suggest some changes to the new product to accommodate the backward-compatible offering.

Simplicity Principle #3: Design with the life cycle in mind

A very broad discipline in the product world is life cycle planning, or thinking about how the product will be designed, manufactured, delivered, used, repaired, etc. The primary elements of life cycle planning that relate to complexity are clustered under a subdiscipline called Design for Manufacture and Assembly (DFMA).

One purpose of DFMA is to design products and processes, whether existing or new, that provide an overall lowest-cost structure to the business. This encompasses:

- **Design for assembly**, which lowers the complexity of products through parts reduction—that is, elimination or consolidation—and enables manufacturers to quantify assembly times and costs. Design teams consider each part and decide if it must be separate from others in the assembly, leading to systematic simplification of design.

- **Design for manufacture**, which provides cost estimates for the manufacture of individual parts. This allows design teams to make trade-off decisions between process and assembly costs and optimized part designs. DFM reviews material selections and makes corrections in tooling approaches.

- **Design for service**, which supplies a method of designing products for efficient maintenance and repair. It establishes a disassembly sequence to service an item, identifies items that must be discarded or replaced for specific service tasks, assesses the degree of difficulty when servicing specific items, and generates a reassembly sequence and time estimate.

- **Design for environment**, which helps to quantify a design in terms of cost and environmental impact, ensuring that products can be disposed of responsibly at the end of their use. It provides assessments of financial returns and environmental impact.

Benefits of Life Cycle Planning and Execution

In simplifying designs and production, DFMA eliminates much of the cost associated with high levels of internal complexity. The benefits include:

- Improved time-to-market, with less time spent reinventing things that already exist, less paperwork/administration required for the development process, etc.

- Minimized opportunities for a defective part or an assembly error

- Decreased cost
  - Reduced inventories and work-in-process
  - Reduced supplier costs and, subsequently, raw material costs from suppliers
  - Reduced maintenance costs and overhead associated with design and bill-of-material revisions

- Greater process flexibility and capability
  - Improved chance to automate the process

- Better use of capital resources

Example: Simplifying brake design in bikes

To help you see how all the commonality and design simplicity concepts come together, here's a simulation developed from some real-life experience. As part of an overall complexity reduction process, the strategic goal of the company is to eliminate non-value-added costs by cutting the number of different components in half (reducing "N" in the Complexity

Equation) but retaining the complete product line from the customer's perspective. A team is assigned to evaluate several bicycle designs and decides to focus first on the brake assemblies to see if this effort would meet the goal of a 50% reduction in complexity. Their first step is to determine just how many different brake designs currently are used and in what product models. The result is shown in Figure 11.3.

Figure 11.3: Module Use Matrix

Brake Module	High-End Mountain Bike	High-End Road Bike	High-End BMX	Intermediate BMX	Intermediate Road Bike	Retro Road Bike	Chopper Series	Weighted Cross-Platform Importance
Model Weight	8	6	8	10	5	4	7	
Talon	8		8					16
Falcon		6						6
Easy Rider					5	4	7	17
Thrasher				10				10

Model Weight factored to include current margins and market growth factor.

This matrix shows seven bike models that each use one of four different brake modules. The Talon brake assembly, for example, is used in both the high-end mountain bike and the high-end BMX bike. The numbers in the matrix come from the "model weight," which represents each model's strategic importance to the company (higher numbers are better).

A few insights jump out right away:

- The Falcon assembly is used in only one product that is of moderate importance to the company (hence its score of "6"). The company should investigate whether one of the other assemblies would work and eliminate the Falcon assembly altogether.

- Both the Talon and Easy Rider have high scores because they are used in multiple products and/or strategically important product lines. They seem like the best options to select as potential standard modules.

- The Thrasher assembly is only used in one product line, but it is the company's most strategically important product. Whether the company keeps that assembly will depend on whether one of the other assemblies would work as well, or if there is a unique functionality or design that makes the Thrasher economically profitable.

The team next created a Pugh Matrix, which is a specialized table where one option is chosen as a baseline, and then other options are rated as the same, better, or worse compared to that baseline on each of the evaluation criteria. It doesn't really matter which option is selected as the baseline, but typically people use their biggest seller, most commonly used option, etc. This team selected their criteria—which included a mix of factors related to complexity and some related to manufacturability—and created the table in Figure 11.4.

Figure 11.4: Pugh Matrix Comparing Brake Assembly Options

Brake Module	Talon	Falcon	Easy Rider	Thrasher	Importance Rating	
Functionality of design to primary+basic design intent	++	+	B	++	10	B = Baseline (all other ratings are in comparison to the baseline)
Stability of design over its life cycle + length of life cycle	−	S	B	−	4	S = Same as baseline
Ability and ease of technology upgradability	+	S	B	+	6	+ or ++ = Better or much better than baseline
Adaptability of the design for other cross-platform uses and interfaces	−	S	B	−	6	
Total life cycle costs	S	S	B	S	10	− or − − = Worse or much worse than baseline
Cross-platform applicability	S	− −	B	−	7	
Multiple functionality	S	S	B	S	5	
Cross-platform manufacturability	−	S	B	−	8	
Fixed cost structure	−	−	B	−	8	
Maintainability	+	S	B	+	7	

A Pugh Matrix is used to analyze the design components of a product or service. The various required design and performance functions are listed down the side, then compared against existing design options.

The team reviewed each row of the Pugh Matrix for conclusions. For example, the higher-end modules provide better stopping power and more control and are easier to upgrade, but are more prone to changes.

The team then brainstormed the positives and negatives of each design to see if and how the negatives could be eliminated and the positives enhanced into a cross-platform module. For example, a major difference between the two concepts was the use of rim brakes in the Easy Rider design and the use of a disc brake system in the Talon design. The disc brake system is superior, but costs are higher. One cost issue associated with the disc brake system is the disc itself. Could the disc somehow be eliminated? Could the rim itself serve as a disc? The team decided to investigate the use of the rim in the same concept as a disc brake.

This kind of analysis continued with other components of the assembly until the team made its decisions. Ultimately, they reduced the cables and linings models from three models to one, reduced cantilever models from six to two, and so on. This equates to a 67% reduction in complexity which exceeds the goal: hence this is a worthwhile project to be considered.

How management can drive product simplicity

The challenges associated with developing simple products and systems more often stem from business norms than from a lack of engineering capability. The problem isn't that engineers *can't* design with modules, increase reuse, etc., but rather that existing processes and guidelines don't encourage that practice (at best) or actively work against it by providing incentives for producing new and entirely different designs.

The practices discussed in this chapter will not become common (so to speak) until and unless management invokes new design standards that encourage use of existing components/assemblies or design of new components/assemblies that have a good potential for reuse in future generations of products. This includes...

- Changing the product development mindset from placing importance on "design" to placing importance on customer-valued innovation

- Establishing ROIC and PCE% as primary metrics (baselining current PCE% and non-value-add cost; defining a goal for PCE and non-value-add cost reduction)

- Developing conventions and standards for designers/engineers including a Complexity Matrix methodology appropriate for each process

- Establishing a library of accepted designs, and a process for approving additions with interaction to all platform teams

- Developing specific design guidelines for products that go through different types of production processes (welding, casting, forging, extruding, forming, etc.)

Improving Design-to-Market Cycle Time

Simplifying the design and delivery of everything you keep will have a profound effect on design cycle time. It's a relationship we can quantify and manage using Little's Law, the equation introduced back in Chapter 2 that showed the relationship between the amount of Work-in-Process, completion rate, and lead times. Here's the equation adapted for product development:

$$\text{Product Development Lead Time} = \frac{\text{Number of Active Projects}}{\text{Average Completion Rate}}$$

This simple equation may not seem all that earth-shattering unless you are a student of Lean. But what it tells us—and what experience confirms time after time—is that the **number one driver of product development cycle time is the number of projects "in process."** There is no quicker way to shorten product developing cycle time than to prioritize the current initiatives, focus on the important ones, and kill off the lower-priority activities.

This calculation gives us the ability to *control* product development time by making decisions about how many development tasks to launch at any given time. With a given engineering staff, an average completion rate can be estimated; and with a desired lead time, the maximum number of active projects can be estimated.

Managing project workload (number of projects that were active at any given time) was effectively responsible for Sun Microsystems early lead over Apollo. Sun used UNIX, and integrated and reused packages developed by others. Apollo took an entirely proprietary path, resulting in high cost and longer time-to-market.[2] As we all know, shorter lead times to market allows a company to be much more responsive to shifting customer needs—and complexity reduction applied to product design and manufacture is exactly the kind of tactic that can confer that competitive advantage. (Sun's later difficulties versus Microsoft are related to matters of strategy and information velocity, discussed in Chapter 3.)

Replace the word "projects" with the word "tasks" in the above version of Little's Law, and you can see the impact that less complexity will have on your staff:

- It will take fewer tasks for engineers to design a product because, for example, they'll be using existing modules.

- Using components that already work, or building off of "near hits" for which there is manufacturing process, will reduce both the risk inherent in anything new as well as the time it takes. The engineers can always talk to the people who designed the part the first time to gain insights the easy way.

Thus tasks that used to take days or weeks can now be completed in minutes or don't need to be completed at all (speeding up the completion rate). Number of tasks goes down, completion rate goes up... and you have a smaller number on the left side of this equation—product development lead time will drop.

Conclusion: Start with the end in mind

With 70% to 80% of the cost of any manufactured product being defined at the design phase—including material, labor, and overhead, which all contain substantial amounts of non-value-add cost—the application of complexity reduction at the design phase should be mandatory for every company. Thus the more complex the offering, the more complex the process... and the more control you have over both, the greater the impact. Either you reduce the cost of complexity, or the cost of complexity will reduce your shareholder value!

Where to start? "If you have no destination, any road will get you there." The strategic vision of a company in terms of shareholder value should set a clear goal for innovation and for the application of complexity reduction techniques to product design to simplify the task of delivering innovation to your customers.

Endnotes

1 Kimberly Watson-Hemphill is a Master Black Belt with George Group Consulting and lead author of their Design for Lean Six Sigma curriculum. She has trained and coached hundreds of Black Belts and Master Black Belts throughout North America and Europe. She has a wide background in all areas of Lean Six Sigma, new product development, and project management, and has worked with Fortune 500 companies in both service and manufacturing industries. She is a certified Project Management Professional.

2 Carliss Y. Baldwin and Kim B. Clark, "Managing in an Age of Modularity," in *Markets of One: Creating Customer-Unique Value through Mass Customization*, ed. James H. Gilmore and B. Joseph Pine II (Boston: Harvard Business School Press, 2000).

CHAPTER 12

Achieving Service
and Process Simplicity

Optimizing work flow with Lean,
Six Sigma, and complexity tools

Imagine that you're a buyer at Lockheed Martin's MAC-MAR procurement operations back in the 1990s.[1] The company is completing the first in a series of mergers, and is still trying to work its way through all the legacy issues.

Your job is to provide purchasing support for up to 14 different sites, which means tracking 8 different sets of requirements, 14 different product codes for the *same* commodity item, compiling information on 14 sets of suppliers, linking to 14 entirely different purchasing processes...

But wait! Maybe help is on the horizon. The company is working to set up a paperless purchasing system that can also establish database links between the purchase requests directly to prequalified suppliers, eliminating the need for a Buyer. Only it turns out that system doesn't work so well... 3 out of 4 requests that make it into the system are kicked out because of errors.

If ever there was a poster child for service and process complexity, the MAC-MAR procurement center was it. A buyer's job was to provide the complexity customers want, which in this case meant letting the sites purchase anything they wanted. The result was internal chaos.

Today the picture is quite different. The *output* is still as diverse as ever—Lockheed Martin engineers can still design using anything they want—but the complexity of dealing with all the sites is nearly invisible to the buyers now. They spend far more of their time on value-add activities like understanding customer requirements, and far less on things like fixing errors in purchase requests. Better still, these and other changes have cut procurement costs by 50% in the past few years.

How the MAC-MAR procurement center got to this point illustrates a variety of tactics that can be used to reduce service and process complexity. We'll explore more of the Lockheed Martin story as well as examples from other organizations as we look at how to conquer complexity in service applications and processes.

One note before we begin: As it happens, the MAC-MAR stories pertain to services delivered to internal customers. But most of the approaches described below work equally well if you're dealing with external customers because, like MAC-MAR, you can make significant changes *without* interrupting services to the customer or asking the customer to change.

Reasons for focusing on services/process complexity

Throughout this chapter we assume that you're interested in simplifying services and processes for one of two reasons:

1) You've done the up-front analysis to determine that what you're trying to do is provide the complexity that the customers you want to keep *are willing to pay for* (that is, the end service or product is creating value for your organization).

2) The up-front analysis shows that an offering or supporting processes are destroying value and you want to see if you can cut down internal non-value-add costs as a way to make it more economically profitable.

Just as we discussed with products in the previous chapter, making these determinations up front will prevent you from wasting time trying to simplify a service or set of non-value-add processes that you'd be better off eliminating entirely.

Complexity and Waste

The starting point is understanding that from the customer's viewpoint, the majority of work in any process is non-value-add. As discussed in Chapter 2, typical Process Cycle Efficiencies for service processes are almost always less than 5 % and often less than 1%.

Making some gains is relatively easy because most service processes have never been value stream mapped. Doing so can highlight glaring problems and a lot of low-hanging fruit in terms of process improvement. Figure 12.1 shows a sample value stream map from Lockheed Martin. There are only four "value-add" steps in this entire process. The rest represent wasted time and opportunity. Most process maps would look something like this, if not worse.

Figure 12.1: Value Stream Map from Lockheed Martin

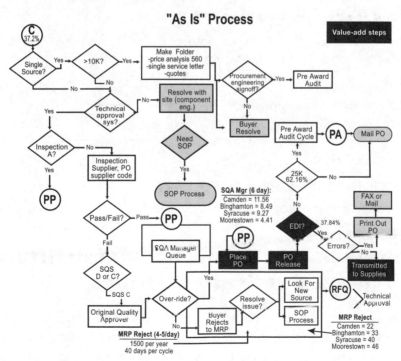

This value stream map looks messy because it depicts the reality of how the process operated at first. What's important is that there are only four value-add steps (in reverse out text)—in other words, 83% of the activities in the process were non-value-add (and hence ripe for improvement).

All of us have worked on processes that were as complex (if not more so) than this Lockheed Martin example. Organizations can end up with complex process flows for any number of reasons—poor quality, lack of process thinking, unclear instructions, or, as in this case, as a consequence of the complexity of customer population (compounded by mergers). The solution can encompass any or all of the following actions:

1) Exploit commonality to reduce duplicative efforts

2) Ensure standardization of tasks (including mistake-proofing)

3) Eliminate the delays and impact of task startup and switching (the "setup time" effect, *see* p. 255)

As you can see, these approaches combine principles of complexity reduction with basic Lean and quality improvement tools.

Revisiting the complexity equation

You may notice that each of the simplification approaches is linked to one or more of the factors in the Complexity Equation, repeated here:

Specifically...

$$PCE = \frac{2V(1 - X - PD)}{N(2A+1)S}$$

- Building common platforms and standardizing work reduces both "N," the number of different items flowing through the process, and "A," the number of activities

- Eliminating delays from task switching attacks "S," setup time

- Error-proofing will reduce the percentage of defective work (X%)

Approach #1: Exploit commonality to reduce duplicative efforts

If you read the previous chapter on product design, you know that *commonality* is a simple but powerful tool for minimizing internal complexity. The basic principle is that you look for duplicative or near-duplicative effort in your organization—places where similar services or outcomes are generated through different processes—and build a single, shared process for as much of the work as possible.

One technique that many companies use that is a close cousin of commonality is Best Practice sharing. At the informal end of the spectrum, Best Practice sharing can be as simple as having teams post the results of their improvement project or process documentation on a shared intranet or website. Commonality comes into play more at the formal end of the spectrum, where a group of people who do the same kind of work agree on a single best way to perform some task or process. That process is then documented, and everyone who performs the work is trained on the new Best Practice. Here's an example from Lockheed Martin:

After the mergers that led to the birth of Lockheed Martin as a single entity in the late 1990s, management recognized that there was a lot of commonality in the work being done at different sites and decided to consolidate some operations. One area targeted for consolidation in the Electronic Business Area sector was quality inspections (still considered "value-add" at that time!) being done at nine facilities. It wasn't just internal complexity that concerned them; maintaining nine separate systems for inspection imposed a lot of complexity on their suppliers, who had to track nine different specifications and Lockheed Martin points of contact for every part.

The staff behind the consolidation knew they couldn't just force a single method on the people from the nine facilities who were being brought together in the new Material Quality Center (MQC). So instead they asked these experienced experts to compare their different processes and define a single Best Practice for the inspection process. That effort launched a rapid evolution in inspection processes and systems, to the point where the MQC itself was disbanded just three years later and virtually all the non-value-add cost of inspection was eliminated and performed by suppliers!

To make this happen, the team first defined a single set of inspection standards that met all corporate and program compliance criteria. Inspection according to those standards was offered to the facilities at a base cost; anything above and beyond would cost extra (remember that "what customers are willing to pay for" phrase we've repeated often?). Guess what? Once they faced the possibility of having to justify a higher cost to their financial gurus, the facilities realized that maybe the base specifications *were* good enough after all! (There were a few exceptions—materials going to NASA operations, for instance, still received a high level of inspection.)

Second, having a standard process with defined criteria made it seamless to add new materials or parts without increasing the complexity of the process.

Third, all testing was centralized in one location. Because all inspections were conducted in one facility, the team had access to more data. What they soon confirmed was that most inspections were non-value-add—that is, the vast majority of material came in, was unpacked, inspected, accepted, repacked, and then shipped out to the facility without any changes being made. That data, coupled with a supplier quality initiative, meant that within three years, more than 75% of the material no longer needed inspection—it all went directly "dock to stock."

Finally, as the benefits of these changes accrued and as evidence mounted that inspection was almost all non-value-add, LM was able to close the MQC facility and shift its efforts to more up-front work with suppliers, using third-party contractors to help them with the *few* exceptions where government regulations or other compliance requirements meant inspection was still needed.

The link between commonality and eliminating variation

As we noted when discussing product design complexity in Chapter 11, we expect that many of our readers will have a background that includes exposure to quality improvement concepts such as driving the need to eliminate variation and standardize work (especially tasks related to critical-to-quality requirements). The outcome of a commonality effort in service processes is similar in that you end up with fewer variations on how work is performed, but the focus is usually broader. Commonality is usually pushed as part of an effort to look *across* offerings, processes, or even departments and reduce duplicative work in the business as a whole. Standardization and variation reduction efforts are more task- or step-oriented, aimed at making sure a process step happens in a particular way time after time.

Approach #2: Ensure standardization of tasks

Depending on your viewpoint, administrative or transactional staff have either enjoyed more creativity than their manufacturing counterparts who were forced to do work in a certain way, or they have paid the price of having too much variability in how work is performed. No matter which viewpoint you choose, what we're now coming to realize is that it's possible to have the best of both worlds. The gains made in cost and time that come from standardizing work frees people to spend more time being creative on value-add work. Just ask the Lockheed Martin buyers whether they prefer their work life *before* all the standardization and other changes—when it would take days to do work they can now do in minutes and they spent most of their time on non-value-added work like fixing errors.

There are many simple ways to build task standardization into a process, such as documenting the process flow, training, error-proofing, automating tasks, etc. None of these are particularly new or earth-shattering, but they *are* underused. Perhaps knowing their link to complexity reduction will provide additional incentives to use them.

Here's a quick example from Lockheed Martin's MAC-MAR center. Several years ago the purchasing process bogged down whenever the buyers had to find and secure suppliers for requested material. So Lockheed Martin put on a big push to increase the number of prequalified suppliers. With the suppliers' information already in the database, the vast majority of purchase orders were placed electronically, with no human intervention at all.

At least that was how it was supposed to work. Data showed that the process had a first pass yield of only 27% (only ~1 in 4 made it through without being kicked out for some reason). Complexity—the numbers of products, different source companies, etc.—played a big role in the 73% failure rate. (*See* Figure 12.2, next page) With a workload of about 10,000 purchase orders a year, this failure was costing MAC-MAR more than 4,600 person-hours a year, or about two full-time staff.

Figure 12.2: MAC-MAR Presource Process Yields

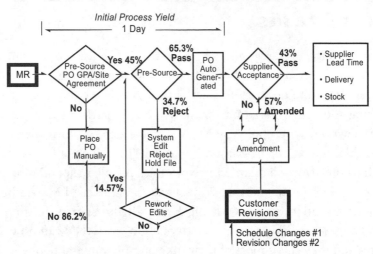

Despite a relatively fast turnaround time of 1 day, the yield from this Lockheed Martin process was very low.

The team attacked the situation with standard problem-solving approaches, defining the problem, using a Pareto analysis to identify the biggest contributors, addressing solutions at those causes, and so on. Resulting initiatives in four areas (technical approval, supplier certification, compliance certification, and scheduling) led to a drop in the reject rate from 76% to under 12% (*see* Figure 12.3); and certified financial results estimated that the combined savings and cost avoidance totaled more than $110K.

Figure 12.3: "After" Results from MAC-MAR Presource Projects

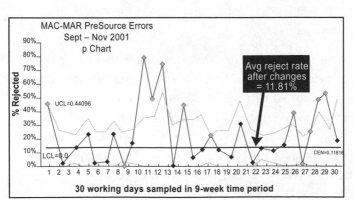

The reject rate stills shows some variation after changes were made, but even on its worse days comes nowhere near the pre-improvement level of 76%. It maintained an average of about 12% during this 9-week period.

Approach #3: Eliminate the delays and impact of task startup and task switching

Most people associate the term "setup time" with total loss of output, and don't consider *reduction* of output as setup time. But judging by business impact, any loss of productivity has the same effect as a complete interruption of work (*see* Figure 12.4). Such losses can occur because when people have to relearn tasks that are infrequently performed, change from one set of instructions to another set, and so on. These ramp-up times will result either in very low productivity levels or in having people collect up a "batch" of jobs before starting the value-add work (such as waiting until there is a stack of invoices before processing *any* invoices).

Figure 12.4: Productivity Loss During Changeover/Ramp-up

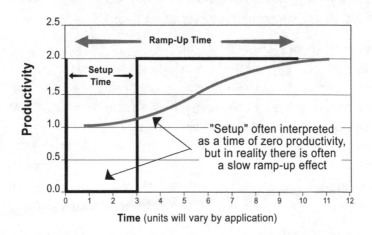

Time (units will vary by application)

Setup time refers to the break between one task (e.g., creating a purchase order for office supplies) to another task (e.g., taking inventory of on-hand supplies to determine if shortages exist). Most people think of setup time as only the period when a machine is actually down or a service process is inoperative. But in fact, there is usually a lingering negative effect on productivity.

Like complexity (N) and the number of activities (A) in a process, setup time appears in the denominator of the Complexity Equation—which means it has an inverse relationship to Process Cycle Efficiency. Setup goes up and PCE goes down. Setup drops, PCE rises. If setup time is reduced to near zero, PCE can approach 100% because that means work is moving directly from value-add activity to value-add activity. Zero setup time would also mean that each activity is infinitely flexible, and it can move from task to task with no drop in productivity.

Thus we have a strong imperative to reduce setup time to previously unprecedented levels, entirely unrelated to any goal of satisfying customer lead time demands.

By whatever name, setup time results in the delays and destruction of PCE, which as we know is linked directly to EP. When you create a value stream map of any process, be it manufacturing or service, you'll likely find comparatively few activities that you think have significant setup times. You will have to be very careful in your observations to even recognize a setup time for what it is: no buyer at Lockheed Martin ever said, "Gee, we are suffering from long setup time."

Our previous book, *Lean Six Sigma for Service*, discussed a setup problem at the Lockheed Martin purchasing operations at some length (*see*, for example, pp. 42 to 46). Here's a quick recap: The core issue was that buyers had to log into the various LM sites and link into that site's purchasing systems in order to process purchase orders; switching from one system to another—the setup time—often took 20 minutes or more. Remember, too, that these sites represented different companies that were joined in the mergers. So each had its own component codes, its own computer screens (different from all others, of course), etc.

As a result of this process complexity, buyers typically processed *all* the orders from one site (which took about 2 days) before moving to the next site. You can do the math yourself: 14 sites, 2 days per site—the lead time to get back to any site was 28 working days. The buyers used the Four Step Rapid Setup method (described next) to cut the setup time to zero and reduce purchase order lead time to less than a day.

The Four Step Rapid Setup Method

The most common approach to reducing setup time is known as the Four Step Rapid Setup Method, a technique that evolved in manufacturing settings but that has since been adapted to be applicable to service processes as well. Here's a quick overview of the method:

Step 1: Observation and classification of setup: Watch the process of changing from one task to another, and record the time and description of each step, be it physical movement or the flow of data or information. Then identify each action within the changeover as:

- **Internal setup**: any task switching where a person must stop producing output altogether or operate at reduced output. "Internal" means the work is an integral part of the process—like switching bits on manufacturing equipment, or logging off one computer system and logging into another.

- **External setup:** things that really could be done before the changeover is commenced. For Lockheed Martin, it meant having information like specifications, supplier qualification, etc. built into the software so the information was "waiting" for the buyer.

- **Potentially external setup**: Steps that currently interrupt or reduce the rate of the flow of work, but that are not part of the value-add stream. An example would include stopping work to go find a purchase request, or having to call a supplier to get lead time or pricing, or calling engineering to get the current drawing. If you examine these steps closely, you'll recognize that the person wouldn't necessarily have to stop working if the required information, tool, etc., were already on hand.

Step 2: Convert potentially external to external setup: Take all the potentially external setup and arrange to have it done so it does not interrupt or slow down the flow of value-add work. Lockheed Martin, for example, drove the number of preapproved suppliers up from 20% to 60%, which meant all the information relevant to the supplier—specifications, delivery dates, etc.—was sitting in the computer "waiting" for a purchase order.

Step 3: Streamlining internal setup: Some residual setup will remain even after you've done everything you can to move other setup off-line or in parallel. Here the methods of complexity reduction enter the process. In services, this translates to changes like delegating some preparatory work. For example, having a research specialist prepare information on a customer prior to proposal generation will greatly reduce the burden on high-caliber business development experts. Technology can be used to provide the staff person with all the information they need in a standard form, so there is no scrambling around at the last minute to compile what's needed to perform the process steps.

Step 4: Eliminate adjustment or "ramp-up": In a manufacturing context, ramp-up would occur, for example, after a die is changed. The operator would then try a piece, measure it, adjust the shut height, press out another piece, measure it, etc. In that example, the "adjustment period" is eliminated by measuring input parameters and determining precision presetting.[2] This same kind of adjustment occurs in all settings, particularly any time someone has not done a task in a long time. They'll likely either work slowly at first or make small errors—and won't reach full productivity for minutes or hours. Administrative or transactional adjustments are often prevented by application of simple technology, such as designing computer screens that won't proceed to the next step in the process until all the information is entered in the correct fields. For example, when you apply for a vehicle registration renewal in Texas, the screen will not let you proceed until you fill in all the blocks containing an asterisk.

If you've never seen the Four Step Rapid Setup method in action, you're probably wondering why we spend so much time on it. The answer harkens back to the simple way to calculate PCE that we introduced in Chapter 2:

$$\text{Process Cycle Efficiency} = \frac{\text{Value-add Time}}{\text{Total Lead Time}}$$

As you probably know by now, the top part of this equation—value-add time—is *very small* in most processes compared to the total lead time (<1% is common; 5% is considered good; 10% to 20% gets you to world class). So we're far more likely to have a big impact on PCE by attacking everything that goes into total time that is *not* value-add. And setup time—changeover time, task switching, whatever you want to call it—is one of the biggest contributors to non-value-add time (which is why it appears as a factor in the Complexity Equation). We've seen the Four Step method applied in almost every environment you can imagine from the factory to office, with amazing increases in process efficiency.

History of the Four Step Rapid Setup method

The Four Step Rapid Setup method has suffered from a lack of clear explanation perhaps more so than any other improvement tool. One of its first descriptions appeared in *SMED: A Revolution in Manufacturing*. In that book, the author, Shigeo Shingo (a renowned Japanese quality pioneer), describes in excruciating detail how he reduced the setup time of a 2700 ton press by a factor of 24 (from 4 hours to 10 minutes). Achieving a setup time just 1/24th of its original level equates to a remarkable 12% increase in PCE (per the Complexity Equation).

Within Shingo's book, buried behind the tepid title and manufacturing "toolsy" exposition, lay a method of immense importance to all business leaders. But with a title like *SMED* and rather uninspiring text, it's not surprising that the brilliant Four Step Rapid Setup method languished in manufacturing obscurity. With the renewed emphasis on improving PCE, this method is now gaining a deserved prominence in service applications.

Conclusion

The demand for ever-increasing proliferation of offerings requires that a firm not only apply the tools described in previous chapters but also use Lean and Six Sigma methodologies to drive PCE levels higher and thereby improve profits. The financial benefits from minimizing internal complexity (for instance, the release of fixed assets) are so great that application of these tools will often drive an organization to lead times (and corresponding PCE levels) that *surpass* goals based on customer needs.

Endnotes

1 We would like to thank Myles Burke, Chris Baeckstrom, James Isaac, George Sanders, Manny Zulueta, and Jim Thomas, all of Lockheed Martin, for their contributions and outstanding work.

2 For more details, see Michael L. George, *Lean Six Sigma*, pp. 211–214, or George, *Lean Six Sigma for Service*, pp. 292–298.

CHAPTER 13

Using Information Technology to Deliver Complexity at Lower Cost

Ask a CIO to name his or her main duties, and chances are "manage complexity" won't make the list. But that's what all CIOs do.... New technologies and continually changing business requirements make it increasingly difficult to control information systems. Complex I.S. processes and technologies increase costs and system-administration requirements, demand specialization among the IT staff, and often impede the quick deployment of new business solutions.

—Executive Report, InformationWeek[1]

Life has gotten too complex inside American. We employ more than 100,000 people... All told, they use hundreds of systems and dozens of technologies... We're focused on the hard work of simplification. We want to look and act like a single organization.

—Monte Ford, CIO of American Airlines[2]

With the emergence of a networked society, ecommerce, and the internet, the last decade has elevated the pressures on Chief Information Officers (CIOs) and Chief Technology Officers (CTOs) of global corporations. It has been both a transformative period of whole new business channels and opportunities, and a rapid-fire period of evolving standards that has resulted in a proliferation of hardware and software systems.

The proliferation race, however, managed in many cases to obscure two critical IT questions: (1) How does your information technology add value from the customer's perspective? (2) If you were to map the processes that IT automates, what would PCE be?

Consider FedEx, whose reputation is built on customer response (being on time and high levels of service) and technology (the ability to track packages, etc.). "Telephone calls to 800-GO-FEDEX that result in a tracking request cost us about $2.30, and we get about 100,000 of them each day," said Robert Carter, CIO of FedEx. "By contrast, on FedEx.com, we're averaging more than 2.4 million tracks a day, and each one of those transactions averages just under a nickel. We're saving about $25 million a month. And best of all, customers prefer doing business with us on the internet."[3]

Customers prefer business that way, and *demand* that business be done that way; indeed the decision to spend money on IT for customer interfaces and channels is the cost of entry for many business segments. "Customers have to be able to have it their way," said Laurie Tucker, a senior VP at FedEx.[4] About 70% of the 3 million packages that move through FedEx's network each day have been processed online.

Under the right circumstances, IT expenditures meet one or all of the following criteria:

- Improve the customer experience through the more efficient capture and dissemination of customer information and transformation into value-add

- Reduce setup time to near-zero, enabling lower-cost tailoring to customers' needs or enabling greater connection to the customer

- Improve the quality of a process by the elimination of human error

- Lead to quantum improvements in the processing cost per transaction through economies of scale

Understanding what it takes to meet these criteria is the subject of this chapter.

Using IT to Deliver Variety (Good Complexity) at Low Cost

IT was integral to Capital One's strategy of "the right product to the right customer at the right time for the right price." From the very beginning, the two founders, Richard Fairbank and Nigel Morris, concluded that credit cards were not banking in the traditional sense, but *information*. "At that point," they said, "we realized that the credit card industry might really be at the forefront of the whole technology revolution."

IT was integral to their strategy. Rather than outsource, Capital One kept it all in-house and built up their IT infrastructure slowly so that by the late 1990s the company had the largest Oracle database in the world, holding the equivalent of 40 single-spaced pages of information on every American. A key benefit, said George Overholser, senior VP of North Hill Ventures (the company's venture capital arm), was

> ...the ability to flex the systems. In other words, going from
> 20,000 customers to a national rollout within three months.
> It's just outrageous. In the early days, we acted as if
> Operations and IT were second class. Now, we view them
> organizationally as heroes because they have created an infra-
> structure that can flex extraordinarily well.[5]

... and that can serve customers better. In the time it takes for the first ring of the phone, the company's computers identify the caller and predict why they're calling (with a greater than 70% accuracy[6]) and what the caller might be willing to purchase. It then routes the call to a customer service associate with the best combination of skills most able to help the customer and make the sale.

Said Fairbank: "We collect lots and lots of information on what the responses to these offers are, and build statistical models to link these results to the data we had on these people. So now, when somebody calls Capital One—instantaneously—we make an actuarial calculation of the customer's lifetime Net Present Value and assess the customer's likely responses. Right on the screen, the customer service rep sees an instant recommendation, such as to negotiate the APR down to 12.9%. That's all instantaneous, totally customized."

The result is that Capital One can offer customized rates and responses, maximizing its own shareholder value without being consumed by huge complexity costs. Furthermore, its investment in IT has resulted in a sustainable advantage—the more tests and offers it makes, the more information it gathers, creating a huge private database of insight on customer behavior that is inaccessible to competitors.

The Cost of IT Complexity

Cost and complexity is our No. 1 problem. It's a hundred times what it was ten years ago.

—Tony Scott, technology officer for GM[7]

Almost all of the IT that we've done over the last 10 to 15 years is pretty neat, but is too expensive and too hard to use. We may have given all these enterprises Lamborghinis…

—Vinod Khosla, venture capitalist[8]

Unfortunately, in the pursuit of delivering the variety customers want, few companies have been as successful as Capital One. Instead many companies in the 1990s created an unwanted and seemingly intractable problem: a morass of internal complexity as multiple (often proprietary) systems were added, layer upon layer.

This is the main beef of the IT Complexity Reduction (ITCR) group, a working group of the Society for Information Management (an industry group comprised of CIOs and other technology professionals). ITCR includes IT executives from USAA, Duke Energy, Kraft Foods, and Prudential Insurance, among others. Its purpose is to reduce the level of complexity in IT systems and make it simpler to integrate systems from multiple vendors. Their data, depicted in Figure 13.1 (next page), shows that IT professionals felt burdened by complexity in multiple areas of their job.

Figure 13.1: IT Grows Complicated

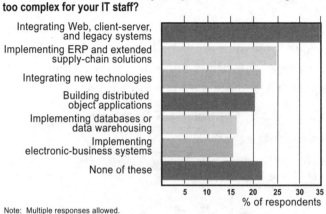

In which areas are Information System processes or technologies becoming too complex for your IT staff?

Integrating Web, client-server, and legacy systems
Implementing ERP and extended supply-chain solutions
Integrating new technologies
Building distributed object applications
Implementing databases or data warehousing
Implementing electronic-business systems
None of these

% of respondents

Note: Multiple responses allowed.
Data: *INFORMATIONWEEK* - RESEARCH SURVEY OF 150 IT MANAGERS

The top three issues identified in this survey all relate to the challenges of dealing with complexity in the IT infrastructure.

The systems integration issues result in both higher unit costs and longer cycle times in implementation of technology, ITCR says. The issue of complexity is so significant to the IT world that it is estimated that 96% of IT managers are now taking action to address it.[9] The drive is to persuade vendors to adhere to more generic (less varied) systems.

In addition to systems complexity, organizations can be hurt by complexity introduced in the development and integration of new applications and processes. At discount brokerage Charles Schwab & Co., products under consideration are vigorously examined against the criteria of corporate and industry standards. "The last thing we want is a proprietary product that requires us to support yet another platform and unnecessary layers of functionality," said James Chong, Schwab's VP of architecture.[10]

The cost of a system is not solely its purchase price but its cost of ownership. "A desktop PC costs $2,000 to buy but $15,000 to run for three years," said venture capitalist Vinod Khosla. Much of the gigantic IT budgets (he estimates 70%) doesn't go to the IT companies, he said, but to internal spending, "to inefficiency. Because these systems are so cumbersome."

Fighting Back Against IT Complexity

So what can companies do? Fortunately, the bursting of the internet bubble and subsequent pressure on IT budgets—and IT vendors—has given many companies an opportunity to realign their technology infrastructure and approach as indicated by data in Figure 13.2.

Figure 13.2: Controlling IT Complexity

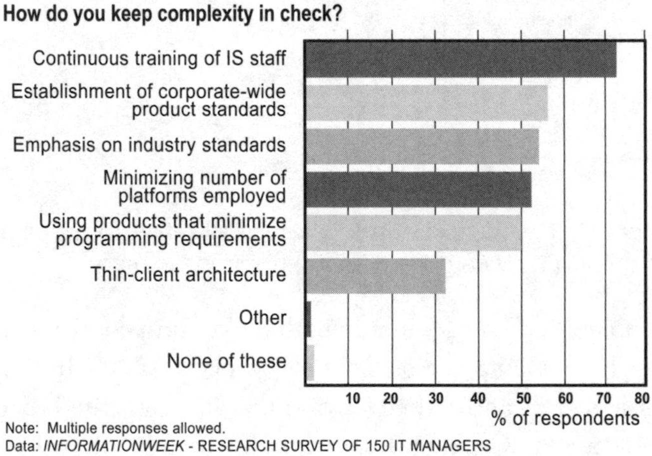

How do you keep complexity in check?

Note: Multiple responses allowed.
Data: *INFORMATIONWEEK* - RESEARCH SURVEY OF 150 IT MANAGERS

Training for Information System staff topped the list of ways to control IT complexity, followed closely by enforcing standards (both corporate and industry), and minimizing platforms (both those developed internally and those from purchased systems).

The smart deployment of Complexity Reduction Principles can help drive the right decisions on your current IT and future IT expenditures. Here are four principles you can use to understand what's driving your IT complexity and simplify its structure:

#1: Don't rely on IT to fix a broken process (it won't!); find and eliminate the non-value-add activities

#2: Reduce the complexity in your systems architecture (your customers won't pay for it!)

#3: Outsource complexity where strategically desirable

#4: Use modularity in your hardware and software

Principle #1: Don't rely on IT to fix a broken process (it won't!)

While IT can generate considerable advantage when integrated into good processes, it is unwise to rely on IT to fix a broken process. To quote Albert Einstein, insanity is "doing the same thing over and over again and expecting different results." Equally, doing the same thing, only automated and faster, is unlikely to yield any better results.

In fact, IT applied to a bad process locks in the non-value-add in the given process, driving up the costs of correcting it. Which is why we have to tackle the complexity in our organizations with a process view to identify the complexity and develop rational, rigorous strategies for taking complexity-related cost out of our infrastructure.

Before you make any move on IT, create a Complexity Value Stream Map of the process, find all the value-add and non-value-add activities and costs, and apply the Complexity Equation to understand the intrinsic PCE. Consider a different IT solution only *after* you have driven up the PCE. Don't be afraid of little solutions. You don't have to buy a $100 million IT system to generate value; once the non-value-add steps are eliminated, you may not want or need to add new IT (which is good news from shareholders' perspective).

Principle #2: Reduce the complexity in your systems architecture (your customers won't pay for it!)

The case to *simplify* IT systems is an easier case to make than the case to *integrate* them (the theme of the 1990s). The process of simplification is one of moving towards common standards and platforms with lower maintenance costs, rather than connecting proprietary systems. If you're one of the companies spending huge amounts of money maintaining cumbersome systems, which solution would you prefer? McKinsey estimates that pruning the number of technologies in use can lead to IT cost savings of up to 20%.[11]

Moreover, reducing the levels of complexity in your IT will establish an important platform for growth, and lower unit costs on future sales. It will also make the function more responsive to future activity, as CIOs and CTOs spend less time battling day-to-day complexity and more on higher-value activities.

The ultimate arbiter of the level of technology required is the question of value. The technology is the tool, not the jewel, in many cases. We need to shift emphasis from considering what the technology does to how it helps our company create value. In *The Process Edge,* Peter Keen says, "Process investment says, 'Kick the benefits habit.' Benefits is a managerial concept; value is an economic concept. A writer may call a firm an exemplar of 'excellence,' laud its use of IT for 'competitive advantage,' … but none of this answers (the question): Does all this excellence actually increase the value of the firm?"

Principle #3: Outsource complexity where strategically desirable

Capital One obviously benefited from keeping its IT in-house, but that's not always the case. A common consequence of a complexity analysis of IT (using a method like that proposed in Part II) is the decision to outsource. And as innovation has accelerated over the last 15 years, so have the demands on corporate IT groups to keep apace. Even when the pace is maintained, it often makes sense to outsource nonstrategic IT functionality that creates complexity costs for the company. In many cases, outsourcing the nonstrategic IT functions frees CIOs and CTOs to focus on the strategic IT applications in the company.

For example, during the late 1990s, FedEx's Laurie Tucker had decided that the company's VirtualOrder software, which had helped hundreds of companies with their ecommerce strategies, was not a strategic strength. The FedEx sales force was better at convincing logistics managers to funnel more packages to FedEx than they were at selling ecommerce software. FedEx would *never* be as determined a player in this field as other new entrants. So Tucker pulled the plug on the IT product, despite the hundreds of thousands of hours and dollars spent in trying to improve it.

This example highlights a common feature of such mismatches: disproportionate effort and spending to compensate for a lack of innate corporate capabilities (both of which could be more productively directed toward strategic strengths). Says Tucker about using outside vendors instead of the internal IT group: "If we had put those dollars into advertising and PR, would we have gained the same credibility and developed the same skills in our IT group [as was present in the outside vendors]?"[12]

Understanding what *is* and what is *not* strategic (aligned to corporate capabilities) is the critical distinction when considering outsourcing. IT systems, like any infrastructure, can become not only an activity trap and a money pit, but also a source of identity. Such was the case with British Airways' BABS booking system, which had soaked up huge amounts of attention and cash over the years, prior to the CEO's recent decision to outsource much of the in-house IT.

Key outsourcing questions

Here are some questions you can use to guide your own analysis of whether to outsource a part of your IT:

1. **Does the IT support a strategic process for the company** (such as it did for Capital One)? Use Core Process Analysis (p. 119) to identify the key areas of strategic support. If the answer is no, consider...

2. **How does the upkeep and maintenance of internal IT drain our resources?** Use the simplified Complexity Equation (p. 30) to determine the size of impact of maintaining multiple systems. Is it a big lever? How many personnel are currently attached to IT support for nonstrategic processes? How many process or quality improvement projects are affiliated with these areas? Put another way, what goals and metrics would be achievable if resources were freed through strategic outsourcing?

3. **Will we ever be as good, as fast, or as cheap as external vendors?** If it's not a core process, and PCE is low, the answer is often no.

4. **What are the full costs of outsourcing?** Beyond the vendor costs themselves, what are the additional costs of monitoring the outsourcing, such as transaction or coordination costs?

5. **What, if any, are the risks of outsourcing?** In many cases, if the processes are nonstrategic, the risks of outsourcing will be limited. However, if outsourcing is done blindly, rather than as a logical consequence of value stream mapping and identifying areas in which the company can create the most value, then all that has happened is that the risks have moved from inside your four walls to outside. But the impact on the customer and shareholder remains the same. The risks associated with outsourcing normally appear because the act of outsourcing is seen as an act of last resort, rather than as a strategic tool.

Says Michael Dell:

> *Outsourcing, at least in the IT world, is almost always a way to get rid of a problem a company hasn't been able to solve itself. The classic case is the company with 2,000 people in the IT department. Nobody knows what they do, and nobody knows why they do it. The solution—outsource IT to a service provider, and hopefully they'll fix it. But if you look at what happens five years later, it's not necessarily a pretty picture. That's not what we're doing at all. We focus on how we can coordinate our activities to create the most value for customers.*[13]

Principle #4: Use modularity in your hardware and software

Chapter 11 discussed how modularity can help reduce complexity in product and service offerings. The same principle of creating standard units that each provide a specific functionality can be used in creating software and hardware.

FedEx applies this principle by looking for opportunities to reuse technology whenever possible. For instance, its call centers use the same application to locate drop-off locations as the one that customers see on the website. Schwab uses the same components and codes in multiple applications.[14]

Another example of using modularity in software and systems is the application of Microsoft's .NET Framework, with its high level of interoperability with other languages, applications, and systems. In essence, it allows for in-house applications and external systems to be stitched together. The ability to support multiple languages means that developers have the choice to use the programming language that's both best suited to the job and in which they have the best capabilities, which improves cycle time and eliminates the costs of multiple specialists.

The modularity analysis should proceed much like that described for products (*see* p. 230), only you would map the software development process, then remove all non-value-add work. Of the value-added elements remaining, consider what development steps are common to all outputs and/or could translate into strategic advantage for the company (and therefore warrant investment in platform design).

Smart uses of technology and an explicit strategy for reusing technology—and preventing the entry of nonstandard components—not only reduces the maintenance costs but also improves the quality levels because of "learning curve" benefits: IT engineers (a) have to learn fewer hardware and software configurations, and (b) they get more experience in the now-standard configurations you do use. In short, they can become experts in what really matters to your company instead of trying to be jacks-of-all-trades.

Using IT to help conquer complexity

Our Corporate Purchasing System [CPS] mainframe was launched in 1990. It consolidated all the existing systems but was really difficult to use. So then we launched a new [materials acquisition interface]—a homegrown attempt at conquering the front end. But it was unintelligible and lacked functionality.

—*Greg Kyler, Lockheed Martin MAC-MAR purchasing*   **271**

Most of this chapter has been about how to simplify the structure of your IT infrastructure. But the other side of the IT coin is using technology to help solve other complexity problems in your organizations. The purchasing examples in Chapter 11 from Lockheed Martin were all cases where IT was able to deliver on the promise stated at the start of this chapter: allowing people to deliver what the customers want faster and more efficiently.

Conclusion

IT is often transparent to the customer (exceptions being in areas like ecommerce). Unless customers touch the IT system directly, they'll be indifferent to whether you're using a billion-dollar system or a million-dollar system. But your shareholders will care!

One of the key principles of conquering complexity in IT is *do not rely on IT to fix a broken process*. A bad process that is automated is still a bad process... and is still one that *won't* add value to customers, that *will* destroy shareholders' wealth, and that ultimately will drive up the complexity of systems and technology in the company.

At this time, many companies are still reeling from a decade of investment in non-aligned systems, or have written off huge sums of money related to IT. But since it requires significant investments to maintain current systems, the pressure on CIOs and CTOs to simplify IT and lower costs is unlikely to lessen any time soon.

Questions that your business needs to answer include:

- **Which processes does our IT support?** Are they core strategic processes or noncore? If they are noncore, is it sustainable to keep these processes in-house, or can we outsource? Remember the Complexity Equation: complexity costs rise as you add more processes. Why invest technology dollars in noncore processes if you are ultimately going to outsource them? In many instances, these noncore processes are supported by multiple databases and systems that have introduced huge levels of complexity and cost into the organization, to the point that many companies are now spending more than 80% of their IT budgets on *maintaining* their existing systems.[15]

- **What is the PCE for core strategic processes?** Before spending millions more on IT, consider how much value-add is contained within even your strategic processes. Value stream maps of these processes will highlight the opportunities to eliminate non-value-add-related cost and capital costs. Moreover, complexity analysis of your offering will significantly reduce or even eliminate the need for IT spending as you identify entire processes that are non-value-add or that support a product/service group that does not meet its cost of capital.

- **Can IT confer a competitive advantage?** Research has shown that on average there is no correlation between a firm's level of IT spending and its business performance.[16] So obviously the issue requires careful handling because throwing money at IT will not create value. However, as Capital One and others have shown, IT *can* confer a competitive advantage when applied correctly.

- **How can I free up capital and ongoing cost currently tied to non-value-add IT systems?** They are of no more value than an empty warehouse. To determine the dollar opportunity requires value stream mapping of the IT-related processes.

Note that the first two bullets don't deal with IT directly but rather with where value is created in your organization. The message is clear: all of your management (and IT executives in particular) need to focus on using information technology *strategically* to create value for shareholders and better serve your customers. There are no prizes awarded for having the largest IT budget, and there is no correlation between that and performance. What is rewarded is the use of technology to cut costs, accelerate speed, or improve quality. Understanding what does and does not create value in an organization is the foundation on which these investment decisions should be based.

Endnotes

1 Karyl Scott, "Executive Report: Battle Complexity to Add Profitability," *Information Week*, September 14, 1998.

2 Christine Canabou, "Fast Talk: The New IT Agenda: CIOs and CTOs offer straight talk about their most strategic investments (and how they justify them)," *Fast Company*, April 2003.

3 *Ibid.*

4 Laurie A. Tucker, "Digital Competition," *Fast Company*, December 1999.

4 Bharat N. Anand, Michael G. Rukstad, Christopher H. Paige, "Capital One Financial Corp," Harvard Business School case, April 24, 2000.

6 *Ibid.*

7 Fred Vogelstein, "Finding a Silver Lining in the Tech Bust," *Fortune*, October 14, 2002.

8 Erika Brown, "Less Is More; Silicon Valley's top venture capitalist has a different view on how to find a winner in technology: Help buyers spend less money on tech," *Forbes*, May 26, 2003.

9 Rusty Weston, "Complexity without a cure," *Information Week*, October 1998.

10 Scott, "Battle Complexity."

11 Frank Mattern, Stephan Schönwälder, and Wolfram Stein, "Fighting Complexity in IT," *McKinsey Quarterly*, May 2003.

12 Tucker, "Digital Competition."

13 Dell and Magretta, "The Power of Virtual Integration" (see chap. 3, n. 1).

14 Scott, "Battle Complexity."

15 Mattern, Schönwälder, and Stein, "Fighting Complexity in IT."

16 Peter G. W. Keen, *The Process Edge: Creating Value Where it Counts* (Boston: Harvard Business School Press, 1997), p. 3.

PART IV

High-Return Investments When Conquering Complexity

CHAPTER 14

Creating a Culture that Can Conquer Complexity

In designing a new model of the Celica sports car, Toyota's styling department suggested a longer front quarter-panel for cosmetic reasons. The change was opposed by the manufacturing engineer assigned to door panels because the panel would be difficult and expensive to produce as a unique component (interpretation: there would be high costs to this added complexity).

The chief engineer, Toyota's equivalent of a high-powered project manager, initially sided with the styling department, but the manufacturing engineer felt strongly enough that he elevated his concern to the general manager of manufacturing. After substantial argument, the two sides reached an innovative consensus that achieved the desired look with a satisfactory level of manufacturability.[1]

If this had arisen in your own company about a product or service, what do you think would have happened? Probably the same thing that happens in most organizations. Two functions become polarized around their respective goals (in this case, manufacturing wanted to control costs; marketing wanted to increase sales). Conflict surfaces in a long list of *if onlys*... *if only* marketing would stop offering customers new products our costs could be lower... *if only* manufacturing would have more vision.... These reactions, part cultural, part incentive-driven, cause both sides to dig deeper into their functional silos.

Under such conditions, true consensus—a decision that everyone agrees on and supports—is a pipe dream. The best that companies can hope for is compromise (one or both sides "giving up" something they think is valuable); and in many cases they settle for a decision based on executive fiat, an outcome neither side may support. Such decisions may leave a lot of the complexity profit pool untapped, as their driving force becomes one of arbitration to keep both sides happy rather than of collaboration to find the best solution that will create the greatest estimated incremental increase in shareholder value.

As the Celica case study demonstrates, however, it is possible to have a culture where conflict drives innovation not wasted time. Conflict is a good thing so long as it is driven by data as much as possible, and by good judgment when data is not available. Yes, Toyota has a powerful set of commonized components and assemblies applied across platforms, but such tools are useful only when there are cultural norms that value the control of complexity and its costs.

Your organization must reach a point where functional silos cease to be an obstacle to conquering complexity, where pet causes are subsumed under the greater good of the organization. This will happen when you:

1. Believe conquering complexity is an imperative

2. Require ongoing executive engagement

3. Target high value-at-stake opportunities

4. Dedicate organizational resources

5. Provide an analytical methodology and toolset

6. Align metrics, incentives, policies with complexity goals

7. Nurture close customer connections

Cultural Ingredient #1: Believe conquering complexity is an imperative

The decision to focus on reducing product and service proliferation has led many companies to identify offerings that could be outsourced or deleted. It has also led companies to withdraw from certain customer segments or markets in the pursuit of higher Economic Profitability and overall growth. Other companies find they need to expand product or service offerings to reap maximum Economic Profit.

These types of changes are dramatic for marketing, for sales, for the company as a whole. Such changes can lead to market leadership and improved economics. But they require significant courage and a strong will to make them happen. Resisting the drive to grow through proliferation (more and more options to the customer regardless of cost) is not easy; guiding expansion into new markets or customer segments can be just as difficult.

To carry it off, you have to believe that conquering complexity is *not* optional for your business. Conquering complexity must be seen as a significant part of your equation for becoming a business with positive-Economic Profit and positive-growth. It must be part of your "*We can't just stay where we are*" message. In today's fast, global markets, this is clearly not a platitude but a cold hard fact.

Another component will be the identification and communication of a "Future-Back" vision: *if we can't stay where we are, where are we going?* It's not just that the status quo will not do; the companies that have conquered complexity are not only efficient and make money, they are **exciting companies with bright futures.** What is your company's Future? What might your company look like in 10 years' time? Now translate that Back: what does it mean for you today? What is the pathway of transformation that other companies have taken? Emphasizing your goals with a Future-Back message negates many of the fears that can arise with cultural change. (There's more on Future-Back visions in Chapter 15, *see* p. 302.)

The ultimate message is "we have to do this to become a great company." At a minimum, greatness implies positive EP, high efficiencies, and ecstatic customers who love your value proposition. Personalize case studies like those in Chapter 1 to your business so that everyone understands that, at a minimum, conquering complexity can only propel the company toward greatness.

Cultural Ingredient #2: Require ongoing executive engagement

Every successful Lean Six Sigma corporate transformation we've been involved in was strictly dependent on top executives supporting the initiative and having a corporate-level Champion to lead and coordinate the effort.[2] But when companies embark on a journey to conquer complexity, they soon realize that *no one person is in charge.*

More so than most other high-profile corporate undertakings, conquering complexity needs the commitment of and action by the CEO and executives because of its systemic and deep-rooted nature. That also explains why complexity cannot be conquered from the bottom up. Decisions about product and service offerings affect sales, marketing, fulfillment, product development, manufacturing, distribution, service after sale... nearly every aspect of your business.

Complexity conquering can't work if you put the burden of complexity control on only one of the functions. The vision or opportunity may arise at a management level below the P&L manager, perhaps in marketing or engineering—and these functions can help to build the case through piloting some of the techniques . However, without senior leadership engagement to address the difficult issues that will arise across the portfolio of offerings, the gains will be limited.

Winning the complexity battle requires all stakeholders to pull in a common direction—an outcome more likely if executive leadership and sponsorship are provided *throughout* the process, not just at the launch. And that's why companies who proceed with complexity reduction without obtaining the engagement of senior leadership and every P&L manager should recall Winston Churchill's words on the disastrous Gallipoli campaign in WWI that cost him a military career and the lives of tens of thousands of soldiers:

> *People in a subordinate position are very ill advised to embark on a major undertaking without their Chief's commitment.*[3]

Some ways for the CEO and top executives to display strong and visible commitment to conquering complexity:

- Clearly and consistently articulate the strategic case for change and the reasons for change

  "The low-cost carriers already ate our breakfast and we're trying to stop them eating our lunch."

  —*Paul Coby, CIO, British Airways, 2002*[4]

  "What is complexity? It's a multibillion dollar opportunity."

  —*Theresa Metty, Chief Procurement Officer, Motorola*[5]

- Realign incentives, metrics, and management accounting policies as needed to be consistent with goals of conquering complexity (details later in this chapter)

- Identify, execute, and publicly celebrate early wins

Consider the somewhat parallel experience of corporations as they execute Mergers and Acquisitions. It is now accepted that a) the integration phase of an acquisition is the most critical to success, and b) Integration Champions or Managers are a critical component to managing the integration process. One of the lessons from General Electric, seen by many as a master acquirer, is that integration management is a full-time job and needs to be recognized as a distinct business function, just like operations, marketing, or finance. Conquering complexity shares many facets of the integration process: cross-functional dynamics, high levels of ambiguity, charged emotions, focus on creating shareholder value.

Another shared dynamic is that many acquisitions are conducted as if they are unique events, and so process infrastructure is poorly planned and lessons once learned are soon forgotten. GE saw the folly of this and implemented a methodology for conducting successful acquisitions. Conquering complexity is of a similar nature: while many companies embark on SKU-cutting sprees, service cutbacks, or brand-extension programs, few incorporate this experience *into the way they do business.*

Having an executive-level leader with authority will help to institutionalize conquering complexity as a management approach. Such leaders have much more room to maneuver than their counterparts with functional responsibilities; in fact, a system-wide purview is their job. Also, they have access to the senior management team so complexity remains on the corporate agenda.

In short, if you want to conquer complexity there must be someone at the executive level—a VP, a Champion, a Chief, a Director—whose job it is to make sure complexity is considered in strategic decisions, who leads the analysis of complexity in your organization, who serves as a central point for deployment of specific complexity reduction projects, and who creates an infrastructure to execute the conquest of complexity. While your President or CEO has the purview of your entire organization, he or she does not have the time or capacity to take on complexity as a daily role, but you should name someone who reports to the CEO.

The executive who champions the conquest of complexity in your organization needs to:

1. **Drive the development of a value agenda through clear fact-based analysis of the root causes and costs of complexity** (working with other executives, often a strategic committee): These agenda decisions usually cut across functional boundaries, require significant authority, and may impose significant change on the organization. It is imperative that this value agenda be based on hard analysis or it is certain to be rejected.

2. **Design and oversee the launch**: including the draft of the initial charter, selection of the senior-level managers responsible for leading teams implementing value-agenda projects, and the facilitation of the early workshops with leaders of the organization.

3. **Manage the portfolio of complexity projects**: including the initial assessment of the corporation for the highest-value complexity targets, and the ongoing monitoring of progress.

4. **Institutionalize "conquering complexity" in the business**: including deployment of complexity methodologies and metrics; sponsorship of senior level workshops and ongoing education and personalization of complexity ("what does it mean to me").

5. **Communicate to the company and beyond**, act as the day-to-day manager of the key initiatives (including regular updates to the

Characteristics of a Complexity Champion

The leader selected to lead complexity efforts should have...

- **Deep self-confidence with relatively few ego requirements**: This may be the ultimate change agent role and requires a strong, confident individual who can drive change in spite of cultural inertia, and without having to insert his or her own ego into every discussion.

- **Respect of the organization**: While a Complexity Champion may have no *direct* authority over the functional areas. Toyota uses its chief engineers in this role because they are individuals who command deep respect within the organization and have the clear backing of the CEO and executive team. Nonetheless they are able to guide great change in the organization through process improvement resources (e.g., Black Belts, Green Belts) within the functional areas.

- **Cultural intelligence and communication skills**: The only other individual in the company who must communicate and work across functions to the same degree is the CEO—so the ability to drive change while working collaboratively with functional leaders is crucial.

- **Project management skills**: While there are clearly many cultural nuances to deal with, this doesn't negate the need for very strong project management skills, akin to launching any new corporate initiative with strong ability to drive things forward.

company), and as the point person for complexity-related efforts and inquiries from partners, customers, and suppliers.

Note: there is no imperative that this person be sourced from a particular function, say, strategy, marketing, product development, or operations. While it can be useful if the individual has spent time in a number of areas, it is more critical that they meet the above requirements. The special role that these leaders play, and the requisite balance of skills as a consequence, can be summed up thus: "Act *like* a CEO. Think *like* a CEO. Report *to* the CEO." In addition, let us never forget the primary leadership qualifications outlined by Warren Buffett in an address to MBA students at Columbia University, his alma mater:

Managers must have honesty, intelligence and energy: and if they don't have the first one, the last two will kill you.

Cultural Ingredient #3: Target high value-at-stake opportunities

When products or services have existed for a number of years, it is easy to believe that those offerings define your company rather than the other way around. Tradition triggers inward-focus and impaired performance. So what is the trigger that will signal that change is required? A key component will be careful selection of the initial areas of focus: Are they high-value areas? Are they visible? Remember our example of Procter & Gamble when they decided to trim their product line by 20 percent. What do you think that kind of action said to the organization as a whole? You'd better believe people knew P&G's leadership was serious!

The question is how to make change really happen: It's about driving the desired strategic improvement down to specific improvement projects that create value. Projects are the "tip of the spear" for driving real cultural change (*see* Figure 14.1).

Figure 14.1: Using Projects to Help Drive Change

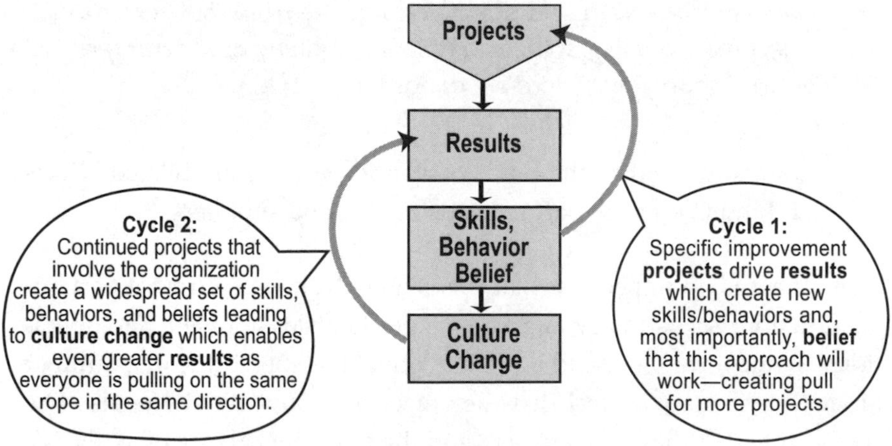

Focused, value-creating improvement projects are the "tip of the spear" for leading real sustainable culture change. Choosing visible, high-impact projects and doing everything possible to ensure their success can start the cascade of cultural change.

Cultural Ingredient #4: Dedicate organizational resources

As the list of complexity-related projects grows on your value agenda, the obvious question is how to get them done. The answer: the same way you would get any other strategically critical project done. Except there's one tweak: Complexity issues often stretch across organizational boundaries. That means teams working on complexity projects should have access to, and preferably guidance from, mid- to high-level managers with broad authority. And those managers, in turn, must be committed to conquering complexity.

Most organizations will contain some project-deployment infrastructure, existing either as responsibilities added onto mainstream jobs (managers, supervisors, work groups, etc.) or perhaps in a parallel structure like that used to deploy Six Sigma or Lean Six Sigma, with Black Belts leading projects, Master Black Belts serving as in-house consultants, a Champion to oversee their progress, etc. Whichever path you choose, avoid creating a separate "complexity silo" of people committed full time to complexity but with no connections to the everyday work of the organization.

Cultural Ingredient #5: Provide an analytical methodology and toolset

Parts II and III of this book outlined both a diagnostic approach and implementation tools that can help you conquer different kinds of complexity and even determine if complexity is the real problem. Not everyone in your organization needs to know all these tools, but you should train a core cadre of people in the diagnostic processes, and deploy specific tools out to the teams working on the various complexity issues. The Complexity Champion must also be able to provide funding from the P&L budget to train personnel within the functional areas in the specific tools needed to capture requisite data and implement specific solutions.

Don't forget that often the issues and decisions you will encounter will likely be contentious and even political in nature. The only way to effectively combat these issues is to bring a sound analytical method to prove your case.

And don't forget to continuously feed new ideas into the front end of the pipeline of this methodology, which will allow you to rapidly couple complexity reduction to market demands and create the fastest growth rate in EP generation. Ongoing assessments of your portfolio— conducted at the highest levels and using the methodology outlined in this book—will keep your focus where it should be.

Cultural Ingredient #6: Align metrics, incentives, policies with complexity goals

Making decisions that *favor* conquering complexity will be a major change for many organizations, requiring people to stop non-value-added complexity they've grown accustomed to and try on new behaviors. How can you design incentives that will encourage the desired attitudes and actions towards complexity?

It may become clear that your incentive system is a key causal factor of non-value-add complexity. If your company dictates that people will be promoted for increasing the proliferation of products/services, you can be sure that you will see such proliferation, whether it is value-creating or not.

The vast majority of companies today approve new product launches based on passing one of three criteria: (a) a projected revenue hurdle, (b) a projected gross profit hurdle, or (c) someone's opinion that "this looks like a winner" or "a customer asked for it." When products or services have to pass a complexity-adjusted EP hurdle, you'll end up with a smaller pool of approved new offerings that are different from, and represent more potential value than, what you've had in the past.

One given is that you must start measuring and projecting the impact of new products on PCE and cost (as introduced in Chapter 2). Using that

Leveraging the lessons of infrastructure

Do companies that have successfully deployed Six Sigma or Lean Six Sigma have a leg up in conquering complexity? Consider that two of Six Sigma's shaping forces are its infrastructure and its focus on data-driven problem-solving. Both are critical to conquering complexity.

Six Sigma infrastructure creates a cadre of cross-functional Black Belts who are trained to look at problems from a fact-based position. Decisions become data-based: data on what customers really want, calculations of the Economic Profit of a given project, statistical linkages of causes and effects. The common vocabulary of data and improvement eases the transition to conquering complexity. The entire infrastructure is focused on the highest-value problems and uses the best talent in the organization. It is organized to drive change in a practical no-nonsense fashion, owned by the line organization with full-time resources focused on solving the biggest problems faced by the business.

Companies that have succeeded in deploying Six Sigma or Lean Six Sigma are used to challenging the status quo, stepping across functional boundaries, and making big decisions that will change the look of the organization. Lou Giuliano, CEO of ITT Industries, when asked what had surprised him about the impact of Lean Six Sigma, responded:

"Because you now have 300+ people working full-time at change, change becomes more comfortable, not only because it's familiar, but it's demonstrating real results. So what happens is, in other parts of the organization the resistance to changes becomes less."[6]

For many of these companies, conquering complexity is the next step: moving beyond the departmental basis to examine the systemic effects across the company; enjoining the strategy to operational decisions; developing a Complexity Value Agenda and then leveraging the problem-solving skills of the Black Belts and Master Black Belts.

Does this mean that deploying Lean or Six Sigma is a prerequisite? Absolutely not. When Porsche decided to reduce complexity by eliminating air-cooled engines, it came face to face with the fact that process improvement could not have solved the problem it faced. To survive, the company had to attack complexity first.

metric to guide development and marketing decisions will prevent you from getting into the wrong businesses in the name of growth.

Where are the roadblocks that can prevent your complexity leader and his/her team from carrying out their work? In the short term, what measures are required to facilitate change? What about long term? Revisit your Complexity Profile. If you're in a product-oriented company, what is the average part count over time? What are your reuse metrics? These were metrics that Toyota, Scania, International Power Machines, and effectively Capital One used in their own war on the cost of complexity to sustain performance. Create your own reuse metric appropriate to your business.

A services-oriented company has the same issues, and the effects are often worse. We worked with one business services company that had undertaken a review of its professional services offerings and found 300 offerings but only 10 to 20 distinctly different practices. In their environment, it was incredibly easy to create a new professional service offering with little thought given to reuse or retiring obsolescent practices.

Many companies' sales and marketing teams are compensated largely or solely on sales, no matter what degree of customization they have to offer your customers, and this compensation plan has produced high complexity levels. It is futile to embark on an offering-reduction program without also tackling the root cause. Conversely, in an operations-dominated organization, if cost becomes the only measure of success at the expense of participation in a new profitable market, incentives are misaligned. Attacking the root causes of incentives and cultural norms is a far more powerful way to attack complexity than looking for a one-time hit. Look closely at any incentives, policies, and practices that drive complexity-creating behavior, and make the necessary changes.

Cultural Ingredient #7: Nurture close customer connections

Clearly one of the reasons that companies become overly complex is that they do not *know* what customers want or are willing to pay enough for to allow for positive EP. A big mistake that companies make is assuming that gathering Voice of the Customer data is a one-time event rather than a continuous process. The establishment or development of strong interfaces to capture the Voice of the Customer is vital to guard against the introduction of non-value-add cost, as well as to tap into potential growth areas. As we discussed in Chapter 3, the increase in the number of communication nodes and layers in your organization can slow the transmission of information from the market. The information is out there and it is in the minds of your customers. The methodologies in Chapter 10 can be very powerfully applied to understand what customers are telling you—what they *value*, not just what they *want*. Establish channels to gather this information on an ongoing basis.

Conclusion

Complexity is spawned in every corner of your organization, and bringing it under control will take systemic, cultural changes. It cannot be conquered by isolated efforts, even if they are led by knowledgeable, committed individuals. Approach complexity as you would any major change, making the imperative clear to everyone in the organization. What does conquering complexity mean to a sales person? Delighted customers, shorter lead times, higher retention. What does it mean to your product or service designers? Less time wasted reinventing wheels; more time available for truly differentiating features. What does it mean to product development? A shorter development cycle, fewer suppliers to manage. Make it relevant to the entire organization and make your commitment visible.

Endnotes

1 Durward K. Sobek II, Jeffrey K. Liker, and Allen C. Ward, "Another Look at How Toyota Integrates Product Development," *Harvard Business Review*, July 1, 1998.

2 See Michael L. George, *Lean Six Sigma*, Chapter 5, or George, *Lean Six Sigma for Service*, pp. 22-23.

3 Winston S. Churchill, *The Second World War, vol. 1: The Gathering Storm*.

4 Kevin O'Toole, "Keeping it Simple," *Airline Business* (Reed Business Information, UK), September 1, 2002.

5 Theresa Metty, "Next-Generation Supply Management" (keynote address from the 88th Annual International Supply Management Conference, Nashville, TN, May 18, 2003).

6 George Group Executive Roundtable, Waldorf-Astoria, December 4, 2002.

CHAPTER 15

Conquering Complexity in Your Product and Service Value Chain

As a small start-up, Dell couldn't afford to create every piece of the value chain. But more to the point, why should we want to? We concluded we'd be better off leveraging the investments others have made and focusing on delivering solutions and systems to customers.

—Michael Dell[1]

Every firm has a value chain that extends from suppliers all the way to customer satisfaction. As a consequence, complexity reaches beyond the four walls of your company, deep into the supply chain where all the interdependencies exist. All segments of your value chain feel the cumulative weight of complexity: Customer service reps struggle to stay up-to-date as new offerings proliferate and make it difficult to provide quality service. Suppliers battle to maintain quality and delivery times with vast diversity in material requirements. High numbers of suppliers create a form of complexity that drives up hidden procurement costs.

Manufacturing itself is a node of enormous complexity in the supply chain, which offers very high returns if properly scoped and managed,[2] or a drag on returns if not. Retailers are forced to make trade-offs on floor space without which they may be unable to market efficiently. And then there's the impact on the customers themselves, who may feel overwhelmed by choice, or underserved, or are simply paying higher prices due to your internal complexity. Until, that is, they find a better alternative elsewhere.

In this chapter, we'll look at how complexity principles should influence how you structure and manage various components of your value chain, especially those that are not under your corporate roof.

Value Chain Configuration: Extracting the full value from conquering complexity

All of us, whether in a services-centered organization or a product-centered organization, depend on upstream and downstream partners in the process of reaching customers. But the pressure is intensifying to select the right links of the value chain in which to participate. More companies are selecting processes to outsource (typically support processes such as payroll, but increasingly value-add operations like manufacturing) and looking for partnerships in areas such as R&D.

Value-chain, and specifically supply-chain, decisions are about cost, but they also are about investment, responsiveness, and growth. Consider what Michael Dell says about growth, and why he believes supply chain choices can influence results: "Suppose we have two suppliers building monitors for us, and one of them loses its edge. It's a lot easier for us to get capacity from the remaining supplier than to set up a new manufacturing plant ourselves. If we had to build our factories for every single component of the system, growing at 57% per year just would not be possible." Dell's virtual model cannot be replicated within every company. But clearly designing the optimal supply chain is a strategic issue of enormous import for shareholder value.

Process characteristics of the supply chain

In an internal process, a complexity focus leads to reducing the number of nodes in the process, because every excess step introduces time and waste (recall the number of nodes or Activities is the "A" in the Complexity Equation). The challenge in the supply chain is minimizing the number of nodes (including your own factories, production facilities, or, in a service environment, customer handoffs, etc.) while ensuring optimal customer reach and responsiveness.

Determined management is going to declare process improvement war and demand unconditional surrender of all the non-value-add activities in their processes, but what of the value-add activities?

What is optimal will depend on the characteristics of the industry, e.g., transport costs vs. labor costs, perishability of goods, duties and tariffs, etc. For example, because they are easy to produce with relative low quality requirements, toys quickly became the domain of Asian manufacturers. Many consumer goods companies, on the other hand, maintain local production sites so as to tailor the product to regional tastes.

There are multiple benefits to reducing the number of nodes through which an offering must pass:

- Every node, like every process step, is a chance for error and introduces additional variability into the system

- Every node takes you further away from the customer

- In many instances, savings follow a step function; if you cut your offering, cut deep enough to generate significant fixed-cost savings, such as closing a warehouse or eliminating a shift. Infrastructure adjustments can generate dollar improvements from product and process complexity reduction efforts. This issue heightens the need for a strong analytical approach to understand the key break points for removal of these fixed costs.

For example, consider the consumer goods companies that make dozens of different varieties of shampoo. To cut just a few SKUs may do little to diminish marketing costs, as the focus often is on the brand not the product. In overhead, the same management and offices are required. You may save labor costs, but they are not the step-change improvement you would get by, say, closing a plant, withdrawing from a segment, or eliminating a shift. This is not to diminish the significant benefits of greater focus, reduced variable costs and reduction in hidden complexity costs. But to lose sight of the end goal is to leave the largest chunks of non-value-add money on the table.

If decisions about optimal supply chain infrastructure—where to locate production facilities, whether to outsource your call centers, etc.—are made on an incremental cost basis, you'll lose a significant opportunity. A far better alternative is to analyze the "value" in your chain from start to end, look at what your company is good at doing, and structure the entire chain accordingly. Without the complexity viewpoint, and the power of the complexity analytics, attempts to optimize supply chain costs are at best ad hoc and directionally correct—and, at worst, cause loss of share and value.

Strategic Sourcing: How complexity drives the make-or-buy decision

A manufacturing engineer at Cummins Engine Company noted that they were:

> *Spending a great deal of time on improvement projects…in an effort to catch up with small machine shops that… could have almost certainly manufactured the same components at lower cost and with comparable quality. Did these improvement efforts, however successful, warrant the time that we devoted to them?*[3]

Conversely, strategic inputs such as fuel systems were being increasingly outsourced. He concluded:

> *A strategy predicated on preserving jobs often results in insourcing parts that are easy to manufacture, largely to make work, while outsourcing those that are hard to make. Over time, fixed costs rise, product differentiation declines, and manufacturing performance remains stagnant… The very survival of the company is threatened.*

A study of major manufacturers found that most were *overinvesting in commodity parts and neglecting the proprietary things that represented the best sources of differentiation and advantage.*[4] It's a course of action with dire consequences:

1. An erosion of capabilities in areas of differentiation relative to competitors

2. A deterioration of skill-level-to-wage ratio relative to suppliers who take on the difficult work

3. A low rate of improvement due to complexity-related dilution of resources across the company

Why would intelligent management make these types of decisions? Complexity often is the product of multiple silo decisions, and sourcing decisions often reflect this problem. Internal competing agendas and lack of coordination between groups can lead to a variety of individual sourcing strategies. Also, many managers are guided by traditional accounting systems that obscure rather than clarify the sources and drivers of value creation. In Chapter 2 we likened complexity to high blood pressure, a silent killer that provides no symptoms through the managerial accounting system upon which management depends. Remember, GAAP accounting is not at issue; it makes no explanation as to how overhead costs are allocated and we therefore have no quarrel with GAAP. But until the cost of complexity is made visible, as introduced in Chapter 2, even the most brilliant executive may not be able to pierce the fog of managerial accounting.

Finally, often there is strong cultural resistance to stop doing things that have become part of the identity of the company, and a fear that overuse of outsourcing will diminish the company. The irony, of course, is that with their current course of action, companies featured in the study above actually are accelerating the deterioration of their competitive position.

In contrast, toy companies with retail sales under $100 million (90% of all toymakers) typically outsource all their production. They deploy their management attention to the highest value-creating tasks: marketing, branding, product development. The need to outsource arises from the nature of the industry: most products have a very short life and are sold in brief, defined seasons; obsolescence risk is considerable. A single product can deliver enormous returns. They operate in an industry with high consumer-driven complexity.

By outsourcing much of production, toy companies—more accurately, toy *marketers*—are able to focus resources on bringing more products to market. The lesson: in markets with high levels of consumer-driven product complexity, the ability to focus on your value-creating processes will lead to a competitive edge

Porsche, after suffering a hit to sales in the 1980s, has learned this lesson well. Today, as the world's most profitable automaker,[5] Porsche outsources nearly 85% of its production,[6] while retaining in-house processes it considers its core strategic processes: engine production, transmissions and final assembly—the processes that define the company to customers and are high value-add components.

Consider the alternatives to focusing on high-value processes: There is perhaps no mindset more likely to leave you vulnerable to competitors than one that says *we need to do it all ourselves.* Strategic sourcing is critical to conquering complexity in the supply chain.

Most companies perform activities that represent something of value to the customer *and* activities that *are just part of the process.* The distinction is critical. The Core Process Analysis introduced in Chapter 7 provides the guidelines:

- Focus on processes and things that you are good at and that are critical to the finished goods and services (strategic processes with high Process Cycle Efficiency, PCE)

- Improve the processes and things that you are not good at but which are critical to the finished goods and services (strategic and functional processes with low PCE)

- Outsource processes and things in which suppliers have comparative advantage, noncore processes with low PCE, such as capability, scale, cost, incentive, which in turn enables you to focus on the processes and things that you are good at

The balance is the optimal level of complexity that leads to value creation.

Focus on core processes

Every company should do what it is good at where there's a large value-creation opportunity: this means selecting high EP products and services and their core processes, and driving high Process Cycle Efficiencies resulting in accelerating shareholder value.

We talked about Core Processes in Chapter 7. In his recent book, Jim Collins infers that these are the processes that, if executed better than in any other firm, will make you a great rather than just a good company. These are the processes that are going to create an "unlevel playing field" in your favor. Warren Buffett likes to use a medieval metaphor:

"Both Coke and Gillette have actually increased their worldwide shares of the market in recent years. The might of their brand names, the attributes of their product, and the strength of distribution systems give them an enormous competitive advantage setting up a protective moat around their economic castles. In contrast most companies do battle daily without any such means of protection."

Coke decided that their bottling plants were not creators of EP and divested them, deploying capital to plants to provide high-value syrup around the world and focusing on brand creation, effectively the last link in the supply chain. Gillette chose the path of product differentiation and vigorous patent defense. What you choose should be more dependent on your store in intellectual capital and competitive advantage than on the legacy of past products, services, and markets.

Managing Upstream Complexity: Strategic supplier segmentation

Managing suppliers can generate enormous complexity costs or can yield enormous competitive advantage for all parties involved. With increased outsourcing, and purchased products now accounting for half of every sales dollar in the typical industrial firm, procurement is a fundamental strategic issue.[7]

Traditionally, the focus has been on reducing the bargaining power of suppliers. One of Michael Porter's "Five Forces" was Supplier Power:

> *In purchasing, then, the goal is to find mechanisms to offset or surmount these sources of suppliers' power...... Purchases of an item can be spread among alternate suppliers in such a way as to improve the firm's bargaining power.*[8]

But as you might suspect, opening up purchase contracts to thousands of vendors creates management headaches. And while it may drive cut-throat pricing, it also drives complexity costs. Consider the impact of having to manage 8,000 suppliers—as British Airways did, prior to its stated desire to reduce the number to 2,000.[9] The alternative is the partnership model, whose aim is to reduce transaction costs and improve performance through cooperation with suppliers—in essence, very low complexity. But what is the cost to set up and maintain these relationships? And moreover, which of the two approaches is optimal?

The answer is a combination of the two, in which you segment your suppliers as you would your customers or offerings, developing close partnerships with some and keeping others at arm's length. **Supplier segmentation minimizes the complexity of multiple vendor relationships while retaining and investing in relationships critical to your differentiation and value-creation.**

Let's discuss General Motors' approach versus the Japanese-style partnerships. General Motors historically has deployed the Competitive Bidding process—or *arm's length* style—sometimes going more than five rounds of bidding. In a study of 453 supplier-automaker relationships featured in *California Management Review*,[10] the authors found that the GM-style relationship was characterized by:

- Short-term contracts
- Frequent rebidding
- Low levels of information sharing
- Low levels of relation-specific investments
- Low levels of trust

These characteristics drive untenable disadvantages. First, the transaction costs associated with managing the large number of vendors outweigh the cost savings. Firms may spend more time and money negotiating and processing a contract than on the differential cost of the item itself. As an example, GM traditionally has employed nearly 10 times as many people per procurement dollar as Toyota to manage its large supplier base. The opportunity also applies to vastly more complex supply problems than automotive production.

Second, having more sources of supply doesn't necessarily mean you get more buying power. By extending continuous improvement to a smaller supply base, better pricing contracts can be more easily achieved with 3 suppliers than with 30.[11]

U.S. automakers claim to have "partner" style arrangements, too. But the authors of the study found that even with preferred partners, the only difference was length of contract. Every other condition remained. By contrast, Japanese-style partnerships result in superior performance because the firms share more information, invest in relation-specific assets that lower cost and improve performance, and rely on trust to govern relationships, which lowers transaction costs further.

What about Toyota? They use elements of both the arm's length and the partner models. Interestingly, the traditional view of Toyota is that all its suppliers are part of the *keiretsu*, a loose conglomeration of companies organized for their mutual benefit. But in fact, Toyota puts its suppliers in two categories: 1) those that provide requisite but nonstrategic inputs, e.g., tires, batteries, or 2) those that provide differentiating strategic inputs, e.g., engine parts, body panels. The management needs are different for each classification.

With nonstrategic inputs, the degree of collaboration between buyer and supplier is low, and the impact on the final value proposition is low, so the need for coordination and investment in relation-specific assets also is low. However, even with nonstrategic inputs, Toyota doesn't simply open up bidding to everyone; instead, they use capability and pricing benchmarks, and then select two or three vendors who are assured of some future business as long as prices remain competitive.

Strategic inputs play a clear role in the value proposition of the product. Therefore, they require a high degree of coordination between buyer and suppliers, and some level of relation-specific investment. With a high level of trust, the buyer's sales group can share marketing information with the suppliers' sales group to ensure that customer needs are being met. The benefits of trust and cooperation can be considerable. For every car sold, GM loses $300, Ford loses $240, and Toyota makes $1,800, and that is before Toyota's cost-cutting moves, such as recent work with suppliers' engineers for suggestions on how to cut costs by 30%.[12]

Wal-Mart also uses stratification in its approach. It is famous for its direct "one-number" negotiations, bypassing the retail norms of rebates and discounts that simply add complexity costs. "It's very pure," said Newell Rubbermaid division president Steven Scheyer.[13] "All the funny money... 1% for this, 2% for that... it isn't there." This arm's-length approach is nonetheless augmented with partnering and the sharing of information with suppliers to streamline the supply chain from raw material to the customer.

"They would rather extract fat from the process than extract their suppliers' profits," said Ananth Raman, a Harvard Business School professor who studies supply chains.[14] The benefits for Wal-Mart suppliers: not only huge volume—Wal-Mart accounts for 15% of Newell Rubbermaid's sales—but *predictable* volume, which translates to profits. *Fortune* cited surveys of Wal-Mart vendors describing the giant as both the best to do business with and the most profitable.[15]

What is the balance? Strategic partnerships should dominate when effective coordination is value-creating, e.g., high complexity and high value-add industries. (Caterpillar not only provides Lean Six Sigma training to its supply base, it also offers it to key customers and dealers, making the process one of revenue growth as well as cost and lead time reduction.) Conversely, arm's-length arrangements should dominate when the value of effective coordination is low, for instance in simple component industries or in declining industries with excess capacity.

Planning for Value Chain Changes

Consider some typical consequences of complexity analysis: decisions to withdraw from certain segments, find alternative delivery methods for certain segments (outsource), or grow certain segments. Now consider your supply chain. You most likely have the right supply chain in place for *yesterday's offerings* and *yesterday's competitors*. For example, you may have facilities focused on producing goods that are rapidly commoditizing, and that you consider less viable for investment. Clearly, your offering decisions (such as the withdrawal of a product) will mitigate the need for these facilities; eliminating them represents considerable freed assets.

Unfortunately, it also is a big task often without clear central authority: any change to the supply chain is a potential risk, with multiple stakeholders involved and detailed planning required. This is why we encourage clients to create a Complexity Champion who reports to the CEO, or multiple Champions in diversified companies who report to the P&L manager. Without such clear chains of responsibility, the supply chain often improves only through a series of local incremental decisions that are operationally driven rather than strategically driven, or else it simply remains "as is," out of step with changes in business strategy.

An alternative is to use our proposed Future-Back strategy to move the supply chain closer to the optimal model for your business, enable growth and cut costs (*see* Figure 15.1, next page). It works through the following series of questions:

1. Based on the complexity analysis, where are we creating value (products, processes)?
   - Which processes and products are differentiated and provide a platform for future growth?
   - Which markets are creating value?
   - Which processes do we excel at?

2. What does this say about the future of our business?
   - Where are the disconnects between "business as usual" priorities and our value-creating areas?
   - What are we willing to do to capture value going forward?

Figure 15.1: A Future-Back Strategy

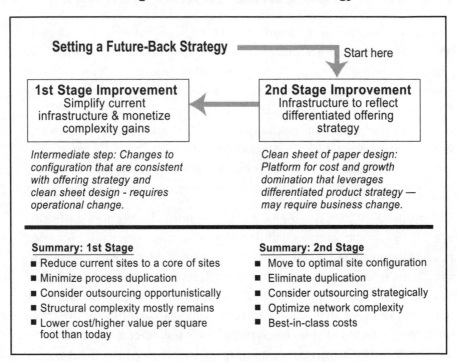

3. What is the optimal design (transformative 10-year vision) for competing on this strategy? [The 2nd stage]

4. What is the appropriate intermediate stretch goal (consistent with the future offering strategy and endgame)? [the 1st Stage]

5. What are the alternative configurations for reaching this stretch goal?
   • What are the value and risks for each potential configuration?
   • What are the migration paths for process relocation?
   • As we transpose the Complexity Value Stream Maps of selected processes onto their targets, what are the points of high risk?

6. How are we currently configured? What needs to change?
   • For what incarnation of our business was our current supply chain right?
   • What cost and lead time advantages can we derive by conquering the complexity of our supply chain?
   • What changes to the competitive landscape can we expect over the life of these assets?

This complexity analysis highlights areas in which you *are* and *are not* creating value, and processes in which you *do* and *do not* have an inherent advantage. The data can change your view of what your business does now and should do in the future. The 2nd stage, for example, can be thought of as the operations endgame, but its importance rests in its ability to align your supply chain decisions to the future strategic goals of the company. The 1st stage improvement goals are rooted in where you are today (and hence manageable) but because they are linked to the endgame view, nonetheless remain consistent with strategic goals.

You are thus liberated to focus on near-term goals, such as creating a tactical plan for increasing value-per-square foot in a production facility or streamlining service delivery. There are other consequences to the Future-Back strategy: short of a decision to radically outsource all undifferentiated product, you may nonetheless decide to group differentiated and undifferentiated products in separate locations for two reasons:

> ### The need for value analysis
>
> Preparing a Complexity Value Stream Map at a macro level—showing the relationships of all major processes—can help you avoid suboptimization. In fact, if complexity analysis is undertaken *without* viewing the Economic Profit created at each node of the supply chain, a value opportunity will be lost that may be grasped by a more agile competitor.

1. Ultimately you may choose to outsource or sell the undifferentiated groupings—you are effectively packaging them at this point as a stepping stone to your "future" organization.

2. Differentiated and undifferentiated imply different profitability levels and different customer requirements. Stratification by type can make less differentiated products more profitable (cheaper channels) and ensure the right degree of focus on growing revenues of differentiated products.

Downstream Complexity: Smashing the retail paradigms

We know that high complexity costs are linked to high variability with many low-volume offerings. In retail, there is natural variability due to end-customer demand. Demand is very product specific and varies by its category, such as functional vs. innovative (toothpaste, chicken soup, and general "basic needs" goods have less "spiky" demand than flat-screen TVs and diamond bracelets). But there is another level of variability that affects products with little customer-driven variation: retail pricing practices, discounts and other options, which in effect create an explosion in SKUs (and cost) that benefits neither side. The untapped profit pool can be the incentive to break through the habits of retail and eliminate this extra layer of complexity.

Campbell Soup Company sees very smooth demand. Only 5% of products are new each year, and they keep enough finished stock on hand to satisfy more than 98% of demand. Yet for years, shipments were very spiked and inconsistent with demand. Why? Price promotions. Every January, for example, Chicken Noodle soup volume dramatically spiked from a fairly consistent 200K to 300K cases to more than 700K cases due to the discounts Campbell was offering.[16] Other, smaller spikes during the year occurred for similar reasons. Naturally, retailers responded by stocking up with thousands of cases (known as *forward buying*), sometimes buying up to a year's supply!

But it was a lose-lose deal. Retailers had to pay to carry the year's inventory, while Campbell struggled to cope with the spike in volume.

Recognizing the problem, Campbell approached its core retailers with a proposition: waive the option of forward-buying and receive the products at an "everyday low price" equal to the average price that a retailer would pay, taking into consideration the discounts.

The results were very good. When you consider that retailers' profits average about 2%, and that a 2-week inventory reduction in retail represents a cost savings equal to nearly 1% of sales, it is not surprising that supermarkets loved the new program. Because retailers make more money on Campbell products, they have incentive to carry a broader line of them and give them more shelf space. And so, after the program was introduced, Campbell noticed that sales of its products grew twice as fast through participating stores as nonparticipating stores.

So both parties went from a *lose-lose* to a *win-win*. Cooperation to remove the complexity that was hurting both parties resulted in financial gains for both parties. The hurdle is overcoming the existing paradigms and short-term fixes that result in value destruction, such as pricing promotions. By pulling demand forward, a company is creating non-value-add cost for both parties and creating a gap in the next quarter, which can be filled only by pulling demand forward again. Thus, the vicious cycle.

Conclusion

The upside of a strong supply chain is enormous. It can yield the biggest gains and establish a platform of cost advantage. What level of advantage? One study estimated that the difference between world-class supply chain management and the average firm amounted to a sustained profit margin difference of 2.5%.[17] We consider this a minimum benefit level of supply chain rationalization for typical firms, most of whom have not applied a consistent methodology of complexity reduction as described in this book.

However, the impact on share price of a 2.5% increase in profit margin can be enormous. The five-year average Return on Invested Capital of the S&P 500 is 5.8% versus a cost of capital of about 4%. (e.g., *see* Ibbotson for industry specifics) and trades at about 3.2 times book value. Thus a 2.5% increase in margins can more than double ROIC. At the other extreme, Michael Dell puts his company's total costs at roughly 50% of its competitors. This results in an operating margin of 6.5% versus 4.3% for his industry, and price-to-book ratio of 14.6—about twice that of his industry!

Dell's competitive weapon is its supply chain, not its technology. Any advantage conferred by innovation or technology can be quickly overwhelmed by the power of a competitive supply chain process—

innovation does not guarantee sustainable advantage. A car or a PC: the principle is the same. Note that Toyota and Dell, two of the world's most successful companies, often are *not* the innovators, but rather the fast followers who overwhelm the competition with the speed and efficiency of their supply chains. They avoid many technical risks and investments, and reap most of the value to be gained.

Is the status quo acceptable? If you're currently cost-disadvantaged, clearly not. And even if you're at an advantage, your competitors are going through the same reasoning process... *"we need to realign our supply chain"*... and are preparing for action. You'd better be doing the same, but to create competitive advantage it is imperative to view the supply chain through the lens of the cost of complexity.

Exemplar organizations rarely treat site consolidation or supply chain overhaul projects in isolation but instead combine them with offering re-organization. Typically supply chain infrastructure changes lag offering changes (if they change at all). Both Procter & Gamble and Unilever undertook major brand and product alignments concurrent with major change in their supply chain configuration.

Changes in the supply chain configuration, switching suppliers, outsourcing, closing facilities, etc., may make the best of managers break out in a cold sweat, as they consider the risk of change... but while risk is uncomfortable, it can be planned for and controlled—especially if you follow our advice to have a strong Complexity Champion. The only alternative to change is the risk of inaction, which grows by leaps and bounds in a global economy.

Endnotes

1 Dell and Magretta, "The Power of Virtual Integration" (see chap. 3, n. 1).

2 See Michael L. George, *Lean Six Sigma*.

3 Ravi Venkatesan, "Strategic Sourcing: to Make or not to Make," *Harvard Business Review*, November-December 1992.

4 *Ibid.*

5 "BusinessWeek reports Porsche's net profit margin as 10.1% versus 6% for Toyota," *BusinessWeek*, January 19, 2004.

6 Gail Edmondson, "This SUV Can Tow An Entire Carmaker; Porsche's hot-selling Cayenne has kept the company rolling as it readies launches of new sports-car models," *BusinessWeek*, January 19, 2004.

7 U.S. Bureau of Census, *Annual Survey of Manufacturers* 1985.

8 Michael Porter, *Competitive Strategy* (New York: Free Press, 1980).

9 O'Toole, "Keeping it Simple" (see chap. 14, n. 4).

10 Jeffrey H. Dyer, Dong Sung Cho, Wujin Chu, "Strategic Supplier Segmentation: The Next 'Best Practice' in Supply Chain Management," *California Management Review*, Winter 1998.

11 See George, *Lean Six Sigma*, Chapter 13.

12 Robyn Meredith and Benjamin Fulford with Jonathan Fahey, "The "Oof" Company," *Forbes*, April 14, 2003.

13 Jerry Useem, "One Nation Under Wal-Mart," *Fortune*, March 2, 2003.

14 *Ibid.*

15 *Ibid.*

16 Marshall L. Fisher, "What is the Right Supply Chain for your Product?" *Harvard Business Review*, March 1, 1997.

17 W.G. Biemans and M.J. Brand, "Reverse Marketing: A Synergy of Purchasing and Relationship Marketing," *International Journal of Purchasing and Materials Management*, 1995, cited in F.I. Stuart and D.M. McCutcheon, "The Manager's Guide to Supply Chain Management," Business Horizons, March/April 2000.

CHAPTER 16

Applying Complexity Principles to Mergers and Acquisitions

Imagine for a moment that you are a consumer goods company and you decide to buy a brand from a competitor. Somehow you have to incorporate the sourcing, the production, the marketing, and the distribution of those new products into your current processes.

In Chapter 2 we learned that if we increase the number of products and tasks with no process improvement, we reduce Process Cycle Efficiency (PCE) and increase cost. The Complexity Equation shows us that, if we double the number of products we had better make proportional reductions in setup time, non-value-add activities, and quality improvement. This is in sharp contrast to the conventional wisdom that adding additional volume will "spread overhead" over more volume. This would certainly be true if no new products were added, but that's seldom the case since the rationale of many acquisitions is the cost "synergies" that will result (read: consolidation of operations).

Failure to understand the impact of complexity on merging processes can lead companies to overestimate synergies and hence overpay for a target company.

But there is a flipside: **the ability to understand where there are huge costs associated with complexity in a target can enable acquirers to harvest synergies greater than the premium paid.** These are both complexity due diligence issues.

The old song "Lookin' for love in all the wrong places" has its parallel: Cost synergies often are sought in all the wrong places—in SG&A rather than in reducing the cost of complexity of the offerings and the supply chains. SG&A can be reduced by the stroke of a pen to eliminate duplications…well and good. But many SG&A costs are related to the future, such as R&D, training and education, marketing development—all the elements of intellectual capital that may be the source of high margins. In addition, the big numbers are generally in Cost of Goods Sold and Asset Reduction in the balance sheet. The costs due to complexity represent a hidden asset that can be exploited.

The intrinsic value of a company is the discounted value of cash flows as discussed in the Appendix. When all is said and done, an acquisition is "good" only if it costs you substantially less than the discounted value of future cash flows… and this is what due diligence should be all about. So the question remains: if traditional due diligence still can result in inaccurate estimation of synergies, what other analyses can we apply?

Complexity Due Diligence

For managers to avoid future problems and to exploit the hidden assets of target firms, the answer is the same: **Complexity Due Diligence**, blending the complexity-value analysis described in Part II with traditional due diligence methods. The methods described in Chapters 6 to 9 can help you estimate more closely the true value represented by acquisition targets, the costs you may incur (in PCE, for example), and whether those costs can be contained or reversed through process improvements.

While most well-run companies perform proper financial and strategic due diligence, they give short shrift to operational due diligence and the impact of complexity. A survey by Lochridge and Associates asked companies which areas they studied in due diligence and which areas caused subsequent failure of the acquisition. The results are quite instructive. About 71% of the due diligence time was spent on accounting, environmental, and legal issues. Only about 13% of the due diligence time was spent on operations and organizational assessments, yet these areas were responsible for 85% of subsequent failures!

The principal reason for this mismatch? The professional organizations involved in due diligence are good at the 71% portion (accounting, environment, legal, etc.) that can be studied in isolation from the businesses to which they will be joined, and bad at or ignorant of operations and complexity evaluation. Operations and organizational assessments cannot be studied in isolation; the integration of new processes into the acquiring business can have profound impacts on the combined business all the way from the suppliers through to distribution and service levels.

Win the Deal, Lose the Synergies

A client of ours was interested in acquiring a marine engine manufacturer that assembled its engines from components produced in over a dozen "focused factories." The total travel length of components in the engine was over 4,000 miles.

We assisted our client in their analysis by looking at two of this manufacturer's plants and determined that PCE was well below 5%—meaning there was likely a lot of low-hanging fruit in terms of cost, quality, and lead time improvements that our client could exploit to drive revenue growth in this well-known brand.

However, we asked to visit at least a sample of the other factories and distribution centers, but were denied permission—and at our recommendation our client subsequently withdrew from bidding. The "winner" of the bidding process saw their investment evaporate within 24 months as the company became insolvent.

Did our client miss an opportunity by withdrawing? We'll never know for sure. We had all wanted the deal—our client for the revenue and brand potential, ourselves for the opportunity to help create an integrated factory and distribution system, and eliminate huge non-value-add costs related to low PCE. But you cannot make a rational decision without the necessary data.

Perhaps our client would have had a better fit than the competitor that won the deal and subsequently lost the synergies. But from a complexity perspective, they made a wise choice. We simply could not gauge how difficult this integration process would be, how long it would take, and when the benefits would in fact result. Expected synergies would be a roll of the dice…and that is not investing, in the words of Benjamin Graham, it's speculating.

There will always be *some* added costs due to complexity in any merger. For example, if two companies were integrated into one common operations with capacity eliminated (a common cost synergy strategy in a merger plan) and the number of products doubled (i.e., no products were produced in common), what would be the impact on PCE? According to the Complexity Equation (Chapter 2), PCE would be cut in half; if the relationship were like Figure 2.1 in Chapter 2, the cost would increase approximately 4%, an unpleasant but predictable surprise. But a combination of product rationalization, setup reduction, non-value-add removal, and so on, could preserve or indeed increase PCE, bringing costs back to neutral or better.

That doesn't mean you should *not* do the merger. Rather, you need to make proper product and process improvements if you want to preserve PCE, and take advantage of lower overhead and management cost.

Complexity Due Diligence leverages the Complexity Equation to enable us to war-game a number of scenarios, and avoid the impact on customers as lead times explode. You'll need to ask and answer questions such as:

1. **What are the synergies in the acquisition proposal?** The majority of acquisitions (70%) are initiated with the clear intent of gaining economies of scale, at reducing unit costs or eliminating excess capacity (e.g., many bank mergers[1]). This requires detailed understanding of both consolidating processes, the impact of consolidation on unit costs, and the opportunities for rationalization:
   - What made the deal attractive in the first place?
   - Which type of synergies are being proposed?
   - What assumptions do they depend upon?

2. **To which processes in your company and in the target do these cost savings relate?** Most deal proposals do not talk in process terms, but synergies are always linked to certain key processes,

e.g., consolidation of back-office operations (merging of A/R processes), or revenues from customer capture (new volume merged into current sales process). By identifying the supporting processes behind the listed synergies, we can evaluate in greater detail the veracity of the estimate.

3. **What 20% of processes contain 80% of the cost savings potential?** In the Due Diligence phase, focus on speed and "where the dollars live" is the priority. In Economies of Scale acquisitions, you cannot realize many of the big gains until operations have been "rationalized" and duplicate systems eliminated. What are the right rationalization targets, and what is the expected timeline and potential barriers to extracting that value?

4. **What is the impact on Process Cycle Efficiency of combining operations?** Merging processes can result in unexpected impacts on PCE, which can lead to longer lead times and financial consequences. Whether you predict negative impact on PCE, you still need to look for process improvement opportunities—leveraging the change mindset to incorporate complexity, Lean, and Six Sigma methodologies.

5. **What are the incremental complexity costs of combining these operations?** As we have shown in this book, there *are* complexity costs. And likely they have not been figured in. What is the impact on variability and cost as your supply chain accepts more low-volume offerings?

6. **What are the danger points?** You may have seen such examples in your own organization: you decide to take on more business, acquiring a product line or consolidating operations. The impact of doing this suddenly stretches out your customer lead times. Customers become upset, and what began as a project to lower unit costs ends up backfiring. So you need to think carefully about

where cost and lead time might suffer. What would such scenarios mean to customers? What is the inventory of management knowledge of process improvement processes in general and Lean Six Sigma and Cost of Complexity in particular? How accepting or resistant is existing management to continuous improvement? What gaps in management exist and how can they be strengthened without loss of key sources of energy and intellectual capital? Is there going to be a new CEO? If so, what must you do to prepare the ground for acceptance and support? What communication plan must we put in place? These are just a few of the danger points that must be explored.

In addition to assessing management, generating a high-level Complexity Value Stream Map of core processes will help you develop a plan for preventing a post-merger meltdown at critical junctures, while identifying the cultural or organizational impediments that may prevent a successful execution of product and process improvements necessary to preserve Process Cycle Efficiency. You can go into the merger or acquisition more fully informed, and aware of opportunities for extracting waste from combined process as well as pinpoint areas that require extra attention.

You may also want to develop a Complexity Profile (*see* Chapter 6) of the target and compare it to your own. For example, one key area of improvement may be in financial reporting. According to benchmarking data, the typical company budgets for 230 line items versus 40 for first-quartile companies.[2] Reporting fewer items both improves the speed and reduces the chance for errors. It also frees managers from looking for data so they can focus on activities that actually create value for the company. This was an opportunity discovered in the upfront diligence process.

Of course, no one disputes that deal activity can happen at a blistering pace. And sometimes you may not be able to get value-stream information *prior* to making a bid. However there normally exists an adequate due diligence window during which analysis can be completed. Moreover, this work becomes de facto part of your integration plan.

Hidden profits, hidden rocks

Remember, the more process disconnects there are (and work required to incorporate the new processes), the harder it can be to realize the cost synergies—short of major process improvement and change. If you're examining an organization that has low PCE and no corrective action underway, that should be an alarm bell—at least triggering the need for early, and significant, integration planning. This is complexity as an indicator of a potential hidden rock in the form of cultural barrier. This can be overcome, but adds a layer of risk.

However, for many companies, process improvement is an institutionalized capability, and the company has developed considerable abilities in "mining" value through Lean and Six Sigma, TQM...it really doesn't matter which. Under these scenarios, complexity due diligence opens up pockets of value that are not evident to other bidders, the seller, or the financial community. Thus, the opportunity for hidden profits.

Addressing Complexity Can Accelerate Integration

A uniform merger success trait is integration speed. According to Cisco Systems' John Chambers,

> *One calendar year (in transition) is equivalent to seven years of normal growth, and so you have to move at an unbelievable pace.*

Studies[3] have shown that speed of integration and eventual cost savings are linked: if done well, most post-merger activities are completed within 6 months to 1 year.[4] Fast integration eliminates stakeholder ambiguity: both customers and employees know where they stand. And there is a compelling financial rationale for fast integration: integration is the mechanism by which an acquiring company can monetize the synergies earlier identified. The longer it takes, the longer the wait for a beneficial cash flow effect.

Let's look at it a different way. On the one hand, fast integration tends to drive value creation. On the other, post-merger integration is the phase that bears the greatest failure risk.[5] In a McKinsey study, it was estimated that a newly merged company experiences a loss of 5% to 10% of its existing customers (beyond normal churn) as a direct result of the merger.[6,7] This is due to customer uncertainty, slips in service and quality, and general loss of focus on the customer. Worse still, the loss can continue well after closing. In another study of 160 acquisitions by

Losing sight of customers' needs in the integration phase

Case Corporation, which manufactures farm machinery, acquired New Holland Corp in 1999 for $4.6 billion.[8] In doing so, the new firm CNH Global, with $11 billion in combined revenue, became the second-place player in that market, next to John Deere (which has been practicing continuous improvement for many years). Almost overnight, CNH started losing focus on the customer and the markets, and revenues were off $2 billion by 2001 (*see* Figure 16.1)

Undoubtedly some of this was caused by macroeconomic stress. But CNH began losing market share to Deere almost as soon as the deal was sealed. The real killer: delays in integration left open customer anxieties. Fearful that CNH would discontinue duplicate products, many equipment dealers switched to Deere, which capitalized by offering special financing programs to lure buyers. All of these potential problems are measurable and preventable. What is the impact on shareholder value? Where would you like to invest: CNH or Deere?

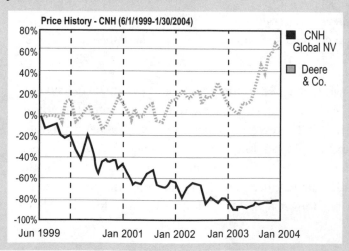

Figure 16.1: CNH vs. John Deere Stock Performance

157 public companies in 11 different industries, on average the acquiring firms grew 4% less than peers during the three years following closing, and 42% of the group lost ground.[9] The size and experience of the acquiring firm did not seem to matter.

The longer the cycle time for integration, the lower the value of the synergies (time can never be regained) and the lower the probability of a successful merger. The longer you lie in the water, the more you look like a dead fish. Complexity Due Diligence can help you accelerate the integration phase. How? Because the work you do in developing Complexity Value Stream Maps, assessing Economic Profit, etc., can provide invaluable guidance for integration.

Among other things, Complexity Due Diligence can help identify cultural barriers to the merger.

Other information from the due diligence will help you develop a detailed integration plan that lays out:

1. **A Complexity Value Stream Map populated with data on the merging processes:** Studying the work flow and process characteristics of the merging organizations will help people define projects in high-value processes that will allow them to achieve world-class PCE. It can also help highlight gaps in management knowledge and capability.

2. **Products and offerings targeted for rationalization or improvement:** These targets are identified in the upfront due diligence process.

3. **Migration paths for transitioning processes:** As capacity is eliminated or as new volume goes through an established process, there is a time of transition. This part of the plan is customer-critical. How will you ensure uninterrupted supply and service to customers? What are the transition costs? What is your risk mitigation plan? How long will it take?

4. **Core Process Analysis and special provisions for Strategic Processes:** As stressed in the methodology defined in Part II, certain processes define your ability to create value for yourself

and your customers. Other processes are less critical. Distinguish between the categories so that you can focus resources.

5. **Accountabilities, timeline, and value-at-stake (by plan component)**: As we know, speed equals success (or improved probabilities of it) while delay drives failure. Just as we would use Value Stream Mapping to highlight areas of waste and time delay, conduct a high-level Value Stream Map of *the integration process* as you've defined it. Can we change the flow? Can we eliminate sign-off delays or other delays?

6. **Complexity metrics to help stay on pace**: This sounds simple enough, but remember that it means putting in place the critical metrics to overcome integration roadblocks, rework, and nasty surprises (such as not achieving projected cost benefits). For example, having defined the processes where 80% of the cost synergy resides, drive those Process Cycle Efficiencies from below 5% (trust us, they are below 5%!) to above 15% in six months.

Making Complexity Due Diligence (and M&A) a Repeatable Process

Data suggest that whether you view the acquisition process as a one-off activity or a repeatable process (like purchasing or billing) plays a role in your success. Private equity firms and LBO shops are renowned both for creating value with deals and for their focus on continuous improvement of their deal methodology. Every deal is a learning opportunity. This contrasts with many corporate experiences.

In an article in *Harvard Business Review* discussing GE's methodology, the authors wrote: "Most acquisitions and mergers are one-time events that companies manage with heroic effort; few companies go through the process often enough to develop a pattern. Thus it tends to be seen not as a process—as something replicable—but only as something to get finished, so everyone can get back to business."[10]

The takeaway here is not that companies should increase the number of acquisitions. Rather, we should apply the principles and lessons of M&A

far more frequently than we will actually do big acquisitions. For example, Complexity Due Diligence is a methodology that can be equally applied in the case of a single process incorporation as in a multibillion-dollar merger. Remember our example upfront: two simple processes are to be merged. We want to put more business through our benchmarked process, but in the past, such moves have lengthened our customer lead times. We need and want to know the following:

- What is the impact on our delivery speed?

- What is the impact on our unit cost?

- What are the areas we need to manage most carefully?

- How can we optimize this combined process?

Conclusion

Mergers and acquisitions can be of enormous strategic importance in extending a company's product and customer strength, and in creating shareholder value.

If there is no interaction between companies, and the companies operate entirely separately all the way from suppliers through the supply chain to customers, then complexity issues do not arise (although duplications, and non-value-add cost, are likely retained). However, if cost benefits are expected to accrue by combining volumes through common processes, the impact of complexity will be critical to the attainment of cost synergies.

Most strategic acquisitions have a significant complexity component that spells either the creation or destruction of shareholder value. Creating value is strictly dependent on management's willingness and ability to embrace continuous improvement and complexity analysis. The lack of focus in this area in due diligence and subsequent executive action is largely responsible for the failure of the majority of strategic acquisitions in meeting cost objectives. By performing Complexity Due Diligence, a company will be better able to measure the challenges or opportunities that people and processes represent, and more likely to make an informed offer that results in value creation.

Endnotes

1 A.T.Kearney, Global PMI Survey. 1998-1999

2 "All Together Now,"by Cathy Lazere, *CFO Magazine*, Feb 1998, citing a benchmarking study by The Hackett Group, a consultancy.

3 Donald DePamphilis, *Mergers, Acquisitions and Other Restructuring Activities: An Integrated Approach to Process, Tools, Cases and Solutions* (San Diego: Academic Press, 2003), 279.

4 Andersen Consulting study, cited in DePamphilis, *Mergers, Acquisitions and other Restructuring Activities.*

5 Kearney, (*see* n. 1).

6 DePamphilis, *Mergers, Acquisitions*, p. 292.

7 James Down, "The M&A game is often won or lost after the deal," Management Review Executive Forum, Nov. 1995, p. 10, cited in *Mergers, Acquisitions and other Restructuring Activities*, DePamphilis

8 Excerpted from DePamphilis, *Mergers, Acquisitions*, p. 292.

9 McKinsey and Company, Inc., Copeland, *Valuation* (see chap. 4, n. 8).

10 Ronald N. Ashkenas, Lawrence J. DeMonaco, Suzanne C. Francis, "Making the Deal Real: How GE Capital Integrates Acquisitions," *Harvard Business Review*, January 1, 1998.

APPENDIX

The Complexity Equation[1]

Anyone who has ever performed a "Do It Yourself" job around the house for the first time, be it plumbing or tile setting, knows that you figure out how you should have done it just about the time you've finished. If you don't do that task again for months or years, you have to go through the same kind of learning curve all over again.

The same kind of effect happens in businesses all the time with tasks associated with low-volume offerings, which by definition are not a usual part of how you do business every day. Chapter 2 showed that an offering with a lot of complexity will involve some tasks that are not performed frequently. These tasks potentially have a much higher cost and lower quality than those that are performed frequently.

To compensate for this higher cost, this book advocates first trying to "commonize" the process tasks or product/service components that make up several offerings (see Chapter 11). The example we explored in some depth dealt with how International Power Machines made all "invisible" or "transparent" components (those the customer wouldn't see or care about) common to the power unit platforms. These efforts cost money, and the question is, what will the return on my investment be? What is the cost of offerings that are seldom produced? Traditional management accounting doesn't provide the answer.

A fiberglass company we know had some very high-volume products that they produced every month, and a few low-volume ones that they would only produce every six months. They did this because there was a significant fixed setup time and startup scrap that they wished to minimize. By amortizing the fixed costs across a batch size that amounted to a six-month supply, the unit cost of the low-volume offering approached that of the high-volume product. The problem, of course, is that 60% of the factory space was used to hold finished goods inventory, and most of it was low volume products!

In our book *Lean Six Sigma for Service*, we documented a service example of this same phenomenon. The commodity buyers at a Lockheed Martin procurement center were faced with having to serve 14 different business sites, each with their own legacy purchasing systems and procedures. Because it took them so long to switch from one legacy system to another, they ended up processing all the requests from one site before moving on to the next. With 14 sites, this led to a 28-day cycle time—so by the time a buyer returned to any site, it had been about a month since they had used that site's procedures, codes, systems, etc., and they'd have to re-learn it all over again. The resulting "ramp-up" time caused low productivity, as depicted in the following diagram.

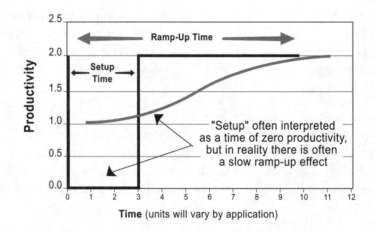

Time (units will vary by application)

What is the cost of ramp-up? Any time an activity in a process has to switch from one task to another, and in so doing experiences a slow down in productivity due to a setup time or ramp-up time, the activity can react in one of two ways:

1. Perform one unit of the task at exceptionally high cost
2. Perform all tasks possible that will avoid another setup or ramp-up

The first approach has been relegated to very high cost "concierge" services, the artisan's studio, or developing nations. The second approach is used universally, from the Lockheed Martin service example to automobile manufacturing. Most people in service applications are so close to the problem that they do not realize that their poor average service times are due to setup time, but the graph above shows that a slow down in productivity in changing tasks is equivalent to a setup time.

The Impact of Setup Time on Lead Time (Average Service Time)

To illustrate how setup or ramp-up time affects Process Cycle Efficiency, we'll start with a tangible case where you can trip over the problem, such as in manufacturing, then generalize to service applications. We will start with the first example of setup time ever attacked, the one that created the Four Step Rapid Setup method (see Chapter 12).

Let's assume that we have a large machine such as a Press that stamps metal parts by pressing a die onto a sheet of metal. We will take a specific example, then generalize the equation:

- When the machine is operating it can produce 5000 parts per hour (the processing time is 0.0002 hours per part)

- The press must produce 20 different kinds of parts, A through T, each with its own unique die

- Let's assume it takes one hour to change from one die to another

- The customer demand for each of the offerings is 230 per hour

Given these data...

- What is the average delay time that this activity injects into the process?

- What is the average lead time to meet a change in demand mix?

- What is the *minimum* number of pieces of inventory that must be held to meet this schedule?

Like all important equations, ours begins with a fairly simple idea. The press begins with product 1, builds a batch quantity B of product 1, then performs a one hour setup, and builds a batch of Product 2, and so on, through Product 20, then it returns to Product 1. It clearly has to build enough Product 1 to satisfy the demand of 230 per hour until it can get back to Product 1 again (which won't be until after Product 20 is finished). Since the demand, setup time and processing time for all parts are equal, the batch size that must be run for each part is also equal, and we will refer to it as a batch size of B parts. (This can be generalized to unequal demands, setup times, batch sizes, etc., as we'll discuss later on.)

The new press begins by performing a one hour setup to change the dies to product 1, then produces a batch of product 1 in quantity B at a rate of 5000 per hour or 0.0002 hours per part. The time it takes it to produce a batch of B parts is 0.0002B. We can show the whole cycle from product 1 to product 20 on an Activity Turnover Diagram (also called an " Inflexibility Diagram" because it shows how much time it will take for a process to complete is production cycle before it can get back to producing any given item):

Activity Turnover (Inflexibility) Diagram

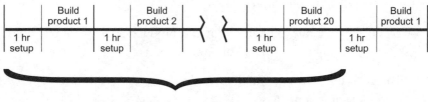

Activity Turnover Time

The Activity Turnover Time is defined as the time interval to produce one full cycle of all 20 products. It is simply the sum of 20 setups and 20 runs of batch sizes B at the rate of 0.0002 hours per part:

$$\text{Activity Turnover Time} = 20(1 \text{ hour}) + 20(0.0002)B$$

We know that the batch size B has to meet the demand of 230 parts per hour for the duration of the Activity Turnover time. Thus we can write:

$$\frac{B}{\text{Activity Turnover Time}} = \frac{B}{20 * (1 + 0.0002B)} = 230/\text{hour}$$

$$B = 230 * [20 * (1 + 0.0002B)]$$

$$B = 4600 + 0.92B$$

$$B - 0.92B = 4600$$

$$B = 57,500$$

We can now calculate the activity turnover time as :

$$\text{Activity Turnover Time} = 20 * [1 + (0.0002 * 57,500)]$$

$$= 250 \text{ hours}$$

$$= 3 \text{ shifts} * 5 \text{ days/week} * 2 \text{ weeks}$$

Each batch of parts is consumed at a constant rate over the two weeks, so on average a part is in inventory for a week. You might think that a week of delay is a long time, but it is not uncommon. All of the cost of transporting, stocking, etc., is captured in the Complexity Value Stream Map and increases the slope of the Process Cycle Efficiency curve. We can make a first generalization of the equation very simply. Let:

N = Number of different products

P = Processing time per unit

S = Setup time

d = Demand per hour for each product

B = Minimum batch size

A = Number of activities in the process

D = Nd = Total number of products demanded per hour

V = Total value add time in the process

$$\text{Activity Turnover Time} = NS + NPB$$

$$d = \frac{B}{NS + NPB}$$

$$B = d(NS + NPB) = NdS + NdPB$$

$$B(1-NdP) = NdS$$

$$B = \frac{NdS}{1-NdP} \quad \text{for each activity in the Process}$$

After Batch B is produced, it is delivered to Finished Goods inventory, where the inventory level approaches zero, at which point a new batch has been produced and is delivered to replenish Finished Goods. Thus the average Finished Goods inventory is approximately half the batch size:

$$\text{Average inventory due to a product} = \frac{NdS}{2(1 - NdP)}$$

And for an Activity that produces N different products:

$$\text{Average total inventory due to an Activity} = \frac{N^2dS}{2(1 - NdP)}$$

But Nd is just the total number of products D delivered each hour, thus we can write the above equation as:

$$\text{Average Total Finished Goods on hand} = \frac{NDS}{2(1 - DP)}$$

The formula for Work in Process Inventory levels can be derived in a similar way. For a process consisting of A activities in series, the total average inventory (WIP + FGI) in the organization is given by:

$$\text{Total Inventory} \quad = \quad \frac{\text{NADS}}{(1 - \text{DP})} \quad + \quad \frac{\text{NDS}}{2(1 - \text{DP})}$$

We can combine these fractions using a common denominator to reach:

$$\text{Total Inventory} \quad = \quad \frac{(2A + 1)\,\text{NSD}}{2(1 - \text{DP})}$$

Now we know from Little's Law that

$$\text{Total Lead Time} \quad = \quad \frac{\text{Number of Things in Process}}{\text{Average Completion Rate}}$$

Since Average Completion Rate= D, then

$$\text{Lead Time} \quad = \quad \frac{(2A + 1)\,\text{NS}}{2(1 - \text{DP})}$$

Adapting the basic PCE equation (from Chapter 2), we get...

$$\text{Process Cycle Efficiency} \quad = \quad \frac{\text{Value-add Time}}{\text{Total Lead Time}}$$

$$\text{Process Cycle Efficiency} \quad = \quad \frac{2V(1 - \text{PD})}{(2A + 1)\text{NS}} \qquad \text{where } \text{PCE}_{max} = 100\%$$

In many instances, it is reasonable to assume that the only value-add time is the processing time. Further, we know that there is a relationship between Process Cycle Efficiency and non-value-add cost that is determined by the Complexity Value Stream Map and is often nearly linear over a range from 2% to 20%:

$$\text{Non-value-add cost} \quad = \quad f\,(\text{Process Cycle Efficiency})$$

$$\text{Non-value-add cost} \quad \approx \quad \frac{2KV(1 - \text{PD})}{(2A + 1)\text{NS}}$$

where K is the proportionality constant.

The effect of scrap is derived in the referenced patents and results in

$$\text{Non-value-add cost} \quad = \quad \frac{2KV(1 - X - PD)}{(2A + 1)NS}$$

Where X is the % of work that must be scrapped and reproduced. (The full equations include expressions for rework, absenteeism, downtime, etc.)

The power of the Complexity equation lies in its ability to determine whether a complexity reduction initiative (attacking N and A) or quality initiative (reducing X) or a Lean initiative (reducing S and or P) will be most effective in reducing cost consistent with other strategic initiatives such as customer satisfaction, etc.

And that's what the simplified form of the Complexity Equation does. From there, we can generalize the equations such that each product or task has its own unique setup time, processing time per unit, defect %, etc. We denote the setup time for the ith product at the jth Activity by S_{IJ}, etc., and end up with some fearsome triple sum notations...but the ideas are the same. The power of the simple form of the Complexity Equation is that it allows management to have an idea of what can be accomplished.

Management Policy as an issue affecting PCE

It should be emphasized that these equations show the best possible intrinsic Process Cycle Efficiency. Management may make things much worse by arbitrarily having larger amounts of things in process. By using the complexity equations, the minimum safe level of work in process (and batch size in manufacturing) related to this intrinsic PCE can be determined and an immediate improvement in Process Cycle Efficiency realized. For example, one of our clients manufactured antenna systems, and their management policy was to release a one-month requirement of each product into the line. A Complexity Value Stream map showed that the setup times were minimal. The Complexity Equation then showed that material could be released in batches of 2 days' requirement with no process improvement. We would refer to this batch size as the intrinsic batch size, as determined by the Complexity Equation. This was increased to 3 days due to demand fluctuations. By implementing a Pull system to put this 3-day cap on material releases, the number of things in process began to fall, which led to an overall reduction in the amount of WIP, decrease in lead time by nearly 90% , and a ten-fold increase in Process Cycle Efficiency over the next six months. This is the most extreme example of the impact of management policy on Things In Process that we have ever encountered. However, it is not unusual to see a 20% to 30% excess amount of Things In Process that can be immediately eliminated. However, recalling Figure 1.5, we would not expect to be able to remove a lot of non-value-add cost until we had removed 60% to 70% of Things In Process.

Effect of Variation

The derivations above do not include the impact of variation in demand, setup times, processing times per unit and reject rates. These phenomena can be approximated by formulas from Queuing Theory, but due to their limited range of application, we prefer to calculate the effects of variation using computer Discrete Event Simulations.

Steps beyond the Simplified Complexity Equation

In Chapter 8, we discussed examples of how the Complexity Equation can be used to estimate the impact of process or product improvements, such as the reduction in the number of different offering or reduction in average setup time, all other things being held constant. But what if you want to know the impact of reducing only the number of low-volume products via commonization or outsourcing, etc.? The derivation becomes a bit more complicated, but the math itself remains in the realm of the second year of High School algebra. **We start by divide the offering into two groups (high-volume vs. low-volume) using Pareto analysis.**

The high-volume group will constitute about 20% of the total number of offerings, and have an average demand of D_H per offering per unit of time. The low-volume offerings (which constitute about 20% of total demand, and 80% of the number of offerings) will have an average of D_L demand. We will use the same nomenclature as above: N_H = number of different offering in the high-volume group, etc. (It doesn't matter if the split is 70/30, we will first derive a completely general expression for process cycle efficiency. We will then apply it to the case of breaking the product line into two groups, then as many as you like. Remember though, or goal is to increase Process Cycle Efficiency, not build models.)

To keep the math simple, we will return to the original derivation earlier in this Appendix. The addition of quality and process complexity complicates the formulas.[2] We start with the definition of Process Cycle Efficiency (numbers correspond to equation numbers from the patent applications):

$$\text{Process Cycle Efficiency} = \frac{\text{Value-add Time}}{\text{Total Lead Time}} \qquad \textbf{(15)}$$

Now the average value-add time is

$$\text{Avg. Value-add time} = \frac{1}{N}\sum_{\iota=1}^{N} P_i \qquad \textbf{(16)}$$

The total lead time is, from Little's law:

$$\text{Total lead time} = \frac{\text{Total Number of Things in Process}}{\text{Completion Rate}} \qquad \textbf{(17)}$$

The components of this equation can be denoted as:

$$\text{Total Number of Things in Process} = \sum_{\iota=1}^{N} TIP_i \quad \text{Completion rate} = \sum_{\iota=1}^{N} D_i \qquad \textbf{(18, 19)}$$

From the Patent[3] using the usual rule for matrix multiplication:

$$(TIP_1 \; TIP_2 \ldots TIP_N) = 2\left(\sum_{i=1}^{N} S_i\right)(2A+1)(D_1 \; D_2 \ldots D_N)\begin{pmatrix} (1-X_1-D_1P_1) & -D_2P_1\ldots\ldots & -D_NP_1 \\ -D_1P_2 & (1-X_2-D_2P_2).. & -D_NP_2 \\ \cdot & & \\ -D_1P_N & -D_2P_N\ldots & (1-X_N-D_NP_N) \end{pmatrix}^{-1} \qquad \textbf{(20)}$$

This assumes that each of the N products has unique demand, processing time, etc. So now lets apply this to the problem we posed, breaking the product line into two segments, with N_H being the number of offerings with high volume demand D_H high volume and N_L the number of low volume products, etc:

$$(TIP_H \; TIP_L) = 2(S_H+S_L)(2A+1)(D_H \; D_L)\begin{pmatrix} (1-X_H-N_HD_HP_H) & -N_LD_LP_H \\ -N_HD_HP_L & (1-X_L-N_LD_LP_L) \end{pmatrix}^{-1} \qquad \textbf{(21)}$$

Now any 2x2 matrix can be inverted according to the rule

(22)
$$\begin{pmatrix} a & b \\ c & d \end{pmatrix}^{-1} = \frac{1}{ad - bc}\begin{pmatrix} d & -b \\ -c & a \end{pmatrix}$$

Thus we have:

(23)
$$\begin{pmatrix} (1-N_HD_HP_H) & -N_LD_LP_H \\ -N_HD_HP_L & (1-N_LD_LP_L) \end{pmatrix}^{-1} = \frac{1}{(1-N_HD_HP_H)(1-N_LD_LP_L)-(N_HD_HP_L)(N_LD_LP_H)}\begin{pmatrix} (1-X_L-N_LD_LP_L) & N_HD_HP_L \\ N_LD_LP_H & (1-X_H-N_HD_HP_H) \end{pmatrix},$$

We can now substitute (23) into (21) and compute TIP_H and TIP_L, use these values in (19), (17) and finally compute PCE in (15). A 2x2 analysis is often an easy first cut at the problem, because it captures a lot that is currently hidden from management. It allows you to vary the number of low-volume parts N_L and compute the impact on Process Cycle Efficiency. From the complexity matrix you can decide whether an initiative related to commonization or pruning (reduction of N_L) or a lean initiative in reducing setup time (S_H and/or S_L) will be most effective in reducing PCE. Given the cost data from the Complexity Value Stream Map, you can estimate just what chunks of non-value-add cost could be removed. Equation (9) in the patent allows us to have a Processing Time per unit P_H for the high volume and a separate P_L for the low volume products, and in fact we would expect $P_H<P_L$, because of the volume and repetition differences, and similarly $S_H<S_L$.

Now if you believe that you need to break the demands into more than two groups to more closely mirror your offering, the math isn't any more difficult…its just bigger, and gets beyond the realm of pencil and paper. The problem of inverting an NxN matrix in a reasonable amount of time used to require mainframe computers. However, Excel™ now has "solvers" with add on packages that make virtually all practical problems within the reach of Pentium™ PC.

Endnotes

1 The equations derived in this book related to Process Cycle Efficiency are protected by U.S. patents 5,195,041 and 5,351,195 and patents pending. For information regarding license of these equations, please contact George Group Consulting, L.P., www.george-group.com

2 *Ibid*

3 *Ibid*

INDEX